Edd Roush

Edd Roush

A Biography of the Cincinnati Reds Star

MITCHELL CONRAD STINSON

McFarland & Company, Inc., Publishers
Jefferson, North Carolina, and London

LIBRARY OF CONGRESS CATALOGUING-IN-PUBLICATION DATA

Stinson, Mitchell Conrad.
    Edd Roush : a biography of the Cincinnati Reds star /
Mitchell Conrad Stinson.
        p.   cm.
    Includes bibliographical references and index.

    ISBN 978-0-7864-4407-6
    softcover : 50# alkaline paper ∞

    1. Roush, Edd, 1893–1988.   2. Baseball players — United
States — Biography.   3. Cincinnati Reds (Baseball team)
4. Chicago White Sox (Baseball team)   5. World Series
(Baseball) (1919)   I. Title.
GV865.R65S85   2010
796.357092 — dc22   2009054315
[B]

British Library cataloguing data are available

On the cover: Edd Roush in his batting stance (National
Baseball Hall of Fame Library, Cooperstown, New York)

Manufactured in the United States of America

McFarland & Company, Inc., Publishers
Box 611, Jefferson, North Carolina 28640
www.mcfarlandpub.com

To my parents, Conrad and Donna Stinson.
Still nurturing after all these years.

Acknowledgments

A world of gratitude goes out to Edd Roush's granddaughter, Susan Dellinger. Despite having her own Roush book on the market, she put the family photo collection at my disposal and offered to help in any other way she could. Figuring that *Red Legs and Black Sox* had run its course, Susan welcomed the idea of another biography about her beloved "Daddaw." In fact, she wouldn't mind if *everybody* wrote one. The more the merrier. I believe two is the perfect number but still applaud Susan's attitude. Over the course of several email exchanges and a couple of face-to-face meetings, she has always been helpful and encouraging. I consider her a friend.

I was also lucky to connect with Susan's son, Jade Dellinger. Not only did he provide great family insights during an interview in Tampa, but he arranged another interview with a long-time Roush confidant and served as my tour guide. I left Florida knowing that I'd met one of the nicest guys in the Sunshine State.

That "confidant" was Kent Chetlain, a former Bradenton sports editor and county commissioner, and longtime pal to Roush during the last decades of his life. An accommodating host, Kent spoke at length about his city's famous snowbird. His input was invaluable for the chapters on the Florida years and he gave an eyewitness account of Roush's death scene at a spring training game. Back in southern Indiana, Bill Marshall was a huge help with the Oakland City years. A longtime resident and local historian, he knew the Roush twins and their town quite well.

Thanks to Tricia Brown, a veteran of the book business who became my adviser on many matters, big and small. She's also my cousin. In conclusion, I have to credit my father, Conrad Stinson, for launching this whole thing some three decades ago. He told me about Edd Roush, took me to meet him and somehow convinced an insecure teenager that he was worthy of talking to the legend.

Table of Contents

Table of Contents

Preface

In hindsight this book seems inevitable. As a teenager I conducted two tape-recorded interviews with Edd Roush and, as an adult, became a newspaper sportswriter. But the idea of authorship actually developed quite slowly.

It wasn't even a consideration when I showed up at Roush's backyard in the summer of 1978. This was simply taking advantage of the opportunity of a lifetime. The old Hall of Famer was a well-known and easily approachable figure in Oakland City, Indiana. Arriving with my parents and toting a tape recorder, I conducted an amateur interview with him. Two years later we did it again. Those interviews are the foundation of this biography.

It wasn't until the mid-to-late 1990s that I gave serious thought to writing a Roush book. Making two research trips to the Baseball Hall of Fame in Cooperstown, I pored over the bulky Edd Roush file and listened to Lawrence Ritter's tape-recorded interviews with Roush from the 1960s. I also researched files on Roush contemporaries, such as Bill McKechnie and Zach Wheat. The Hall of Fame museum proved informative, too.

Providing a more personal research touch were my lengthy interviews with Roush's great-grandson (Jade Dellinger), a close companion from his golden years (Kent Chetlain) and a hometown family friend (Bill Marshall). Briefer input came from a few other acquaintances and distant relatives.

Incalculable hours went into newspaper microfilm research. My primary sources, in order, were the *New York Times*, *Cincinnati Enquirer* and *Chicago Tribune*. Evansville, Indiana, newspapers became major resources, too. Roush played in or near that city for most of his minor league career. His hometown paper, the *Oakland City Journal*, was a treasure trove of information about life in that rural town. Obituaries proved a great source for Roush family history, as did the nationally renowned genealogy department at Willard Library in Evansville. For Edd Roush's extremely brief Kitty League stint in Kentucky, I found fantastic coverage in the *Henderson Gleaner*.

A pit stop in Nebraska's state capital is followed through the sports pages of the *Lincoln Daily Star*. The *Indianapolis Star* and *Newark Evening News* fed the narrative for Roush's foray into the Federal League. At every stop I tried to provide a feel for the local community and its background, whether it came from history books or contemporaneous newspaper accounts. Most information was mined from visits to library microfilm departments or inter-library loans. Some came through Internet sites. I stumbled across one site that carried a full run of *The Sporting News* and another that provided a partial run of *Baseball Magazine*.

Courthouse records provided information about a lawsuit filed against Roush and his pool hall in Oakland City. I also discovered divorce proceedings records on his brother, Fred Roush. By itself, the divorce wasn't really pertinent but the testimony provided information about Fred's minor league baseball career.

I read or re-read many articles and books relating to Roush's time and the teams he played for, as well as biographies of some of the more well-known figures he encountered — John McGraw, Christy Mathewson, Babe Ruth, Shoeless Joe Jackson, Casey Stengel and Gil Hodges. Some works provided a backdrop to Roush's experience. Of course, stories about the 1919 World Series were required reading, though my information about the Black Sox World Series comes almost exclusively from extensive research of several newspapers and magazines, along with Roush's insights from 1980. Reading other works simply gave me a broader feel for the subject through repetition, and confidence that I hadn't omitted something important.

The Glory of Their Times has an Edd Roush section included among the many narratives from old-time baseball players. It's the first book I read while researching my own. The last was *Red Legs and Black Sox*, a 2006 release written by Roush's granddaughter, Susan Dellinger, focusing on the 1919 World Series as Edd saw it. Readers interested in the Reds' side of the Black Sox story — a group that would presumably include most who read this preface — are heartily encouraged to find a copy.

Prologue

He is splotched and daubed and fairly dripping with color. He uses a most eccentric bat: heavy, cumbersome, but short. He handles it in an eccentric way, poking at the ball like a chop hitter, only he doesn't choke. On the contrary, he swings from the handle like a slugger.... His manner of standing in the batter's box is the maddest, freakiest method in vogue anywhere on the Major League diamond. There seems no rhyme or reason in his curious gyrations. On the contrary, he seems to violate the accepted rules of stance. — Baseball Magazine, *1927*[1]

It was the summer of 1978 and the mighty Cincinnati Reds were trying to reclaim their throne. They'd won back-to-back World Series championships in '75 and '76, then missed the playoffs the following year. Now the "Big Red Machine" found itself embroiled in a tight race for the National League's Western Division title. Its roster still read like a Who's Who of big league stars: Pete Rose, Johnny Bench, Joe Morgan, George Foster, Tom Seaver, Ken Griffey Sr., Dave Concepcion and venerable manager Sparky Anderson — all fabulously famous during the glorious '70s.

Few of their adoring fans knew about the aged ex-outfielder who set the standards for Reds stardom early in the century. Six decades after brashly bursting into major league prominence he was alive and well, and considerably disillusioned by what had become of his beloved game. The old guy lived about 170 miles west of Cincinnati in the sleepy, southern Indiana town of Oakland City.

That's where this story begins, with a carload of strangers dropping by the legend's house on Main Street and finding him in his backyard. There he was in all his emeritus glory — Edd J. Roush, 85 years old, sweating through khaki work clothes while mowing the lawn. Not on a riding mower, as any good cardiologist would recommend, but by good, old-fashioned push power.

It wasn't the same 5-foot-11, 170-pound specimen that endured almost two decades of grinding pro ball. Yet for somebody his age, it came surpris-

The author as a teenager interviews 85-year-old Edd Roush in 1978 (photograph by Donna Stinson).

ingly close. His head bore an impressive resemblance to portraits of yesteryear, when that taut face was framed by grinding jaw ridges and high-perched cheekbones. Old photos showed thin lips, a sharp nose and a piercing squint perfect for focusing on pitchers or deer — both his prey. Age and gravity joined every new pose, now though Edd elbowed them to the background. He was heavier but not fat, his hair thinning but not bald, way slower yet an active octogenarian who walked everywhere. Nestled between the nose and each cheek were the beginnings of two vertical ravines that flowed downward, just past the corners of his mouth. The rest of the face seemed relatively smooth, with no deep wrinkles. Baseball's elder statesman could have passed for someone in his 60s.

The visitors waited while he wrapped up his yard work, then sheepishly approached after the mower went silent. A 14-year-old boy emerged from the group, nervously clutching a bulky tape recorder. He wanted to ask questions about old-time baseball and record the answers. Left unsaid was the fact he felt too intimidated to show up alone. After all, this was a genuine pioneer of the national pastime, a contemporary of Ty Cobb, Babe Ruth and Rogers

Hornsby. The kid couldn't have been more awestruck if Buffalo Bill Cody trotted across that freshly trimmed yard on horseback. A light mixture of green and blue, Edd's eyes glowed with country charisma as he projected a relaxed, yet commanding aura of self-assurance. Back in the old days, New York Giants manager John McGraw pegged him perfectly: "That Hoosier moves with the regal indifference of an alley cat."[2] A lifetime later, Edd still looked secure in his fur.

Earthy and approachable, he sat on a backless stone bench while guests gathered around. This day's audience consisted of a mother, father, grandmother, sister, cousin and your author — the tape-recorder boy. Without hesitation or reservation, Edd took them all on a time machine to yesteryear. Every so often a freight train would pass slowly by on tracks that lay a stone's throw away and its warning whistle drowned all talk. As if by prearranged signal, everybody went mute simultaneously, waiting patiently until the din faded. Other audio intrusions occasionally sprang from the brush, where hidden cricket orchestras alternated between dramatic crescendo and dead silence. It was all part of country-town cadence, a charmingly slow beat that Mr. Roush embraced for the better part of eight decades.

Speaking over insects, between train intrusions and under clotheslines, he reminisced about fast times in a bygone era. The teen read questions from a hand-written list and the icon dipped responses from a bottomless well of colorful recollections. There hadn't been an exchange this lopsided since the Lou Brock–Ernie Broglio trade.

"Who was your best friend on your team?"

"Oh, you never had any great friends on a team. They were all against ya if ya was good and if you was bad, they were all your friends. No, we were all friends after the ball game. You know, same way with the fellas on the other club. After the game was over, why we used to go down some place and get a soft drink or a beer or something like that and we're all friends. But when that ball game started, all friendship ceased. And I said, 'If ya don't want to get hurt, stay out of my way.'"

One query, one wonderful reply. Just like his playing days, Edd Roush didn't need much time to warm up.

"Did you notice Ty Cobb being really rough or mean?"

"By God, back in those days you didn't play Ping-Pong out there! You played baseball to win. Your strike zone was from up around your neck (to) down here (motions to knees) and they threw at you. Why, I hit the dirt a'many a time. I got 'em off of me because I started in on the infielders. I started (spiking) the infielders out of there. Well, it wasn't long till they got pitchers off of me, of throwin' at me, see?"

"Which team did you like to play on the best?"

"Well, they were all alike. Back in those days you played for the money.... Of course, I played the longest in Cincinnati, but when you're away from home, what's the difference where you're at? I was always glad to get home in the fall of the year to start in huntin'."

At one point the young interviewer went blank and fumbled with his list, mumbling, "Let me see here ... look around here ... hmmmm." Then came reassuring words from his new hero. "Take your time. There ain't no hurry about this situation."

Edd wasn't just politely accommodating this boy; he truly enjoyed their interaction. The interview continued.

"Who was the toughest pitcher you ever faced?"

"Well, I never saw a pitcher in my life that I couldn't hit. I always figured they was all tough. As far as hitting the ball I could hit any of them but they didn't all go safe. That's where the hard part is."

How about legendary fireballer Walter Johnson?

"If you held your bat way up here against Walter Johnson, by the time you got around to swing, the catcher'd be throwin' it (back) out. You talk about being fast. Well, thunder! That's the way Walter Johnson was. Now I hit Walter Johnson all right in the spring of the year because I always had my bat down. *That's* all, *that's* all."

What about Tinker to Evers to Chance, the old Chicago Cubs double-play combination that was immortalized in poem?

"They weren't so good. No! It was something some writers started.... They were good ballplayers, don't misunderstand me, but they weren't as good as they thought they were. Thunder!"

Dizzy Dean?

"He was with the St. Louis club in the spring of '31 and they told me about him. They said he was wild but he had a lot of stuff, and I said, 'Well, I seen a lot of them guys who had a lot of stuff and was wild.' He only had three good years and they put him in the Hall of Fame. Why? He was a talker on television, that's how he got in there."

Leo Durocher was dismissed as good field, no bat, and all mouth.

"That's all he could do was talk. He was a pretty good fielder but he couldn't hit. I told him, 'You're the worst I ever saw.' Of course, you got to swing. I said, 'Thunder! Ya can't hit anything if ya don't swing. If ya get three swings, ya might hit the ball.'"

Edd liked to go off-script, too, and that was a good thing. He could carry an interview without prompts from a questioner.

"There was always about five or six of us that drank beer and at the ball game it was hot out there in that sun all day. And I'd say, 'I'm gonna get beer after the game is over.' I always got three bottles. The first bottle went down pretty fast, the second one purt near as fast, and then you could take your time on the third one and that was all I was gonna drink anyway, see, and then go to the hotel. They used to say, 'Here comes Roush and his three beers.'"

He punctuated the punch line with a throaty chuckle and wide smile. Edd loved that story. It's all the more amusing because he played most of his career during Prohibition. Some of those conversational side trips covered exciting ground; most didn't. Yet even small talk proves engrossing when big men reflect on small things.

"Four kids wanted my autograph today. Well, I give it to the mailman when he come along. I give it to him to take it up and mail it, see? If they don't send me a stamped envelope, I don't do anything about it. I just throw it in the wastebasket. Thunder! It's got so it's 15 cents. Why good Lord almighty. Used to, when it was only three cents, I'd just put a stamp on it and send it back to them. But now it costs so much I say fizzle on that."

Or ... "You know I fell down there one day, right just inside the garage there.... I missed the last step on the ladder and I thought I was gonna fall. When I start to fall, I just turn loose and fall. If you try to hold on to something, you're liable to break your arm."

Or ... "In the fall of '17, that's when they had the big snow, the big snow. That's when the quail all died. My dad went out looking for them to feed them and good Lord almighty, he found the whole bunch of them dead. They couldn't get under the snow. See, the snow was so heavy. Well, up there it rained on top of it. Froze it, see? Now the rabbits, they'd dig themselves in there but the quail couldn't get in there."

When the cassette tape ran out, it seemed a good time to end the interview. They never really discussed that infamous bribery scandal that soiled the 1919 World Series. The boy never heard of it, the Hall of Famer didn't bring it up, and the boy's father broached the subject too late to get anything recorded. All in all, however, things had gone tremendously well. At one point the boy could not believe it when Edd said he'd never heard of Rod Carew, the six-time American League batting champ, one season removed from a .388 batting average. To a teenage sports nut in the late '70s, that was like saying he'd never heard of Jimmy Carter. But Edd disliked modern baseball and didn't keep tabs on its latest crop of stars. They were all second-rate compared to his era's standouts. Send those present-day hitters back in time and they couldn't handle the bigger strike zone, foreign-substance pitches or worn-out baseballs. Not to mention the superior competition.

Though his message often sounded negative, Edd's blunt delivery usually brought a laugh. Homespun humor sprinkled through a delightfully dizzying personality that was gregarious and engaging, yet obstinate and a tad

Edd took a break from lawn mowing to talk baseball to a group of strangers that dropped by unannounced. Clockwise from left are Christia (Stinson) Ward, Conrad Stinson, Mitchell Stinson (author), Roush, and Ruth Potter (photograph by Donna Stinson).

cantankerous. He held the small audience in the palms of his calloused hands. Once, Edd waved both arms to emphasize a point and one came close to the head of a female listener. He paused, then playfully swung the arm back into the same place, flashed that million-dollar smile and said, "Look out!" He was a charmer, this guy.

Resilient, too. It had only been a couple months since Edd's wife died, yet he held his head high, laughed freely and showed warmth toward total strangers. All that while dealing with his own health issues. Edd suffered a stroke years earlier and it still affected his speech. "See, after I had that stroke, some of these names doesn't come to me right quick," he explained. "(But) I never lost any cuss words, I know all of them.... I had the stroke on the wrong side."

In addition to a cassette full of magic, the boy left with two autographs — one on a baseball, the other adorning an Edd Roush postcard, issued by the Baseball Hall of Fame. Always prepared for signature hunters, Edd rarely left the house without a stack of those cards in his shirt pocket.

A couple years later, the kid returned for another round. Much of the conversation sounded familiar: the strike zone was from here to here; Roush and his three beers; when the game started all friendship ceased. He broached different subjects, too, most notably the Black Sox World Series when several Chicago White Sox took a dive against the Cincinnati Reds. Eight were eventually banned from baseball.

"Yeah, so what? Maybe they did and maybe they didn't. Course, they put eight of them out of it. Maybe they did. Back in those days they threw ball games. Things happened back in those days.... I think we would have beat them anyway and right dang quick.

"...What the hell! Nobody knows what in the hell was goin' on then. As I was told, they was supposed to throw the first ball game to Cincinnati and they didn't get the money (after) the first ball game and after that they went out and tried to win. They don't tell you that. They don't tell you that in anything, but that's the way they told me, see.... Now there's been all kinds of stories about it and nobody knows what in the hell it is."

Owner of two National League batting crowns, Roush was a 26-year-old wunderkind back then. Like others in the baseball community, he'd heard rumors about a White Sox conspiracy, but also got tipped off that gamblers were going after Reds players. A Cincinnati pitcher confirmed the rumor, saying he threatened to deck the lowlife who offered him a $5,000 bribe. This was sensational stuff from an eyewitness to the most infamous episode in baseball history.

The old guy proved crankier during the second interview. Attacks on modern baseball carried more venom and things just generally bothered him more. He bemoaned the pervasive presence of black major leaguers. They were an unskilled, overrated lot. But then again, so were the whites. What about the old Negro league stars from Roush's era? Good within their own group, he answered, but damn few could've played with the big boys.

Edd cursed a lot in this interview, something that didn't happen much in 1978. His eyes seemed permanently bloodshot and he moved with an unsteady gait. Two years is a lot of time for a body succumbing to it. Out of the blue, he accused listeners of doubting his word.

"They come in here and ask me this, that and the other and I tell 'em. Goddamn it, you ain't going to pay any attention to it to start with. When I tell you the strike zone is from here to here and when I played it was up here, you look at me like I'm a nut, (like) something's wrong with me."

And ... "Well, anyhow, it's no use telling you guys anything because you don't pay any attention to it. Course, back in those days they didn't have television. If they'd have had television you'd see all of it. But they didn't have any television. That come along in the '30s. So you listen to me talk and you say, 'That fella's nuts.'"

And ... "Now a lot of this stuff you think is a lot of baloney. Stuff that I know. When I played the goddamned outfield, I played that outfield. I went and got the damn ball. What in the hell are they doing today? Ah, so what?"

Maybe a little venting was good for Edd. A closer look at his unbridled side might've illuminated the audience too. Regardless, the rants wounded no feelings and created only minor awkwardness, a small price to pay for a mostly cordial and exceptionally educational exchange. Besides, it was fun when he aimed that sharp tongue elsewhere — toward baseball executives, for example. "They didn't know what the hell the score was, to tell ya the damn truth. They didn't know what the hell a ballplayer was. They were the god-damndest people I ever saw. They'd go out and buy somebody and he ain't worth a shit. Good God almighty!"

Or sportswriters: "The writers, they don't know their ass from a hole in the ground, them goddamned writers. They don't know anything about a ballplayer to start with. They're writers. But they put you in (the Hall of Fame). I told 'em, I said, 'Writers? What the hell do they know about base-ball? They're writers!' Fizzle!"

Or the faster pace of games during his era: "(Pitchers) got up there and threw the goddamned mother. They didn't sit back there and dig out a god-damned hole and then come in and look at it and so on. (The umpire would say) 'Get in there and pitch or else.' And what in the hell have you got today? If they played a game in an hour and 15 minutes, they couldn't sell anything."

By the end of this interview, Edd couldn't find his balance to walk. Sitting in that backyard so long had thrown off a fragile equilibrium, so the visitors kept him upright as he slowly shuffled toward the front door of his three-bedroom house. Five decades earlier, he'd bought it for $4,500, then spent another $4,500 on extensive remodeling. It became a landmark of sorts — home to a nationally renowned ballplayer, his wife Essie, and daughter Mary. The Roushes were as much a part of that neighborhood as the dirt it rested on.

Edd and Essie would slowly become old there. Still vibrant in the latter stages of life, Edd took community leadership roles, serving on the town board, school board and volunteer fire department. He owned property just out of town and regularly hosted big cookouts at his cabin.

The Roushes embraced Florida in the '50s, building a house in Bradenton and spending their winters there. But they always returned to their beloved Oakland City when the seasons changed. It was a good life, a good *long* life. Time's inevitable decline was showing by 1980, however, and Edd needed help to get through his own front door. A neighbor peered over and asked if "Mr. Roush" was OK, her voice a mix of concern and foreboding. She seemed only partly reassured by the answer that he was simply woozy.

Toting the tape recorder in one hand, the teen-age interviewer used his other to balance Edd by the shoulder. They slowly entered the once-bustling home, thick with memories but sadly quiet without its matron. Entering his living room the former speed demon eased into a comfortably padded reclining chair, then kindly assured the concerned visitors he felt fine. Both sides exchanged cheerful goodbyes, one gushing gratitude for the other's company. Mister Roush smiled broadly throughout and kept smiling as the door closed.

The old charmer was back.

1

Roughs in the Diamond

We like to believe, in Indiana, that we have developed a certain type of prominent citizen who has acquired the wisdom and gloss which come from living in town, without surrendering the homey virtues and the horse sense which are the heritage of those born out in the country ... men large enough to hold their own in any company and yet, each one of them, as common as an old shoe when walked up to on the human side. — American Magazine, *1922*[1]

Think of Indiana and the big orange ball comes to mind. Buried somewhere beneath the state's rich basketball lore is that little spheroid from the national pastime.

Sure, Hoosiers like baseball as much as the next guy. They'll make road trips west to watch the St. Louis Cardinals, east for the Cincinnati Reds and north to catch the Cubs or White Sox in Chicago. But their history and passion, so the theory goes, are etched indoors on hardwood floors.

After all, Indiana produced two strong candidates in the "greatest basketball player of all time" argument before Michael Jordan settled the question. Or did he? Some hardliners still believe Indianapolis native Oscar Robertson deserves the imaginary crown. If that's true, Jordan wasn't even the best guard of all time.

In an era when referees still enforced traveling rules, Robertson dominated the game at every level. He led Crispus Attucks High School to two state championships and won three national scoring titles at the University of Cincinnati. Then came an amazing professional career, highlighted by a 1961–62 season that remains the gold standard of individual achievement. It unofficially changed his name to "Oscar Robertson, the Only Player to Average a Triple-Double for an Entire Season." (That's double figures in points, rebounds and assists.) It remains his name today; even "Air Jordan" couldn't change "only" to "first."

In the '80s, another Hoosier great ascended into the national spotlight.

It was Larry Bird, "the Say Hayseed Kid." Today, it may seem like a stretch nominating Bird for greatest, but the concept wasn't far-fetched when he guided the Boston Celtics to five NBA finals and three championships. In addition to his uncanny shooting touch and court awareness, the self-professed "Hick from French Lick" owned an intangible quality that separated him from the pack. It became part of *his* name — "Larry Bird, He Makes the Players Around Him Better," which basically means the man was a remarkable passer.

Greatest college coach? Case closed, the honor goes to a Purdue All-America who played high school ball in Martinsville, a town located just south of Indianapolis, the state's capital and geographic center. John Wooden led UCLA to a staggering 10 NCAA titles, including seven straight, from 1967 to 1973. Oscar Robertson, Larry Bird and John Wooden — three immortals who are only the shimmering tip of a Hoosier hoop iceberg. But look beyond the ice and diamonds come into focus. Baseball ruled Indiana when basketball was still in diapers and peach baskets.

The state produced scores of big-time big leaguers during the old days, including a pair of elite pitchers who were born about 50 miles apart in the 1870s. Amos "The Hoosier Thunderbolt" Rusie hailed from Mooresville, near Indianapolis. Armed with a frightening fastball, he became a star for the ancient New York Giants, winning 233 games from 1890 to 1898. Mordecai "Three Finger" Brown gained fame and an unforgettable nickname from a childhood farming accident in rural Nyesville. He lost part of an index finger when his right hand became trapped in a feed chopper. Yet a silver lining sprang from the cloud of catastrophe; that stump imparted unusual spin, which led to unfathomable ball movement. With Brown as ace of their pitching staff, the Chicago Cubs played in three straight World Series, from 1906 to 1908, and won two of them. He finished a 14-year career with 239 wins.

One of baseball's earliest home run kings was practically neighbors with Rusie and Brown. Big Sam Thompson came from Danville, slightly west of the state capital, where he eventually made a name in minor league ball. Joining the National League in 1885, he cranked out 128 home runs over the next 14 years and retired with the second-highest total in that circuit's short history. Thompson stayed at No. 2 until Babe Ruth stormed past him in 1921.

Oscar Charleston emerged from the Indianapolis sandlots to become a Negro league superstar of the 1920s and early '30s. Some old-timers called him the finest black player of all time, better than Josh Gibson, Satchel Paige or Cool Papa Bell, which makes Charleston a legitimate candidate for best *ever*, regardless of color.

Yes, Indiana is baseball country; it's as much a part of the Hoosier landscape as corn stalks and coal mines. Along with crops and black rocks, those fields would harvest a steady stream of pro ballplayers. The southern soil proved especially fertile for growing major leaguers. Terre Haute, for example, was the birthplace of Pittsburgh Pirates star Max Carey and talented Giants pitcher Art Nehf. Carey won a championship with Indian Springs native Vic Aldridge, Pittsburgh's ace hurler during the 1925 World Series. Born east of Vincennes in tiny Sandborn, Grover Lowdermilk spent nine years in the bigs and pitched one inning for the losing side of the 1919 Fall Classic. A rowboat ride away from Louisville, New Albany saw the life debut of Billy Hermann, a future Chicago Cubs hero who played on three pennant winners during the Depression.

In addition to the esteemed, many more saw brief and undistinguished tenures but at least made it to the mountaintop. Look hard at the tapestry of baseball history and a lot of Hoosier red comes into focus. As the decades rolled by, new Indiana stars sprouted, particularly in the extreme south. Born during baseball's heady days in the roaring '20s, Petersburg's Gil Hodges would become a Brooklyn Dodger legend and then champion manager of the 1969 "Miracle Mets." Near the end of Gil's days, a baby with a future was born in Evansville. His name was Don Mattingly, who became the best Yankee first baseman since Lou Gehrig. When "Donnie Baseball" wound down, another chosen one came into the world at Jasper. This one answers to Scott Rolen and some called him the most talented third baseman of all time. He's the latest torchbearer in that proud pipeline to the majors, a geographical lineage that's produced some of the finest performers in baseball history.

Standing atop them all was an iron-jawed Oakland City boy named Edd J. Roush. In a baseball bible, he'd rest somewhere between the Old Testament and the New. Edd was old when Dizzy Dean and Joe DiMaggio were new, new when Honus Wagner and Christy Mathewson were old. His career reads like a pastime fable. He traded epithets with John McGraw, won Ty Cobb's respect, earned Rogers Hornsby's praise, and ran a footrace against Jim Thorpe. He could throw with either arm and catch barehanded, and he swung the heaviest bat in the majors at 48 ounces. Back when owners had all the power, Edd leveled the field through hard-nosed holdouts and unyielding stands at the negotiating table. Winning two batting titles and nearly taking a third, he became the National League's preeminent hitter during the last years of the Deadball Era.

Every Roush plate appearance started with a homage to restless leg syndrome; he moved around the batter's box like a caged lion, looking for that perfect moment to break out and claw his captor. Even with a pitch in flight, the body remained in motion. It was a frenetic approach that no coach would ever teach and no manager could ever change. Edd did things his own way.

Then there's the biggest claim to fame of all: a young Roush tanned handsomely on mega-watt exposure from the 1919 Black Sox World Series. It remains the most notorious Fall Classic ever, and he played a leading role for the good guys. History would better remember the disgraced eight, who were indicted, acquitted, and then banned from baseball by a wild-haired rookie commissioner named Kenesaw Mountain Landis. But Edd towered like a giant in 1919 as the best player on the first major league champion in Cincinnati history. His fame continued to soar during the 1920s, right along with his batting average. Renowned baseball men sat up and took notice. In a 1927 syndicated column, Grover Cleveland Alexander wrote, "Of all the batters I have faced ... Edd Roush and Ross Young(s) are the trickiest. I won't say they are the hardest hitters but they are the trickiest, smartest."

On the downside of a 20-year National League career that produced 373 wins, Alexander had faced some of history's greatest hitters. Wagner, Hornsby, Frankie Frisch, Paul Waner, Pie Traynor. They all ranked behind Edd for sheer craftiness. (And Youngs, too, but that's a book for another day.)

Veteran pitcher Fred Toney considered himself quite adept at finding holes in the swings of National League hitters. When he encountered that Roush stroke, however, the towering Tennessean came up empty. "He must have a weakness, they tell me every batter has and most of them don't hide them very well," Toney said. "But if this baby has one, I, for one, am free to admit that I don't know what it is. I know he hits about everything I throw at him."[2]

In his 1962 autobiography, *Casey at the Bat,* legendary manager Casey Stengel named Willie Mays as the best center fielder of all time. Edd Roush ranked second. "He was a great player with the dead ball and played very good when the lively ball came in. He could hit the ball, he could go and catch it."[3]

Edd became the Ty Cobb of the National League, an elite athlete who ran fast, played hard and carried a tough-guy chip on his shoulder. He saw opponents as enemies and had no qualms about using cleats like base path bayonets. Cobb lived that credo for a decade before Edd arrived in the majors. Both were cut from the same rough-hewn cloth, with similarities that extended beyond the ball field. They grew up rural, honed young muscles with farm work, and became avid hunters. Both had fathers who died prematurely, brothers who played the game with far less talent, and investment portfolios that allowed them to live well from outside income.

On the diamond, they expected to run between bases without interference, and infielders risked injury by getting in the way. Both subscribed to a "scientific" hitting method and detested the all-or-nothing home run swing that Babe Ruth popularized. They taught the old method as coaches, with hitters improving under their tutelage. In their old age, Edd and Ty criticized

Roush's playing style reminded many of Ty Cobb, above. Long after their careers ended, Cobb urged voters to put Edd in the Hall of Fame (Library of Congress).

modern baseball, assuring everyone within earshot that their generation was better. Sometimes it's hard to tell one man's words from the other's.

On playing the outfield:

COBB: "To protect against deep drives over our heads, we had to perfect a knack of taking a look at the ball, turning our backs, then running at breakneck speed to haul it down.... I've raced back for many a ball on an educated guess where it'd come down."[4]

ROUSH: "When that ball was hit, I knew where it was going. I didn't have to watch that ball all the way. When the ball was hit over my head, I'd turn around and run till I got to where the ball oughta come down and I'd turn around and catch it. Do you see many of them doing that today?"

On the toughness factor, past versus present:

COBB: "That feuding spirit made baseball the idolized game it once was. That spirit is all washed up now.... Love and kisses have replaced crossed swords."[5]

Roush: "Yeah, back in those days, it was a game of the best man stood up, that's all. And they didn't excuse themselves every time they run into ya. When they run into you, they'd (say), 'You better stay out of my way or next time I come in here I'll cut your ears off.'"

On the inferiority of modern players:

Cobb (circa 1960): "I believe that a lineup featuring such as Bob Feller, Joe DiMaggio, Stan Musial, Mickey Mantle, Ted Williams, Willie Mays and Duke Snider would stand little show with the men of my era."[6] (Cobb's career spanned the years from 1905 to 1928.)

Roush (in 1978): "Well, I'll tell you the honest to God truth. Each club's got maybe two or three ballplayers that could have played back in my day and the rest of them wouldn't even have been hardly in the minor leagues."

On metaphor:

Cobb: "When I played ball, I didn't play for fun. To me, it wasn't Parcheesi played under Parcheesi rules."[7]

Roush: "By God, back in those days you didn't play Ping-Pong out there."

As ballplayers, they shared so many similarities of thought and deed. As men, profound differences separated the two. When fans mailed self-addressed stamped envelopes to an elderly Edd, he'd send back an autograph. Old Ty used to peel off the stamps for personal use and burn the letters in a fireplace. Edd's family never stopped loving him; it's unclear whether Cobb's ever dared start. The "Georgia Peach" was practically a stranger to his children and his wives would accuse him of cruelty during divorce proceedings. Edd's one-and-only marriage lasted 64 years and his daughter always remained fiercely protective of her father. Grandchildren and great-grandchildren would always speak fondly of their "Daddaw."

Cobb had his Coca-Cola stocks, millionaire status and a reputation as perhaps the best baseball player of all time, but was destitute in the realm of human relationships. Teammates, opponents, fans and people in general — all obstacles on his base path of life. Few could stand to be around him. Edd, on the other hand, seemed universally respected in the baseball community. Sure, he played a rough brand of ball and there were times when opponents wanted to belt him in the jaw. But lots of players went about business the same way; it was a tough game. Unlike Cobb, Edd could leave warfare on the field. Fans were fond of Roush and sportswriters gushed over his skill. Here was a special player, a rare talent who could beat teams with the glove, bat or winged feet.

Through it all, Roush remained a proud, if not humble small-town guy, never putting on any airs but also never taking any off. Carrying confidence that bordered on swagger, the former farmer stood tall in alien environs. He moved among big-city folk, battled their gladiators in the arena and demanded gold from the sport's emperors. At season's end he'd sheath his sword, break out the hunting rifle and rejoin the rural folk of southern Indiana. Life slowed to a peaceful pace during autumn and winter, and then the battlefields beckoned again in spring. Edd mastered that cycle for nearly two decades. Strong in mind and body, he became a symbol for the virtues of the country way.

2

Cow Teats and Horsehide

I was borned and raised out here and I've been here ever since. Why in the hell would I go someplace else?[1]

On May 8, 1893, Laura Roush gave birth to twin boys in Oakland City, probably at the family farmhouse just outside of town. The blessed event received passing mention from the "News in Brief" section of a fledgling newspaper called the *Oakland City Journal.* "Will Roush is practicing a Da-Da song to two new boys." Mama's role went unreported.

The first-time parents chose names that were simple and lyrical — Edd, Fred. Not Edward and Frederick. Edd and Fred. That's why they spelled Edd with two Ds; the second was equivalent to a stop sign. His full name was Edd J. Roush and it would always be a mystery what the middle initial stood for. That's because it stood for the tenth letter of the alphabet, nothing more. He had one grandfather named Joseph and another named Jerry. By selecting "J" for the middle moniker, the Roushes saluted both sides of the family and favored neither. Fred got the "J" too. William Roush's side had roots in Virginia and its lineage traced back to the days of the American Revolution. His wife was a first-generation American whose father emigrated from Ireland. They say the family tree probably has an Indian branch, as well.

The twins came into a changing world, with one foot firmly entrenched in a provincial past and the other shyly testing the waters of modernity. Less than three decades removed from the Civil War's end, America still ached from the loss of more than a half-million of its bravest souls. Some 21,000 former Union soldiers belonged to an Indiana–Illinois veterans organization that held annual reunions in Indianapolis, and Oakland City sponsored local Grand Army of the Republic gatherings. Meanwhile, a new nationalist fervor had the next generation spoiling for wars to call its own and the country would soon flex its growing muscle, raising the stars and stripes over distant lands.

Out west, the legendary cattle drives continued, although their days were

The Roush twins would've been about five years old when this classic family shot was snapped around 1898. Pictured, from left, are Laura, Edd, Fred and Will (Roush Family Collection).

numbered. Buffalo Bill Cody and Annie Oakley performed feats of marksmanship in their traveling Wild West Show and Wyatt Earp was still going strong, a dozen years after the Shootout at the O.K. Corral. In the sports world, Gentleman Jim Corbett continued his reign as world heavyweight champion, eight months since taking the crown from boxing's first king, John L. Sullivan.

Grover Cleveland sat in the White House and his wife gave birth there. Of course, baby Esther couldn't compare with the darling Oakland City twins, but both sets of parents seemed happy with their lot. Also born in 1893 were a big-beaked tot named Jimmy Durante, silent film diva Mary Pickford and future Hitler henchman Herman Goerring. Down at Ellis Island young Knute Rockne emigrated from Norway, never dreaming that he'd eventually migrate to Notre Dame and become Irish.

In 1893, the earth was less than 20 years removed from invention of the telephone, phonograph, electric light and gas-powered automobile. Once these epic advancements reached the masses, the world would never be the same. In the meantime, life still moved at a leisurely pace for the average Joe. Unless, that is, he joined the growing numbers who left their rural roots to settle in the big city.

Nobody could mistake Oakland City for a metropolis, but it wasn't exactly "Bumpkinville" either. Sure, horse-drawn hearses trotted through town, but even in New York horses remained a major source of transportation. Big-city traffic often congested into a quagmire of trolleys, cable cars and beasts of burden.

Edd's hometown was just 37 years old when he became an infant resident.

Named Oakland for the stunning grove of oak trees that covered part of the landscape, it later added City to differentiate itself from a settlement with the same name. The town hosted an annual fair that featured horse races, band music and walks along the midway. Built above a store was an opera house that played host to high school commencements, lectures, plays and even an occasional opera. Relatively speaking, Oakland City was a happening place. At the local shaving parlor a fellow could get all gussied up for 40 cents — the package price of a shave, haircut and head cleaning. A college opened in 1891, lending higher-education prestige to the area. Sponsored by the General Baptist Church, it proudly presented its first graduating class in 1894, handing out four diplomas.

Edd's father, Will Roush, is shown here in a baseball portrait from 1895 (Roush Family Collection).

This was the society little Edd and Fred entered, on sands that would continue shifting throughout their childhood. Ahead lay the creation of radio, air travel, the World Series and a splendid little war with Spain. Yet even when progress shook the outside world, the Roushes remained on stable ground. Rhythms of country life continued as they always had — early to rise, early to bed, hard work in between. Growing up on their dad's dairy farm, the boys woke before the sun and grew strong from outdoor chores. They milked cows twice a day. That squeezing motion built powerful forearms, along with vise-like grips, both handy assets for swinging a bat. Milk delivery provided a full-body workout, though the family horse and wagon eased their burden somewhat. They say the twins used to make deliveries on the way to school, and then send "Daisy" home unattended. She knew the way.

Bolstering their sense of identity and belonging was a colorful, tight-knit extended family. Grandpa Jerry Harrington was a small child when he departed his Irish homeland and barely more than a kid when he enlisted in the Union Army's Eighth Kentucky Cavalry Regiment. His Civil War record would include the words, "distinguished service." Grandma Mary Johnson Harrington was one of Oakland City's earliest natives, her parents both moving there from different states.

The Roush side didn't migrate to Indiana all at once. First came a short move to east Ohio, not long after grandpa Joseph's 1867 marriage to Caroline Grim in their native West Virginia. He eventually took his family to Oakland City and ran a restaurant there for several years.

William married Laura Harrington in 1891, became a dad two years later, and after his father's death in 1901, settled in as new Roush patriarch. Meanwhile, Edd developed an unusual affliction that stayed with him the rest of his life — he was left-handed. It put him among an underserved minority, with southpaw baseball gloves almost impossible to locate in rural environs. As a result, he trained himself to perform as a righty. The twins never had to sneak off to play ball with their chums because, as a former semi-pro player himself, William approved of that particular diversion. There's an old photograph of him, clad in ancient baseball garb and posing for a portrait. Lean face, sharp nose, solid chin ... take away the mustache and it could double for Edd; not Fred, who looked more like stout mom than dad.

The Roush boys were not identical twins. They shared a similar lifestyle, one that centered on family, farm, school and worn footpaths to nearby Oakland City. Turning 16 years old in 1909, they saw the town turning into something quite different — oil country. Surrounding fields produced about 2,000 barrels a day, along with significant output of natural gas. Of the 40 wells drilled since the discovery of black gold, 24 found oil, nine showed gas, and seven were dry.[2] Oil companies signed deals with farmers to drill on their land, and then brought in workers for the extraction. A new and vibrant subculture melded into Oakland City, and on April 11, the *Journal* welcomed a couple incoming power brokers: "W.H. Heydrick, managing partner, and Jack Lash, superintendent for Michael Murphy & Co., have moved their families to this city. They inquired the conditions of citizenship and were told they must subscribe for the *Journal* and vote the republican ticket. Both had complied with the first condition, and are non-committal on the second. They seem to be all right, however."

The public school year wound toward a close in early May, with a large crowd attending commencement ceremonies at the local Methodist Church. A newspaper tribute displayed waist-up portraits of all high school graduates, including 11 boys dressed in suits and ties and 12 girls in virginal dresses that reached the chin. Included among the dark, grainy photos was a shot of Essie Mae Swallow, Edd's future bride. An Oakland City version of the cultured uptown girl, she played piano at a local theater, sang in a school quartette, and seemed a central figure for social get-togethers with other upright young folk. The second of four children, she followed in the footsteps of an older sister who performed as pianist and vocalist at the nickelodeon.

A grittier type of entertainment was taking place at area diamonds, where summer baseball would soon reach full swing. One day, late in the season, Oakland City's town team found itself short a player and a suggested solution rang out from someone in the crowd: Why not put in that Roush kid? He'd built a good reputation playing with and against other youngsters. Though not rejecting the idea, Edd was much too shy to join the chorus. The manager waited a few more minutes, hoping his regular would arrive but eventually gave in and told the greenhorn to put on a uniform.

Thus began the first step of an epic journey. Four-and-a-half decades later, the memory seemed fresh during Edd's interview for *The Glory of Their Times,* Lawrence Ritter's masterpiece of remembrances from old-time ballplayers. "I went out and had two base hits out of four times up and played a pretty good game in right field.... So I was their regular right fielder for the rest of that season, which didn't have too long to go."

The last sentence casts doubt on a popular theory that Edd's debut occurred in 1909 when he was 16 years old. The season "didn't have too long to go," yet newspaper reports have the Roush name in several mid-summer contests. Unless it's a different Roush, he appeared in a 15–8 loss at Princeton on June 20. With that closer to the beginning of the season than the end, maybe Edd's big break came in 1908 when he was 15. He subtly hinted toward that scenario while

The Roush boys (Edd, left, and Fred) posed for this portrait as teenagers. They're obviously not identical twins (Roush Family Collection).

filling out a National Baseball Hall of Fame questionnaire in 1970. "I started playing with Oakland City (Walk-Overs) town team in 1908. I was 15 years old."

There's more. In *The Glory of Their Times*, Edd says he got his start "around" 1909, when he was "about" 16. But the following quote didn't make it into the book: "...then when I was 15, I think it was, I played with the big team." It's there for all to hear at the Baseball Hall of Fame, which owns a copy of the author's tape-recorded interview with Roush. A complete newspaper record would remove all doubt, but in those days local game stories were less comprehensive and lacked box scores. It's sufficient to say he started young.

Listed as a first baseman, Edd proved he could play multiple positions during the 1909 campaign. On June 27, a big crowd turned out to watch the Walk-Overs' first game at a new city field and "Roush" was the winning pitcher. Henry Geise played solid defense at second that day, though his tall frame and discomfort with grounders would eventually precipitate a position trade of Roush to second and Geise to first.

A side story circulated that the victory over Winslow was aided and abetted by a local oilman who sat in the stands. He flirted with the girlfriend of a visiting player, she flirted back, and the player noticed. The off-field distraction led to on-field errors, and then the two worlds collided. Winslow would have to find a replacement for its disturbed Romeo, who abruptly left the game to retrieve his best gal. The tale apparently aggravated some supporters of the defeated team. After a loss to Mount Carmel in early July, the *Winslow Dispatch* decried, "There was no sensational oil man and pretty girl story to lose the game and no pin heads present to manufacture one."

The Walk-Overs won a lot of games that summer and young Roush became a key contributor. He scored the lone run in a big 1–0 road win against the Oxford Indians, doubling in the top of the ninth and coming home on a Geise hit. This triumph had the *Journal* crowing for its "invincible" squad and calling it the best amateur team in southern Indiana.

A contentious September 5 contest ended in a no-decision against Petersburg. Though held in Oakland City, the game was officiated by a Petersburg ump who supposedly made some raw calls against the home team. Already feeling cheated of a run in the first inning, the locals were in no mood for what happened during the top of the 10th. Arguing that a Petersburg runner never tagged up before scoring the go-ahead run on a sacrifice fly, the Walk-Overs walked right off the field and took all the gate receipts with them. The dispute became a cause célèbre, receiving mention in newspapers across southern Indiana. Pundits expected a court battle over the 60 percent winners share of that controversial contest but the two sides soon reached an out-of-court agreement, with their game declared a tie and 50–50 division of gate receipts.

The Oakland City Walk-Overs (here in 1910) formed one of the finest amateur baseball teams in southern Indiana. Roush is in the back row, second from right (Roush Family Collection).

Edd's stock continued to rise in 1910 and caught attention from Aggie Grant, boss of Evansville's Central League club. He needed a second baseman and a tryout was arranged, but the prospect failed this early audition. Roush remained on a town team that hit new heights that year.

With his squad sporting a 14–1 record through late June, manager Claude Trusler issued a challenge through the *Evansville Courier*. Championing the Walk-Overs as contenders for the amateur championship of southern Indiana, he asked for games against other strong teams. The nonspecific casting-call approach was fairly common practice.

Trusler's troupe continued racking up victories, most by comfortable margins. Suddenly a talented challenger climbed into the ring, the Owensville Athletics. It would be a matchup of geographic extremes, with Owensville situated on the west side of Gibson County and Oakland City at the far east. Owning a 12–3 record as of mid–July, the Athletics provided a source of pride to a town in need of it. Reported the *Owensville New Echo*, "If Owensville cannot have water works, a city building, traction line, etc., we can have a base ball team."

The combatants having split two earlier games, the third was played on neutral ground in Princeton. It seemed important to the host city, too, and the *Princeton Clarion-News* hyped the July 31 contest with front-page coverage. Two special trains arrived in town, unloading fans for this Sunday afternoon battle at Coal Mine Park, and a record crowd of 1,400 descended on the facility. Grandstand and bleacher seats filled quickly, and a standing-room throng spilled onto the field, barely staying in foul territory. Oakland City didn't respond well to the attention, struggling early and finding itself in a 5–2 hole as the game entered the latter innings. Said Princeton's sportswriter, it "looked like the canteloup boys had put one over on the oil diggers."

The Walk-Overs hit a gusher in the top of the seventh, however, scoring three times to tie the contest. Up came Edd Roush, with two outs, the game knotted at 5–5, and a go-ahead run scoring position. He promptly pounded a long fly ball that was misplayed by the right fielder, allowing a sixth run to score. Oakland City held on for a 6–5 victory.

The kings of southern Indiana carried their imaginary crown to Kentucky for an August 7 showdown against the Owensboro Grays. Played in front of 1,500 spectators, it ended in a 4–4 tie after 11 innings. The game couldn't go any longer or Oakland City folks would miss their return ferry ride across the Ohio River. A rematch was played on the same site at the end of August, with the Grays taking a 4–1 decision. This time, the crowd estimate reached 2,000, many of them Hoosiers. Dedicated fans traveled near and far to support their hometown boys, especially when those boys played ball like the mighty Walk-Overs. The 1910 season was a good year.

At some point Edd enrolled at Oakland City College, even though he never graduated high school. Sources say the college president kicked Roush out when it became apparent he came only to play sports and held no interest in academics. A team basketball photo shows he made it at least as far as picture day in 1911. The year before and after, both Edd and his brother posed for pictures with the town hoop team.[3]

Though baseball season beckoned again, different kinds of statistics made headlines in the spring of '11. These came from the 1910 federal census. Oakland City checked in at 2,370 residents, 379 more than in 1900. That made it one of the biggest towns around, outnumbering such baseball rivals as Petersburg (2,170), Winslow (932), Patoka (657), Owensville (1,237) and Fort Branch (1,182). Of course, Evansville remained the unchallenged king of southern Indiana population, at nearly 70,000. In an April 23 exhibition game, the Walk-Overs hosted a Central League team from that metropolis.

Even at full strength, it would've represented a big jump in competition, but Oakland City's pitcher never showed up. With no Plan B to fall back on, the team recruited a hurler from the opposition, and not just any hurler. It was "Dr. Sullivan"—graduate physician, former member of the St. Louis Cardinals and current minor league standout. The big southpaw tossed a two-hitter but was undone by a boatload of errors behind him, as Evansville grabbed a 6–1 decision. The Walk-Overs took some pride in scoring against a team known for shutouts, Sullivan got an unexpected workout, and visiting batters honed their preseason swings against a quality thrower. It was town baseball at its unpredictable best.

Then there were the things you could always count on, such as a heated rivalry between Oakland City and the Gibson County government seat of Princeton. In some ways, it resembled a feuding relationship between brothers. Princeton was bigger (population 6,448) and older (founded in 1814) and got to do everything first. As a young man, Abraham Lincoln came there to get some wool carded and wound up spending the night. Princeton had the fancy courthouse, Interurban train station and broad tax base. Not to mention a baseball facility that everybody wanted to use.

A dozen miles east, Oakland City played the role of a younger sibling with an independent mind. It had those cerebral college types, determined oil chasers and one whale of a ball team. Beneath it all, both towns were tied together as neighbors, Hoosiers and Americans, who would surely rush to each other's aid in a crisis.

A year earlier, the former Princeton Cubs opened their baseball season with new uniforms and a new name. They became the "Rexalls," a title suggested by the guy who bought the uniforms, Floyd J. Biggs, owner of Rexalls drugstore. Oakland City's team was something of a human billboard too. Residents knew "Walk-Over" as both a footwear brand and the name of certain footwear stores. Of course, the dictionary definition of "unopposed or easy victory" gives it a flattering twist.

In an early spring matchup at Princeton's Coal Mine Park, Oakland City trimmed the Rexalls, 9–8. The visitors would later return to administer a 12–1 whitewashing and Edd contributed to the rout with two extra-base hits. But the most dramatic blow came off the bat of a teammate named Reed, whose prodigious home run landed in a distant coal mine water tank. This was a signature shot, something to rub in Princeton faces from 1911 till the end of time.

Back home for a matchup with Huntingburg, the Walk-Overs took to the opposing pitcher's curves "like a duck to a dough pile" and pounded out a 15–4 win. Edd laid the biggest lick—a bases-loaded homer in the third inning—and a fellow named Fred Roush contributed a double. The overshadowed sibling had talent, too.

After an ugly, contentious game resulted in a Princeton forfeit at Oakland City, the two teams scheduled a rematch, this time in Rexalls territory. To prevent favoritism or accusations of such, the two-man officiating crew

Edd Roush, left, and Pete Lowe were stars of the old Oakland City Walk-Overs town team in southern Indiana (Roush Family Collection).

would consist of one ump from each city. Anticipating a huge and energetic crowd, officials arranged for police presence and strung wire around the field to prevent fans from encroaching into ballplayers' territory. About 650 people paid their two bits admission fee on game day and approximately 150 more arrived through indiscreet fence-climbing. This was heady stuff in cornfield, coal mine territory, the game of the year.

Unfortunately, the Walk-Overs would have to play without their two best players. Roush and pitcher Pete Lowe appeared in a July 3 box score, the former delivering three hits and the latter striking out 12 batters. After that contest, they vanished. In their absence, Princeton reclaimed county pride with a 6–4 win. Now it was time for some braggadocio from the other side. The *Clarion-News* reported:

> It was good to be there, it was refreshing to see the way the Rexalls handed defeat to the proud, haughty and chesty Walk-Overs from Oakland City. Some moons ago an Oakland City fan dreamed that the O.C. team was never to suffer defeat. He told his dream to the other O.C. fans and they believed in it. Believing, they became chesty and at times, hard to get along with. The dream shattered yesterday and now a Princeton fan will meet an O.C. fan in tongue bouts with less fear and trembling.

Responding with a figurative "Oh yeah?" the *Journal* fired buckshot at the county seat: "Princeton fans are gloating over a victory from the Walk-Overs Sunday like a small baby over a tinseled toy. They lost their hobby horse and elephant on wheels in two preceding games played with the Walk-Overs this season, and now they are liable to forget that this little bauble handed them by the fates and never taken by ball playing will be easily broken."

Oakland City wasn't accustomed to defeat, and it stung. Yet the team suffered a far greater loss before the game began when Edd took a seat on the Princeton bench. He was a Rexall now, and Princetonians gushed over their good fortune. They'd lured Lowe, too, though neither he nor Edd took part in the big showdown. Why the sudden change of loyalties? The answer was simple enough: Money. Some of the Walk-Overs were getting paid a few bucks for their efforts and Edd wanted similar compensation. He "raised Cain" about it but to no avail, so the pride of Oakland City jumped to Princeton for the princely sum of $5 per game.

On August 6, the unthinkable happened when Roush played second base for Princeton against Oakland City. To make matters more surreal, the game took place at the Walk-Overs home field. A lifetime later, Edd reflected on his defection. "Don't think that didn't cause a ruckus.... A fair amount of hard feelings were stirred up, to say the least. I think there are still one or two around here (who) never have forgiven me to this very day."[4]

Knocking heads with his former teammates, Edd played poorly that day.

How poorly depends on which town newspaper you believe. Princeton had him going 1-for-3 at the plate and committing two errors, while an Oakland City box score put the figures at 0-for-4 and three errors. Despite an off day from its prized recruit, Princeton still left town with a 4–1 victory.

The Rexalls' coup would prove short-lived, however, because Roush soon took a shot at something bigger. On August 16, he traveled south to join a Kitty League team in Kentucky.

3

The Kitty League

The pleasures I have felt in Henderson, under the roof of that log cabin, can never be effaced from my heart until death.—John James Audubon[1]

Word spread about the talented young farm boy. A primitive grapevine carried that Roush reputation through southern Indiana, across the mighty Ohio River and into the northern tip of western Kentucky, a trip of some 40 miles. Here lay the city of Henderson, where local baseball men seemed determined to upgrade their entry in the K.I.T. circuit, better known as Kitty League. The acronym stood for Kentucky-Illinois-Tennessee, though Indiana deserved a letter, too. It was a Class D minor league, the lowest rung on a long and slippery ladder.

Henderson possessed pioneer status, fielding a Kitty entry from 1903 to 1905 and supplying one of the league's first presidents. After a five-year absence, the city rejoined in June of 1911 when the McLeansboro franchise folded. City authorities passed a "no Sunday baseball" ordinance in that southeast Illinois town and team officials predicted the coffers would run dry without games on the Sabbath. It seemed like raw treatment for the defending pennant winners. Exit McLeansboro, enter Henderson.

Hopkinsville owned an insurmountable lead in the standings but the Kitty League operated on a split-season format, and the second 63-game campaign kicked off in mid–July. Henderson fans had high hopes for season two, though that optimism dimmed when their Hens fizzled to a 10–17 start, 11 games out of first. On August 8, the team's board of directors unanimously agreed to pursue better talent. Their quick fix formula was simple: release mediocre players and lure better ones from other low-level circuits, such as the Cotton States, Michigan State or Three I (Indiana, Illinois, Iowa). Sending out feelers via telegram and telephone, Hens management received encouraging responses from some relatively accomplished athletes. There were also the unproven commodities from the sticks, amateurs who excelled against questionable competition.

"On Monday a nameless backwoods wonder will arrive to try out with the team.... He is a fielder and may be a Ty Cobb or Joe Jackson. We hope so." If the *Henderson Journal* wasn't referring to Roush in that August 15 tidbit, it should've been. Most people came from rural stock in those days, so "backwoods" wasn't the worst insult in the world. Besides, Edd didn't exactly share an inkwell with Laura Ingalls; the family farm lay close enough to Oakland City that he'd run between them while courting his girl. Henderson was far bigger, its population listed at 11,452 in the 1910 census. That was about five times more people than back home and 5,000 more inhabitants than Princeton.

Separated from Evansville's outskirts by the wide river, Henderson had a southern feel and northern latitude. Practically flood-proof, it rested above the southeastern bank of a twisting, horseshoe bend in the Ohio. Henderson was once home to the great naturist John Audubon, who arrived by flatboat in 1810.[2] He found an ornithologist's heaven — nesting areas for countless migratory and native birds. Charles Dickens spent a layover in the town while traveling by passenger steamboat in 1842. City founder Richard Henderson had hired Daniel Boone to blaze a wilderness trail from Tennessee to Kentucky.[3]

As a result, Henderson had some flavor by 1911, not all of it palatable. The northern border was a Civil War–era dividing line between free and slave, though not between Union and Confederate. Kentucky chose neutrality as its official stance and sympathies shot both ways in Henderson County. When rebel General John Hunt Morgan led a raid across south central Indiana in 1863, Edd's grandpa Harrington was among the bluecoats who gave chase. He'd probably enlisted in Henderson, site of the nearest Union recruiting post. A half-century later, the Irishman's progeny followed in his footsteps while answering an entirely different call to duty. Barely 18 years old, Edd arrived by passenger train, a wooden bat his only weapon.

On August 16, 1911, the *Henderson Daily Gleaner* trumpeted news that another horsehide mercenary had accepted terms with the "Chickens." His name was Roush. The article made no mention of a first name, but this was the custom of old-time sportswriters — they identified athletes by field position, and "second baseman Roush" was one of the best hitting infielders in independent baseball. Edd's pact called for $70 a month and the paperwork survives to this day, with a handwritten "seven" drawn over a "six." He apparently bargained a $10 concession in his very first contract negotiation.

Further reports had him arriving on a hot Wednesday night. Temperatures had boiled higher than 100 all day and a drugstore thermometer reportedly registered 98 degrees at 10:30 P.M. If Edd's body clock still ran on cow-milking time, he was probably snoozing by then. When he woke the next day, opportunity accompanied the rising sun; young Roush would get his first true taste of professional ball during a fairly significant showdown against a strong team from Cairo, Illinois. Bringing a solid 17–10 record into town, the Swamp Angels stood third in the Kitty standings, 4½ games out of first place and a half-game from second. A few wins over the lowly Hens and Cairo could climb the ladder.

But this wasn't the same team opponents had been thumping all summer. Henderson won, 3–1, and the *Gleaner*'s beat writer deemed Edd's debut a smashing success. Star of the game honors went to spitballer Tommy Wright, who slobbered his way to a three-hitter and went 2-for-3 with the bat. Yet the new rookie got just as much ink: "Aside from Wright's superlative heaving, the fine playing of Roush, the new second baseman, pleased most. Roush handled himself like a 24-karet pippin, making the territory around second base look like the strongest section in the infield. He also delivered a hit, which was more than Dummy Hughes could do yesterday."[4]

Hughes was the hotshot first baseman for the enemy. A standard nickname for deaf-mutes, "Dummy" probably wasn't inscribed on his birth certificate. The article goes on to provide an in-depth description of Edd's involvement in a pivotal 4-6-3 double play in the ninth inning. He also made a clutch contribution at the plate, driving in the go-ahead run with a fourth-inning single. According to newspaper accounts, the uprising started when "Enlow swatted the ball for a roost on the middle station." He doubled, in other words. Edd's RBI was "another instance that illustrates the necessity of using the bat when it will do some good." A clutch hit, in other words. The original lines read better, however.

Give the ancient sportswriters their due. Though slanted and overwrought by modern standards, their style still captivates the reader a century later. That's the measuring stick for prose that transcends time and these scribes scribbled well. Just look at the last sentence and its self-conscious, yet pedestrian attempt at alliteration. Old-timers would've expressed the same sentiment with far greater skill.

Hens baseball received major league coverage from the city press, with extensive daily game reports, short sidebars, full box scores and tidbits columns. When they showed just an inkling of success with that win over Cairo, the *Gleaner* praised business manager Jake Zimbro for spending a whopping $25 on telegrams and phone messages while beating the bushes for talent. "He succeeded in securing, judging from yesterday's playing, three star players in Enloe, Roush and Jordan. All have signed their contracts and will be held over for next season unless sold or drafted by some higher league. It looks like these three men should bring the club a thousand dollars if sold or drafted."[5]

Barely 24 hours since crossing the Ohio, Edd floated neck-deep in expectations. That hype carried through the next day when Henderson whipped Cairo, 6–1. Though both went only 1-for-4 at the plate, the press paid regal homage to its new middle infielders — Roush at second and Enloe at shortstop.

On Saturday, Henderson would go for the sweep, an ignominy that Cairo had yet to suffer in 1911. By Sunday, everybody would be talking about the game's incredible ending. Henderson led, 4–3, with two outs in the bottom of the ninth when a Cairo player belted a prodigious drive. Right fielder Morgan sprinted after it in what seemed futile pursuit. The *Gleaner* chronicled the rest of the story in fable-like form, resembling a cross between "The Tortoise and the Hare," and "The Little Engine That Could." The ball lands far away and rolls, rolls, rolls. It travels through weeds and other rough terrain while Morgan pursues. Meanwhile, the batter is gleefully prancing around the bases, basking in the glow of his game-tying homer. Just as he passed third base, Morgan finally got hold of the ball and rocketed a throw to his first baseman. The relay toss beat the runner by a foot — game over, sweep complete. Fans swarmed onto the field in celebration.

Excitement had returned to Henderson baseball and nobody showed more enthusiasm than a local beat writer, who taunted the vanquished with an in-your-face lead to Sunday's game story: "The chickens made worms of the Swamp Angels and then ate them completely. Anyone able to find any shreds left on the lot where the ball cavorts is requested by (Henderson manager) Ollie Gfroerer to send them to Cairo by express."

A heckler couldn't have said it any better.

With three straight wins over a good team, the Hens suddenly looked respectable. Not that the squad was without merit before; a Cincinnati Reds scout had recently sent a letter inquiring about first baseman Stelle and left fielder Spair. But when that duo found itself surrounded by new talent, things got interesting. Were the Hens for real? They'd soon get a chance to prove it when league-leading Fulton (Kentucky) came to town for a three-game set.

The series opener wasn't the only athletic endeavor of the day. Two Evansville men announced they would run from their homes to Henderson that morning. They planned to stop long enough for a ferry ride across the Ohio River, and then proceed on foot to the local YMCA. Little did those guys know that the trek would become commonplace 80 years later, with several hundred hoofers taking part in the annual Arts Fest River Run, a 12-kilometer race that began in Henderson, crossed the U.S. 41 Bridge, and ended on Evansville's downtown waterfront. Diminutive Africans dominated the event and gathered the prize money, causing seismic tremors from countless Confederates and copperheads spinning in their graves.

Things were simpler in 1911 when the Hens settled in for a Sunday thriller before 1,000 fans and prevailed, 1–0. Edd finished 0-for-3 on the afternoon, threw out three runners and committed an error. Nothing special for the Hoosier expatriate, but a win was a win. And what a win this was, besting a powerhouse that brought a gaudy 22–7 record into town.

A packed house witnessed game two on Monday and didn't leave disappointed — Henderson 5, Fulton 0. Spair crushed a two-run homer and, in an apparent case of fashionable exaggeration, a sportswriter reported the ball traveling 700 feet before bouncing off a tree. He'd supposedly circled the bases and swallowed a fresh cup of water by the time it was returned to the diamond.

Edd's stats looked similar to his Sunday output, going 0-for-4 with one error, and he threw out three runners. Still, he fielded well and was becoming quite popular with the fans. As the two teams looked toward Tuesday's series finale, Fulton's manager predicted a face-saving victory.

"I know that I am up against it here, as Henderson has the fastest team in the league at present, but I am going to try hard to win the last game, and will win if I possibly can. (Pitcher) Humphries, whom I consider a wonder in this league, and who beat Henderson every game that he had pitched against them, except last Sunday, will pitch for Fulton, and I think that he will get away with his game."[6]

That's just one of the quotes attributed to Manager Rainey. It's hard to imagine those stilted sentences pouring out the breathless mouth of a baseball chief. Maybe managers talked like that 100 years ago, and maybe journalists had a gift for recreating lengthy quotes before the advent of portable recording devices. Or maybe sportswriters took some revisionist liberties.

Tuesday rolled around and, even on a weekday, there was competition for Henderson's entertainment dollar and 25-cent admission cost. The local nickelodeon showcased a film of the first Indianapolis 500. For the price of a nickel, folks could watch excerpts from the May 30 competition when the winner averaged a death-defying 74.6 miles per hour. Other films would be shown, too, but that fledgling race was the centerpiece. None of it conflicted with the big game, however, because "picture" watching was an evening activity. Afternoon belonged to baseball and a huge crowd could be expected on the home grounds. Henderson collected only five hits but made them count in a 4–0 triumph.

With 29 consecutive scoreless innings from their pitching staff, the Hens had become the Kitty's hottest team. Unfortunately, the same could not be said for young Mr. Roush. During that glorious sweep Edd recorded nary a knock, going 0-for-10 at the plate. He was just 3-for-19 since joining the team, and management took note of his productivity, or lack thereof.

Next up for the high-flying Hens was a southerly 75-mile road trip, where they would launch a three-game series against the league's second-place team. Already winners of the first-half flag, Hopkinsville trailed by four games in season two. The *Hopkinsville Kentuckian* predicted bad things for the invaders. "The Henderson 'Chickens' will be served in three different styles — Wednesday broiled, Thursday stewed and Friday fried. Come on cockerels and take your choice."

More than 1,000 locals showed up for the community broil-out and they did, indeed, see a Hens streak come to an end — the streak of scoreless innings, that is. Henderson rolled to a 10–1 triumph, putting its consecutive-win mark at seven. The next day's contest went to extra innings after "Hoptown" tied things up with a run in the bottom of the ninth, but the Hens struck back in the 10th and took a 5–4 decision.

With eight consecutive victories, the Hens were smoking and their bandwagon grew larger by the day. When the *Gleaner* posted inning-by-inning updates of the latest road games, hundreds crowded the sidewalks around the newspaper's office. After taking care of business down south, the team returned home to a hero's welcome. Approximately 1,500 fanatics greeted their train at Union Station, with players emerging to a deafening din of shouts, tin whistles and cow bells. A band belted out happy tunes that were barely audible above the noise.

Showered with warm words and pats on the back as they slowly edged through chaos, the conquerors joined their supporters in a procession uptown. Musicians marched out front alongside the athletes and performed "Hail, Hail the Gang's All Here," with vocal accompaniment by hundreds of cheerful voices from behind. As the group moved west on Second Street, fireworks climaxed the tribute. Darkness practically disappeared for the rest of the journey, as a series of "skyrockets" lit the night sky.

The throngs grew larger when residents poured from their houses and lined the parade route for a closer look at the revelers. It ended at Kingdon Hotel, where the band performed that melancholy standard, "My Old Kentucky Home." A few more cheers, some final curtain calls, and the clamor finally faded.

The Hens took a day off, then launched their next homestand with a 5–1 triumph over red-hot Vincennes, Indiana, winner of 12 of its last 16 games. Spair provided all the necessary offense on one swing of the bat, launching a two-run homer into the distant trees of left field, and Edd recorded the first multiple-hit game of his Kitty career. He went 2-for-4 but also made a couple errors, raising his total to five in six games.

A couple months earlier, the Hens called Illinois home and tried to squeeze a living from a little town of about 2,000 people. Less than two weeks previous, their prospects for contention looked depressingly bleak. Now they'd won nine straight, owned a 19–17 mark, sat a half-game out of third and a full game from second. Fulton enjoyed a six-game bulge over its nearest competition and seven over the Hens. Still, Hendersonians expected to make a run at the flag and, with a win on Sunday, their boys could leapfrog two places in the standings.

It was exciting stuff, to be sure, but lost all relevance for Edd. By Monday, he was a plucked hen. Management brought in a veteran outfielder from the Cotton States League, Spair moved from left field to second base, and young Roush's services were no longer required. A Tuesday blurb explained his demise: "Roush and Morgan have been released. Neither could hit hard enough and to cap the climax, Roush was getting punk in his fielding."[7]

Punk fielding? Lousy hitting? Only 10 days earlier Edd was praised for fast glovework and a clutch bat. The *Gleaner* immediately sang praises for the latest lineup shift, claiming the Hens looked "50 percent" stronger with Spair at second and Tommy Copeland in left field. In another ten days, Henderson signed a new second baseman from the Texas State League who became the next big thing.

What a whirlwind for Edd Roush, starting with his hometown team, followed by a brief fling in rival Princeton, then high praise in Kentucky, followed quickly by termination with extreme prejudice. Now August was almost over and the end of baseball season was in sight.

Edd rejected overtures to rejoin his hometown Walk-Overs in 1912. Instead, he went right back to Princeton, where organizers planned a move to the Ohio Valley League. Coal Mine Park was changed to Ohio Valley Trolley League Park, a nightmarishly long title for headline writers, but it signified advancement on all other fronts.

Joining an organized circuit was a great leap forward from town ball. Princeton once fielded a Kitty team and the memory seemed a source of civic pride. Structured as an amateur association with small player payments permitted, the O.V. League would include other Hoosier cities, such as Evansville, Rockport, Boonville and Mt. Vernon, plus Owensboro, Kentucky. Officials expected a short, manageable season, consisting of around 24 games played on Sundays and holidays.

Community excitement grew as a countdown continued and it seemed that all conversations inevitably shifted to baseball when sporting folk gathered in Princeton. But the team would have to share spring headlines with an international disaster at sea after the British ocean liner *Titanic* hit an iceberg in frigid Atlantic waters, some 1,600 miles northeast of New York City. An early report had all passengers safe, with the ship still afloat and getting towed toward eastern Canadian shores. A couple columns east of that April

15 front-page story was a report on Princeton's exhibition game opener, a 7–0 victory over the Evansville Goldblumes. Roush scored the franchise's first run after doubling in the first inning and stealing third.

One day later, the *Clarion-News* plastered its front section with multiple accounts of an unfolding tragedy. By now, everybody knew the *Titanic* rested on an ocean floor and about 1,500 people lost their lives. It was the story of the century.

Edd rediscovered his batting stroke in Princeton and the team proved itself a consistent contender as the season approached its six-week mark. But it all proved moot when the Ohio Valley League folded in early June. Princeton was one of four teams that pledged to remain intact and play independent ball. That scenario was better than nothing and probably more pragmatic, because those time-honored regional rivalries always put fannies in the seats. A late July date saw the Winslow Tigers come to town for a ballyhooed doubleheader and 1,200 people attended, with many arriving on a special train from little Winslow and points in between. According to one report, there were so many automobiles in the park that they had to be organized into two rows.

Good players could still get noticed on town teams. A man contacted Edd one day, trying to recruit him for Evansville's new Kitty squad. The Roush response was, "How much?" He liked the answer.

4

Blossoming in Evansville

When I started playin' ball here in Evansville in 1912, I got 80 dollars a month and that was a heck of a lot of money. Nobody had any money. Thunder! Used to come to town on Saturday night with a nickel. Maybe I'd have a nickel and my brother would have a nickel. That was it.[1]

I asked Eddie if he had ever played outfield and he said he wouldn't make an outfielder in a hundred years but that he would help out in a pinch. I told him the town was raring to see him bad and it didn't make much difference where he played. The next morning he was on hand.— General Manager Eddie Sisson[2]

Undaunted by his recent failure in Henderson, Edd took another shot at the Kitty League, this time on the Indiana side of the Ohio River. With borders along Kentucky and Illinois, Evansville was the big kid on a tri-state block and, like an aquatic railroad, the river represented a major source of commerce and transportation. A thriving furniture industry acquired raw materials from easily accessible timberland, with well-traveled logs floating to a collection point at city wharves. Twenty-one factories churned out so much product that Evansville anointed itself the world's largest manufacturer of medium-priced furniture. Also calling the city home were such major companies as Hercules Buggy, Bucyrus Steam Shovel and Fendrich Cigar. As far back as 1904, Coca-Cola established a bottling plant there.

It was a multiple newspaper city and sportswriters purred Kitty stories in 1912. The Evansville Yankees became the newest addition to a streamlined circuit that dropped Fulton, Jackson and Vincennes. A year earlier, Evansville belonged to a superior breed of minor league ball — the Class B Central League. Nicknamed "Evas," that franchise floundered to an ignoble end, not long after its players went on a one-day strike for unpaid salaries in late July. Leaving a mountain of unpaid debts behind, the team transferred to the other end of the state, landing in the Central League president's hometown of South Bend. Those home white uniforms wouldn't make the trip, however. A groundskeeper kept them under lock and key, refusing to hand over his hostages over until he was paid the $97 he was owed.

With the city now starting over in Class D Kitty, nobody knew how fans would react to the downgrade. Attendance was shaky during the early-summer months and word circulated that the Yankees might fold. Appealing to civic pride, team president Benjamin Bosse pushed for more support from the masses. His gift of motivational gab would soon make him mayor, but for now he used it to keep a baseball club afloat.

Though Edd's last Kitty experience ended in unceremonious rejection, round two proved quite different. The Yankees gave him room to run, moving the athletic 19 year old to right field and rarely requiring appearances at second base. Yet the wide pastures exposed a weakness — Edd threw with his weaker arm. It didn't matter much when making those short infield flings, but now he had to heave it long distance. It was time for a new glove, one that fit over the *right* paw. In a long overdue transaction, Edd went to downtown Evansville and bought an appropriate mitt for a buck and change. Roush the righty was no more and that powerful left limb, now unshackled, would make a good player even better. The milestone purchase is typically reported as a 1912 happening, but it might have occurred the following year. An elderly Edd said 1913 in at least one interview. Either way, he became a reborn southpaw at League Park and baseball would never be the same.

Joining a team in third place with a 30–28 record, Edd quickly made a name for himself in his 1912 debut. Never mind that newspapers misspelled it; everybody knew who it was. It was that newcomer who scored twice, knocked in a run, stole two bases and caught three fly balls during a July 26 blowout of visiting Clarksville, Tennessee. The following Monday, "Rausch" went 3-for-7 in a

Edd played Kitty League ball for the Evansville Yankees in 1912. He's in the top row at the far right (Roush Family Collection).

doubleheader. Then came August 2, the day one newspaper started spelling his name correctly: "Roush's Home Run Wins Game in Fourteenth Frame" screamed a headline from the *Evansville Journal-News*. It happened with the Yankees and Cairo tied at one apiece and though the ball didn't clear the deep outfield fence, his drive earned a place in local lore as one of history's longest on the local lot. "Roush's hit was the kind you do not field and if it had not been for the center field fence, which the pill hit on the first bound, the ball would have never been found.... Roush was safe on the home plate long before the ball reached the infield. In fact the majority of the Cairo players had started for the bench before the ball hit the ground."[3]

Clarksville was running away with the pennant, which proved an inspirational story in itself. Kitty doormats a year earlier, the Volunteers now sat 20 games over .500. The only remaining drama rested in the battle for second, with five teams in contention. Henderson occupied the runner-up spot, one game ahead of Evansville and two up on Hopkinsville.

With three weeks remaining in the season, stories began circulating that the Yankees would join a different circuit in 1913 — probably the Central League, possibly the Three I. If it came to fruition, Evansville could join a long list of solid baseball cities from Indiana, Michigan and Ohio. This speculation proved K.I.T. competition had only whetted the thirst of local baseball brokers. Before even finishing the drink in front of them, they clamored for something with a stronger kick. For the time being, however, the Yankees seemed contented Kitties. Though out of the pennant race, they had a shot at second place, and that seemed to matter. It certainly did in 1911, when Henderson newspapers trumpeted their team's rise and stall. Now the Hens found themselves in a similar position, trying to hold off Evansville for runner-up honors.

On August 11 the two teams began an important series in Kentucky, marking Edd's return to the city where he'd been tabbed as both a rising star and unmitigated dud. Here was his chance to prove Henderson should've gone with its first impression. When the Sunday opener kicked off at 3:00 P.M., he saw few familiar faces in the opposing dugout. Edd had played alongside Henderson's starting pitcher during 1911, but strangers occupied all other positions. Even Ollie Gfroerer was gone, denying him the chance to show up his former manager. One powerful naysayer remained, however, and he continued to trash Roush's reputation. In an earlier conversation between management, Evansville's boss heard harsh assessments from the Hens leader.

"I tried Roush out a year ago and you'll find he is only a flivver," Jake Zimbro said. "He can't hit left-handed pitching or low fast ones. You'll turn him loose in a week."[4]

Eddie Sisson watched with amusement when his young protégé drilled a low liner through two outer fences. After losing the opener, Evansville went to extra innings in game two. Hens Nation saw little to worry about when Edd approached the plate with two outs in the 10th inning. The go-ahead run stood at second base, but Roush was a lowly 1-for-8 in the series thus far. Then came the stroke that produced a run-scoring double and launched a career. He was thrown out trying to stretch the hit into a triple, but the damage had already been done. Evansville won, 3–2, and Edd's big blow ignited a weeklong tear that put him on the baseball map.

Over in Henderson, the *Gleaner* focused on the ex–Hen angle. Naturally, a misspelling accompanied his name: "A tall, lank, slim youth who goes by the cognomen of Rausch, a Henderson castoff, released from the Kitty club last year because of his failure to deliver the goods, 'came back' with a vengeance Tuesday, and proved the undoing of his former teammates."[5]

Edd went 2-for-5 and scored once in the following contest, as Evansville grabbed a 5–2 decision in front of about 250 fans. After a slow start, he'd helped his new team take two of three from his old one. The Henderson series marked the end of a long, grueling and mostly losing Yankees road swing. Next came a breakout performance on August 15, with Roush going 4-for-4 while leading the Yankees to a 7–2 win over visiting Hopkinsville.

Beginning August 21, he suddenly went cold, and was held hitless in nine consecutive trips to the plate. He sat out a couple games, then returned to the lineup with a 1-for-5 effort in a 3–2 loss to Clarksville. Only a hundred fans showed up at that home contest, but a diphtheria outbreak might've been responsible for the attendance dip. Thirteen cases were reported on game day and seven more had been added by noon on Tuesday. An area health official said large gatherings could be causing the rapid spread and pointed an accusing finger at county fair crowds.

With the season winding down, Evansville owned a sub–.500 record and trailed second-place Henderson by a bunch. But the two teams had nine more head-to-head matchups on the schedule, and if the Yankees won seven, they could still move up. Edd rose to the occasion during an August 28 doubleheader, belting a homer in the opener and two doubles in game two, but the Yankees could only earn a split. They lost again the next day, all but ending their runner-up aspirations.

Edd posted solid if unspectacular final statistics: a .284 batting average and 17 runs scored in 41 games. His team finished the season at 46–53 and, despite all the trumpet calls for a charge at second, barely avoided fourth. Evansville and Paducah finished in a virtual tie for third with .465 winning percentages. Clarksville outclassed the league, posting a 68–29 record that was 17½ games better than Henderson's 52–48.

In October Edd dusted off his glove and joined some familiar faces for a memorable exhibition game. He'd spent a short stint on the Washington

Grays town team during the summer and now they'd scheduled a contest against the Cincinnati Reds. With three Evansville players bolstering their lineup, the Grays took an 8–7 decision from the barnstorming National Leaguers. Starting a seldom-used pitcher and novice catcher, these weren't exactly the same Reds who went 75–78 during the recently completed season. But the victory still resonated for folks of that Hoosier hamlet, located north of Oakland City.

The off-season saw constant speculation about a Yankees upgrade to greener pastures. Not that they set the Kitty world on fire, but pride demanded something grander. An opportunity soon arose and the franchise did indeed defect to a faster circuit in 1913. Faster paychecks arrived as well, with Edd pulling in a cool $100 per month. The Yanks now belonged to a reorganized Central League that cut back from 12 teams to six. A host of new player-managers took over, five with previous connections to the major leagues.

Evansville welcomed back "Punch" Knoll, a local hero who'd managed its Central League entries in 1907, '08 and '09, delivering a championship in the middle year. He'd spent the last three seasons as skipper of the Central team in Dayton, Ohio. Knoll needn't have worried about how Yankees veterans would react to his return. With wholesale housecleaning of the squad's roster, there was no such thing as a Yankee veteran. The name no longer existed; newspapers now called the team "Punchers." Only one player — Roush — appeared in the box scores of the 1912 finale and the 1913 debut. Knoll put him in center field, which was roughly akin to plopping Wolfgang Amadeus Mozart on a piano bench. Edd would become one of the greatest to ever patrol the middle pasture and it all began on an April afternoon in 1913 when boss Knoll filled out a lineup card at the Louisiana Street ballpark.

Also returning from the previous year's team was Slim Turner, a promising young pitcher who turned 21 in the offseason. Other players owned the usual low-minors origins. Hard-hitting Merton "Moxy" Meixell arrived from New Orleans and the Cotton States League. He'd been drafted four times by major league and Double-A clubs. Down in Tennessee, pitcher Rube Merchant threw two no-hitters against Appalachian League competition before joining Evansville, and third baseman J.W. Kibble came off a respectable season for an Oregon team in the Northwestern League.

Evansville's roster took shape in late March and early April. Now, if the players could only make it to southern Indiana. Standing in their way was horrible Midwestern weather and a historic flood. Every Central League city felt Mother Nature's fury, some more than others. A hundred miles north in Terre Haute, the conditions spawned a tornado that killed 18 people and injured 250. Meanwhile, a "miniature cyclone" damaged the grandstand at Grand Rapids, Michigan.

At the top of the list was four days of lethal flooding in Dayton, Ohio. The *New York Times* ran a series of front-page articles on it, detailing the devastation and its aftermath. Stories of widespread drownings, marooned refugees, martial law, food shortage and buildings destroyed by fire were commonplace. Even when fatality estimates were greatly reduced, Dayton stood alone as the queen of woe. The Cincinnati Reds offered use of Redland Field to their Ohio brethren, at least until things returned to normal.

Fear and floodwaters rose in direct proportion near the Indiana-Illinois border, where the Wabash River pawed at earthen banks around Terre Haute and Vincennes. Farther south, the bloated Ohio stopped at Evansville's doorstep. Beyond were submerged fields with only the tops of old corn stalks visible, along with abandoned houses, with water approaching their window ledges. The city became a refugee center for many of the displaced, offering an island of relief to the soggy downtrodden.

Amidst all this, the baseball team opened spring training March 30. Only four players showed up at League Park that day — city residents Punch Knoll and Dick Grefe, plus Moxy Meixel and Rube Merchant. Management had hoped to have 20 players in town by then but conventional transportation modes proved inadequate. As one writer put it, "The aero plane is about the only means by which the many players on the Eva roster may get into this old burg." He might as well have said spaceship. Ten years after the Wright Brothers' breakthrough at Kitty Hawk, aviation was still in its infancy.

The Ohio reached an unprecedented high of 47.95 feet on April 3, edging past Evansville's old record from 1884. A day later it was 48.3. Every small increase seemed to produce disproportionate damage, with floodwaters creeping or pouring into more and more homes. It was the same with city streets — fine one day and inundated the next. Still, the worst was over and Evansville escaped 1913's great flood without serious harm.

Sporting a skeleton crew at the end of March, the Punchers soon saw enough players trickling in to form a practice squad. Most training took place in-house, as a slate of exhibition games were cancelled on account of thin rosters, bad weather and unreliable train service.

With the Central season opener just a few days away, management had some important decisions to make, especially in the pitching department, where eight moundsmen competed for five jobs. The infield seemed set but a battle was brewing in the outfield and even Edd wasn't assured a slot. Of course, Knoll penciled himself in as starter, but three men had to fight it out for the remaining two positions.

Mayor Charles Heilman declared a half-day holiday for the April 23 opener and agreed to throw out the first pitch. The festival atmosphere had become customary among Central League cities and Evansville was no exception, as organizers planned a mammoth opening day parade. Since the "holiday" didn't apply to public schools, youngsters came up with excuses to miss class. Most settled on the old "dead grandparent" standard, then planned a mass wake at the ballpark.

The *Evansville Courier* reported, "There was terrible mortality among the grandmothers of the pupils of the high school. In fact there were so many people being disposed of in such a ruthless manner that Principal Wiles felt it was his duty to end the slaughter and school was therefore dismissed at 2 o'clock to allow the students to witness the opening game."

Some 3,500 fans watched the Punchers drop a 4–1 decision to Grand Rapids. It still proved a great day for young Roush, who rapped two singles in four at-bats, stole a base, scored his team's lone run, caught two fly balls and cut down a runner at home.

The opposing center fielder had a memorable afternoon as well, redeeming an 0-for-3 start with a three-run double in the pivotal eighth inning. Another victim of the minor league revolving door, he'd be gone by the next time Grand Rapids came to town. Those Roush cleats rested on more stable ground.

Dropping the opener was no big deal but the Punchers suffered a greater loss when Edd went down with an ankle injury. He didn't play the next day during a bounce-back win and was still missing when Evansville beat visiting Fort Wayne in front of 3,000-plus spectators. Then came an April 30 news nugget that must have produced a collective "whew" among local fans: "The Princeton boy's ankle has been restored to shape. Roush is anxious to get back in the fray." Truer words were never written ... except for the "Princeton" part. He was, and would always be, an Oakland City boy.

Returning to action on the first of May, Edd belted two doubles and an over-the-fence home run at Grand Rapids. Three days later, he delivered a single, double and triple during an 8–5 win. Hits kept coming and coming for the Central League's newest wunderkind. As an 85-year-old he still had fond memories of those heady days, recalling, "I only hit .556 the first month of the season. Every time I swung, the ball went out there someplace."[6]

Welcome to stardom, Mr. R-O-U-S-H. Sportswriters were spelling his name correctly and, coincidentally or not, the "c" in "Rousch" disappeared about the same time he began knocking the cover off baseballs. Of course, he hit a few bumps along the way. As a left-handed swinger, Edd sometimes struggled against southpaw pitchers and that shortcoming fueled a brief slump that made him look mortal again.

Evansville fell into the Central League basement with a record of 7–14. Ravaged by injury, the team lost four-fifths of its infield to one malady or another. Roush was a rare bright spot and, even after his slump, still led the league with a .426 batting average. As a Sunday crowd of 2,682 watched every move, he enjoyed a 3-for-4 outing and led Evansville to a 5–2 victory over Dayton on May 18. Now batting in the leadoff position, Edd opened the bottom of the first by belting a missile past the left field wall. "...[T]he ball going at a clip that would skin the combined speed of a dozen aero planes," wrote the *Evansville Press*. "There is no evidence that the ball has fallen yet for it was never recovered." Forty-four years before *Sputnik* orbited the globe, a sports scribe credited Roush with launching the first man-made satellite.

A scout named Dick Kinsella arrived for that weekend homestand. He worked for the mighty New York Giants, the two-time defending National League champs. Edd's Sabbath performance should've piqued their interest; he fielded flawlessly in center and, after the rare leadoff homer, drilled an RBI double and a single. In later years a story circulated that Kinsella came to Evansville for a look-see but never went near the ballpark. He supposedly gave up on Edd the minute he heard a false barbershop tale that young Roush was an unnatural lefty, forced to use the weaker wing after breaking his right arm. Three Evansville newspapers, however, reported a Giants scout sitting in the stands for multiple games and two mentioned the man by name.

In Fort Wayne, league president Louis Heilbroner fielded a major league feeler from Cincinnati. He crafted a reply on May 20, telling Reds president Gary Herrmann that Roush was hitting hard and advising him to take the matter up with Evansville's club. The Detroit Tigers showed interest, too, though their town probably wasn't big enough for two Ty Cobbs. Still, it stokes the imagination to think of that pair as teammates. As things turned out, it was Chicago White Sox scout Ted Sullivan who swooped in to sign young Roush, buying his contract for a princely sum of $3,000. He would continue to hone his craft in Evansville, and then get a late-season call-up to the big show.

Edd committed just in time, for that sizzling stick cooled considerably over the coming months. He remained productive and continued to display dazzling overall talent, but several players passed him in the batting race. By mid–July he ranked sixth, with a .329 mark, and his team had a 30–58 stranglehold on last place. Edd could've hit .800 and it wouldn't have made much difference for this spunky but overmatched bunch.

After delivering a couple singles in an August 8 game at Terre Haute, he disappeared from Evansville box scores for good. The country boy was headed for the big city — Chicago, to be specific. Charles Comiskey wanted a look at his prospect, up close and personal.

5

Major League Audition

Hog Butcher for the World, Tool Maker, Stacker of Wheat, Player with Railroads and the Nation's Freight Handler; Stormy, husky, brawl- ing, City of the Big Shoulders.— Carl Sandburg

Onward and upward, past Vincennes and Terre Haute, into the far reaches of northwest Indiana. The Wabash River is a traveling partner for some 150 miles, then turns right for a separate journey northeast. The path continues another hundred miles, overtaking Crown Point and Hammond, before approaching the southern shore of Lake Michigan. As the crow flies, that's the trek from Evansville to the outskirts of Chicago, the third-largest city in the United States.

The forecast called for mild Wednesday weather on August 20, 1913, and that was welcome news to the South Side baseball fans. They'd suffered enough without Mother Nature piling on. Somewhere in the home locker room, Edd Roush wrapped a stuffy wool jersey around his torso. A huge "S" adorned the front. Nestled in the top curve of the letter was a small "o" and in the bottom an "x," spelling "Sox," as in "White Sox."

Edd finished dressing, went through the standard pre-game preparations, and then pushed his hand into a small pancake glove and trotted onto the field at Comiskey Park. If only for a day, he was the starting center fielder for a major league baseball team. At the tender age of 20, he'd reached the mountaintop. This was the Windy City, a bustling metropolis of more than two million people, and the Sox played under a colossal spotlight. So did their northside neighbors, the Cubs.

Edd walked in the footsteps of the American League's greatest stars; whether playing with or against the home team, they'd all passed through Comiskey at one time or another. A couple holdovers still remained from the Sox team that won the 1906 World Series, just a few seasons after the A.L. joined the majors. This place radiated prestige, yet it had that freshly minted feel, too. A modern monolith, built from steel and concrete, the stadium was barely three years old.

Like the ballpark, young Roush became property of the baseball icon Charles Comiskey. Rising from player to player-manager to owner, he was the kind of self-made mogul that the country adored. To call him an American League pioneer would be an understatement. He cleared the trail that pioneers rode across. Two people are generally credited with breaking the National League's monopoly on big league ball: Comiskey and A.L. president Ban Johnson.

A decade later, some Hoosier greenhorn would try to catch the boss's eye. Edd wasn't part of the White Sox family yet; management just wanted to introduce the kid to major league competition and see how he fared, a common practice when the season is winding down and a team has no pennant hopes.

Roush played alongside some of the same men he would face as opponents in the 1919 World Series. At shortstop that day was a young Buck Weaver, who went down in history as perhaps the most unfortunate selection to the list of banned conspirators. Also on the 1913 roster was Eddie Cicotte, the prime catch for Black Sox gamblers. After coming over from Boston the previous season, he was still trying to find a fit in new environs. Cicotte cut his teeth with the Red Sox in 1908, about the time pioneer pitcher Cy Young was losing his. That's the legend Cicotte shared a dugout with during his first full season in the bigs.

He would become a great hurler in Chicago and it all started in 1913, with an 18–12 record and a 1.58 ERA. Cicotte went on to win 166 games for the White Sox before ending his career in disgrace. That's the future legend Edd Roush shared a dugout with during his introduction to the majors. Six years later, they sat on opposite sides for the most infamous World Series of all time, the batting champ at one end and the 29-game winner at the other.

Cicotte was a choirboy compared to teammate Hal Chase. One of the most fabulously gifted first basemen in history, Chase is better known as the most unrepentant game-thrower who ever wore a big league uniform. Coming to Chicago in an early summer trade with the New York Yankees, he wore a Sox uniform for most of 1913 and part of the following season.

Edd also crossed paths with fellow youngster Ray Schalk, destined to become a squeaky-clean bastion of integrity during the Black Sox series. After seeing limited action the previous year, the 21-year-old catcher approached completion of his first full season. It marked the start of a noble 18-year tour, 17 of them in a White Sox uniform.

With his team residing 14½ games out of first place, manager Nixey Callahan decided to take a look at young prospects. Edd Roush would start against the defending world champions, the Boston Red Sox. Mired in fifth place among A.L. teams, the champs fizzled in '13 but still wore imaginary crowns. These were the same players who had reached baseball nirvana. Manning the center field post was Tris Speaker, a 25-year-old Texan already recognized as one of the game's greats.

In 1913, Roush briefly became the property of Charles Comiskey (pictured) and the Chicago White Sox. He got a late season audition before being shipped out to Lincoln, Nebraska (Library of Congress).

Edd had a lot in common with Speaker — both were left-handed, fleet-footed, and stood a tad under six-feet. Other similarities surfaced later when the Hoosier earned a similar reputation with bat and glove. As an old man, Edd grudgingly admitted that Speaker's defensive skills rivaled his own. Spoke was not a better fielder, he emphasized, but as good. In 1913, the star and star-to-be met in undramatic fashion, with Speaker delivering one single in three at-bats, Roush going 0-for-3, and both catching a couple fly balls. The pitchers stole the show on that day, as Chicago workhorse Jim Scott outlasted rookie Fred Anderson in a 1–0 victory.

Edd's first experience was a winning one, even if his personal contribution proved modest. For one hour and 50 minutes, the Oakland City kid played with the big boys. He received a kind appraisal from I.E. Sanborn of the *Chicago Tribune*: "(Roush) fielded everything within reach cleanly and easily. At bat he grounded out three times, which was better than some of the (White Sox) could do. Some of them struck out."[1]

A day later, Edd earned a second start. This time he faced another rookie, Bob Shawkey of the league-leading Philadelphia Athletics. Individual results proved similar; Edd went 0-for-3 with a strikeout and caught one fly ball, but the collective outcome was a 7–1 Philly blowout. Shawkey tossed a five-hitter while giving a glimpse of the skill that propelled him to 196 wins over the next 15 years. Despite his hitless outing, Edd recorded a couple significant milestones: he threw out his first base runner and executed a sacrifice bunt. After a baby step the previous day, this was a footprint in the snow, overt evidence that Roush was here and made a difference.

Second baseman Eddie Collins led the winners, going 4-for-4 and scoring twice. He finished the season with a league-leading 125 runs and placed fourth in hitting at .345. Collins wore a White Sox uniform in 1919 but on this day he remained the sparkplug of a great Athletics team that would win the World Series, its third in the past four years.

These were the kinds of men Edd Roush faced during his second day in the majors. He never started for the White Sox again. Over the next 22 days Edd made five appearances as a pinch-hitter and two in a pinch-runner role. When the Washington Senators came to town with legendary Walter Johnson, he watched the opening game from the bench. Years later he'd face Johnson's famous fastballs during spring training, but for now could only marvel from afar. The Senators brought a future Black Sox with them in first baseman Chick Gandil. Dealt to Chicago in 1917, he became a central figure in negotiations with gamblers.

Edd scored the first run of his career during game two of the Washington series. Entering as an eighth-inning pinch-runner, he took over after a fastball plunked the knee of team captain Harry Lord. Edd eventually came around to record the first of 1,099 career runs.

With playing opportunities becoming rare, Roush found himself thrust into the leadoff slot for an August 30 game. It was just an exhibition contest, played against amateurs in nearby DeKalb, but he represented the Sox well by drilling a home run, scoring three times on three hits and stealing three bases. The bench awaited him when Chicago resumed its major league schedule. Making a pinch-hitting appearance the following day, Edd was credited with a sacrifice during an 8–5 loss to Ty Cobb and the Detroit Tigers. A week into his major league trial run, he still didn't own a base hit. Worse yet, his brief and sporadic appearances provided small chance for refining a batting stroke.

Edd finally broke through on September 11, rapping a single in a ninth-inning appearance at Philadelphia's Shibe Park, home of the reigning champions. It came against Chief Bender, a Chippewa Indian who rose from reservation ball to become one of baseball's all-time greats. Mixing a swift fastball and sharp curve, he compiled a 212–127 record over 16 years. Though his career was winding down by 1913, Chief still had enough stuff to win 21 games that season. Yet rookie Roush stared him down and won their private battle. He was batting 1.000 against the mighty Charles Albert Bender.

Beyond Edd's milestone the game proved uneventful for the Sox, who managed only two hits before starter Bob Shawkey exited for a pinch-runner in the seventh inning. That set the stage for Bender's entry and Roush's quiet appointment with history. The big Indian surrendered three hits during his two-inning relief stint but held Chicago scoreless and closed out a 4–1 win.

One day later, Edd made his final trip to the plate as a member of the White Sox. It was another ninth-inning, pinch-hitting appearance, this time against Athletics rookie Bullet Joe Bush. He went down quietly, making an out against the young hurler who was destined for a long and unremarkable career. Philadelphia won, 7–5, moving 40 games above the .500 mark, while the White Sox dropped to 70–68.

That was the end of Edd's brief flirtation with the American League, and his final ledger left no inkling of what lay ahead. Appearing in 10 games, he produced one hit in 10 at-bats, scored twice, made three put-outs, recorded two sacrifices and struck out twice. Sox management had seen enough and sent him to its farm team in Lincoln, Nebraska.

Roush became an Antelope, which didn't quite have the ring of "Yankee" or "Pirate" but resonated nonetheless. The shorthand version "Lopes" appeared more often in pages of the *Lincoln Daily Star*, a Nebraska evening newspaper that bestowed broad coverage on its minor league team. From Evansville to Chicago to Lincoln, the Hoosier had become quite the traveler.

Nebraska may not conjure colorful images but it was exotic baseball territory in 1913. The major leagues extended no farther west than St. Louis and a majority of its teams were based in or near the eastern seaboard. New York, Boston, Washington, Philadelphia, and Pittsburgh represented the heart of the game, with arteries stretching to Chicago, Detroit, Cleveland, Cincinnati and Saint Louis. The Western League resided half a continent away in Kansas, Colorado, Iowa and Nebraska. Along with Lincoln, owners planted teams in Denver, Des Moines, St. Joseph, Omaha, Sioux City, Topeka and Wichita. It was a proud circuit, with distinct regional identity.

Arriving without fanfare, Edd joined the Antelopes for a September 21 doubleheader at Des Moines and crafted a sparkling debut in the opener. Playing right field and hitting second, he legged out an infield single in his first at-bat as a Westerner, then doubled during a three-run fourth inning. His final stat line in the 4–3 win included 5 at-bats, 1 run, 2 hits, 1 putout, no assists, and no errors.

Comiskey Park aside, Edd Roush made a habit of strong first impressions, though not so far from home. Never mind his hitless outing against a dominant pitcher in game two; the Indiana newcomer had officially arrived with a bang. In addition to its game coverage, the *Daily Star* made brief mention of Edd in "Sporting Review," a column filled with various tidbits from the baseball world. "Mystery—Who Is Roush?" read the briefest of briefs. He'd apparently slipped in under the sports staff's collective nose.

A couple months earlier, some fellow named Cobb played right field for the Antelopes—not Ty, but his younger brother Paul. The junior Cobb enjoyed moments of glory, most notably a tape-measure home run in a road loss at St. Joseph, Missouri. Some said his bomb was the longest ever launched at that park. Paul's highlights, however, proved too few and far between. With a batting average hovering around .250, he eventually lost his starting spot and then disappeared altogether. It makes great reading to say Roush took a job from Ty Cobb's sibling but that's not entirely accurate. In truth, he replaced the guy who replaced the guy who replaced young Cobb. Paul was long gone by then.

Lincoln fielded an above-average team in 1913 but the race was settled by the time Edd arrived. Forty games over .500, Denver led Des Moines by 10 games and the third-place Lopes by 17. Though they assembled a decent hitting attack, the Nebraskans lacked depth on their pitching staff.

With attendance lighter than expected, the franchise offset losses by selling a third baseman to the White Sox and a catcher to the Detroit Tigers. Edd went the opposite direction by starting in Chicago, and then getting shipped out to a remote outpost of organized baseball. Nebraska was a relative newcomer to the stars and stripes, becoming the 37th state shortly after the Civil War, and it always had difficulty shaking a reputation as primitive prairie country.

Frontier days remained fresh memories when Edd disembarked, and the state's entire population numbered about half of the city he'd just left. Lincoln was no sodbuster town, however. Located near the eastern border with Iowa, it stood apart as a state capital, hub of manufacturing and food distribution, and home to the University of Nebraska. Civic promoters proclaimed the city one of the greatest educational centers in America, with more than 20,000 students attending schools and colleges.

Exciting things happened at Lincoln. In August, the sheriff arrested an eight-foot giant for shooting craps and a midget arrived at jail to secure the big guy's release. They were, of course, comrades in a traveling circus. When the state fair commenced in early September, thousands arrived at Lincoln's fairgrounds by train, streetcar, automobile and buggy. From dawn to dusk, visitors could enjoy everything from horse racing to "high class" vaudeville attractions.

A mid–September controversy erupted when the university athletic department announced its intention to raise grandstand admission prices for the big football game against Minnesota. Tickets sold quickly, however, even at the exorbitant rate of $2.50 a pop. The young sport already held a special place in Nebraskan hearts and minds.

Yet baseball found a niche, too. Newspaper coverage reflected affection for the Antelopes, though it often took the tone of a disappointed parent. The team was good but not championship caliber, fan support seemed lukewarm, and the season dragged on way too long. The usual suspects caught blame for the "Lopes" mediocrity: bad pitching and worse umpiring. On July 10, "Sporting Review" addressed a loss with all the charm of a rancid outhouse: "When a team continually gets the worst of the judgments it would seem that there is a nigger in the woodpile some place. If the dusky gent can be located, something should be stirred...."

Edd still wore an Evansville uniform when that column appeared, but he would soon face the poison pen himself. After his doubleheader debut, he returned to the lineup on September 24 and went 1-for-5 in a loss at Sioux City. That solitary hit was a clutch one, however, driving in two runners and tying the game at 4–4. Another doubleheader followed in the same city with Edd going 1-for-6, and then he posted an 0-for-2 outing during a 10–3 loss to Omaha. As Roush and the Antelopes continued their struggles, fans became increasingly grumpy. This squad needed an upgrade on the pitching staff and a commitment to veteran position players. Nobody seemed particularly impressed with kids like Roush. "Youngsters are all right for sale purposes but we would rather have a veteran of Davy Lloyd's caliber in right field than a cartload of Roushs and Red Smyths," complained a *Daily Star* sportswriter.[2]

There it was again, the impatient slap in the face by local press. Never mind that a major league team thought enough of Edd to give him a couple weeks in the big time. Forget his excellence at Evansville.

"...Roush batted .317 in the league he came from, a low class affair. Tom Carney, a .260 hitter in the Western, went into a league of the same class and hit at a rate of over .700 until the pitchers would not trust him and passed him every time he faced them. According to these figures Roush will hit something like .075 in the Western. For a right fielder this is pretty slim sledding."[3]

Make that two smacks in the face and more were on the way. "Sporting Review" proclaimed that outside of pitching, only one position — right field — needed improvement next year. Roush was a fair enough defender but couldn't hit Western League pitching. He'd be better off in some lower class league or with a Western-level squad that already had plenty of hitters. Edd did nothing to dissuade those notions in the last week of the season, delivering one hit in 13 at-bats while frustrated followers voiced their disapproval.

Edd missed the season-ending doubleheader, replaced by someone who went hitless on the day. Lincoln split that twin bill against cellar-dwelling Wichita, a fitting end to a so-so season. Finishing with an 87–80 record, the Antelopes placed fourth in a field of eight. Denver dominated the pennant chase, posting 104 wins in the lengthy 166-game season, a slate of twelve games more than the majors.

Roush completed his Western stint with a sickly .171 batting average. Playing in 10 games, he delivered six hits in 35 at-bats, caught 14 fly balls and committed no errors. The locals were entirely unimpressed by their Hoosier import. He paled next to Antelope .300 swingers, such as Bill McCormick, Donald Rader and Willis Cole. He couldn't compare to beloved third baseman Louis Barbour, who got a late call-up with the White Sox and was never expected to return.

Funny thing about those guys ahead of Edd — add their bright futures together and it would look like flint sparks next to a Roush bonfire. A few Lincoln players got the proverbial "cup of coffee" in the majors, while some had already tasted it and were sliding toward retirement. None ever made an impact on the big leagues, nor did the Western League's best hitters of 1913, with the possible exception of Omaha's Bunk Congalton, who belted .320 for Cleveland back in 1906.

With baseball coming to a close on October 5, Lincoln sports fans could focus entirely on football and a two-week buildup toward the game of the year with Minnesota. When the October 18 showdown approached, it was lead-story, front-page news. Hundreds of Nebraska alumni flocked to Lincoln and shouted full-throated support for their alma mater. Incoming trains were packed with supporters, school banners hung high above the streets of downtown Lincoln, and pedestrians wore cream-colored armbands with the letter "N." This wasn't your typical rivalry; the Cornhuskers hadn't beaten mighty Minnesota in 11 painful years and the losing streak gnawed at them.

Nebraska broke a scoreless tie in the fourth quarter, hitting paydirt on one of those newfangled forward passes, but Minnesota fought back in the waning minutes and reached the Cornhusker 5-yard line. Then came an inspiration that sounds more like myth than reality, but was presented as fact. Music apparently tamed the Gophers' savage breast — more specifically, a school band's melody that floated across a hushed stadium. The *Daily Star* reported:

> Down the field, the Nebraska men desperately defending their goal line, comes the sweetly plaintive notes of the "Cornhusker." There is a haunting sadness in the strain, for the boys are playing their very hearts into the music. They have reached the chorus and this is the message they are crying to the defenders of the lines: "For Nebraska and the Scarlet. For Nebraska and the Cream."[4]

The Cornhuskers responded with a goal-line stand, stuffing one run and recovering a fumble on the next. A wild celebration followed Nebraska's upset victory, which shut down streetcar traffic in some areas, and the university band led a mob of raucous rooters through the streets of Lincoln. Later that evening hundreds of undergraduates built a huge bonfire at their football field, the flames glowing through darkness while countless shadowy silhouettes danced and gesticulated against the dramatic backdrop. Yes, this was football country.

Edd Roush never returned to Lincoln.

6

Breaking the Chains

When I jumped (to) the Federal League I got $2,000 over there. That was for five and a half months, see? That was a lot of money. Good Lord, almighty! That fall, when I come home I bought a Ford car. It cost $225 ... a model T Ford.[1]

Edd was riding what appeared to be a slow train to the majors. In 1914 he jumped the tracks entirely, ignoring his indentured obligation to the White Sox and joining a new circuit that trumpeted itself as the third major league. They called it the Federal League and Edd landed back in his home state with the Indianapolis entry. After a brief and undistinguished tour through Chicago and Nebraska, he'd found happiness about 120 miles northeast of Oakland City.

The Feds made a fairly quiet debut the previous year, setting up shop as an independent minor league with no designs on wooing players from the majors. A "fairly" qualifier is applied because they *did* invade four big league cities in the Midwest, along with a minor league metropolis named Indianapolis. But the newcomers seemed to be little threat to the status quo. In 1912, the United States League (USL) tried the same thing and lasted barely a month. These kinds of upstarts had passed through baseball for the past 30 years — the Union Association in 1884, the Players League in 1890, and a somewhat successful American Association exited in 1891 after nine seasons as a major circuit.

Undaunted, Fed entrepreneurs quickly climbed over USL corpses to stake their claim. Avoiding conflict with the entrenched powers, their inaugural season passed peacefully, but the placid landscape would soon turn bloody. With one season under its belt, the Federal League hired a new, aggressive president and recruited prosperous businessmen into the ownership fold. The reorganized circuit decided it was ready for the big time and asked to join the National Agreement between the American and National leagues. They weren't storming the castle just yet, only requesting a warm room inside. From Organized Baseball's perspective, it looked more like some feeble home invasion attempt by a 98-pound weakling. Responding with a collective "harrumph," pastime power brokers slammed their door in the intruders' faces.

The Feds declared war, brashly proclaiming themselves a third major league. No longer striking the pose of harmonious coexistence, they declared the reserve clause invalid and lured big leaguers with promises of salary hikes. The castle was now officially under siege.

It became known as the "outlaw" league, a telling description for unwelcome outsiders. Cocky, presumptuous and predatory, they bore a striking resemblance to a group that invaded baseball in 1901— the American League. Nobody fumed about the latest interlopers more than A.L. president Ban Johnson, yet he drew the blueprint they followed. It started in 1893, the year of Roush's birth, when Johnson took over as head of the Western League. He quickly developed it into the nation's top minor circuit, and then declared baseball war in 1901, placing franchises in three National League cities and three more in towns that had recently been abandoned by the majors. The new American League circuit proclaimed itself major, prompting a collective "Pshaw" from National League magnates.

The usurpers had deep pockets, however, and two years of costly bidding wars convinced the entrenched powers to push for peace. Under the National Agreement of 1903, the N.L. and A.L. would function as separate but equal major leagues; roster raiding stopped.

By 1914, Johnson saw things from a different perspective. He owned a piece of the castle now and could barely contain his disgust for the barbarians at the gate. A dozen years earlier, they would have been kindred spirits, but Johnson never acknowledged the irony. He was too busy pouring boiling oil from the towers, threatening to blacklist any A.L. player who jumped to the outlaws. Sincere or not, the warning proved a strong weapon in the major league arsenal — that and the dismal longevity record for upstarts. The Feds offered more money, but what good was that if they went belly up? The majors stood on solid ground but paid far less. It was the eternal conundrum, pitting immediate gratification against long-term security, high-risk romance versus platonic pecks on the cheek. Would any notable major leaguers take a chance?

The answer came quickly when two legendary figures switched allegiances during the winter of 1913. On December 28, sports pages hyped the news with large headlines — Joe Tinker and "Three Finger" Brown were jumping to the Federal League. Signing on as player-manager of the Chicago Whales, Tinker returned to the city where he'd achieved immortality as part of the "Tinker to Evers to Chance" double-play combination. A smooth-fielding shortstop, he wore a Cubs uniform from 1902 until 1912 and played on two Worlds Series champions, all of which made him a bona fide box-office attraction.

Like Tinker, Brown was approaching the end of a glorious career that saw four pennants and two world titles in Chicago. Pitching for the Cubs from 1904 until 1912, he became the ace of those champion staffs, racking up 20-win seasons before anybody ever heard of Walter Johnson. But those glory days seemed distant memories while he toiled for the lowly Cincinnati Reds in 1913. Then came an offer he couldn't refuse: take a pay raise and become player-manager of the Fed team at St. Louis. In addition to that pair of aging legends, the Feds landed a young pitching sensation named Tom Seaton. The 24-year-old came off a breakthrough sophomore season that saw him lead the National League in victories while throwing for the Philadelphia Phillies. His 27–12 record gave him two more wins than Christy Mathewson, the great New York Giants veteran.

Tinker, Brown and Seaton represented three heavy fish that landed in the Federal League net, but they looked like minnows compared to the whoppers that got away. Tinker put a hook deep into Walter Johnson's mouth before the flame-throwing pitcher spit it out. After committing to the Whales, he had a change of heart. Penning a somewhat apologetic column for *Baseball Magazine,* Johnson later explained his conundrum, saying Senators boss Clark Griffith guilt-tripped him into reneging on a three-year Fed deal that called for $17,500 per season, with a $6,000 advance up front. "I did not treat the Federal League right. I broke my contract with them. But I broke it only because I was convinced that by not doing so, I would be doing an even greater injury to Washington."[2]

How much did it take to get Johnson back in a Senators uniform? He didn't mention a dollar figure but claimed it was less than what the Whales offered. According to baseball legend, Charles Comiskey subsidized the deal because he didn't want Johnson in Chicago. That kind of star power could siphon Sox fans away and turn them into Whales watchers.

The Federal League also made overtures to superstars Ty Cobb and Tris Speaker, who eyed the bait but decided to stay put. With new bidders in the marketplace, they leveraged fat pay raises from their A.L. owners. In Baltimore, a young minor leaguer was offered $10,000 salary plus a $10,000 signing bonus if he would jump to the city's Federal League entry.[3] His name was Babe Ruth and he resisted, worried that organized baseball might retaliate by banning him for life. Returning home from a world baseball tour, John McGraw had a $100,000 offer waiting in his mailbox.[4] Foregoing the financial opportunity of a lifetime, he declined.

A few established players landed in Federal League ballparks, among them Felder Jones, a 13-year veteran outfielder who eclipsed .300 six times but hadn't played since 1908, and outfielder Davy Jones, who scored an impressive 101 runs in 1907 but never hit .300 during a 12-year career. Venue change was a low risk for those who had slipped through the major league cracks and stood little chance of returning. Others, however, were taking big chances. Falling into the latter category was a group of young defectors who had hit big league pitching at a .270-.290 clip — good enough for a second look if they'd stuck around.

On the pitching front, few Fed neophytes performed well in the majors and precious few would be missed. The same, however, could not be said for a veteran N.L. double-play combo that left Philadelphia for the Baltimore Terrapins. Though light hitters, second baseman Otto Knabe and shortstop Mickey Doolan were legitimate major league starters and a nice catch for the outlaws.

For little-known Edd Roush, it was a no-brainer — he took the money. Of course, his contract paled compared to what the Federal League offered the big boys, but it still made for a hefty raise. Lincoln paid $150 a month, the White Sox contract called for $1,500 per season, and Indy offered $2,000. Making the choice even easier were the slim chances of seeing that major league money anytime soon. Edd wasn't exactly the toast of Chicago or Lincoln, for that matter. Nobody beat a path to the Roush door and that included the Hoosiers. So he took the initiative, contacting multiple Fed managers and offering his services. Three-Finger Brown didn't need any additional outfielders in St. Louis, nor did Joe Tinker in Chicago, but Bill Phillips rolled out the welcome mat at Indianapolis. Responding via telegram, the Hoosier skipper invited Edd to come talk it over. They haggled a bit over salary, with Roush holding firm for two grand and getting it. On March 2, the *Indianapolis Star* announced his arrival and even spelled the name correctly: "Phillips believes Roush has the goods to hit hard in fast company and believes the youngster will force some of the veteran gardeners to travel fast to retain their jobs."

That was his role in a nutshell — a hungry youngster biding time until an adult seat opened. Not that the lineup was set in stone; few returned from the group that dominated the Federal League's maiden season in 1913. But that was minor league ball and Feds aimed higher now by revamping their lineups with better talent. The "Hoofed" seniority system went out the window, replaced by an overall experience odometer. Unfortunately, that Roush kid had barely been around the block.

He became one of about 15 Federal League greenhorns who had made brief and undistinguished major league debuts in 1913. All were good enough for a call-up, yet their full potential remained a mystery. Not quite 21 years old, Edd was the youngest of the bunch and his 10 at-bats were the fewest.

Though the Hoosier roster listed few big league vets, everybody was older than Roush. As the "baby" of the family, cracking the starting lineup would not be easy.

Indy's biggest ace in the hole was an ace on the mound in Cy Falkenberg. Though winding down his career, the 33-year-old hurler had just come off an outstanding season for the Cleveland Indians, going 23–10 with a 2.22 ERA. No other Hoosier came close to those credentials. Vin Campbell owned one of the most impressive resumes among position players. In 1912, the former Boston Braves outfielder recorded a league-high 624 at-bats, hit .296 and scored 102 runs. A year later, he totaled zero plate appearances.

After averaging 186 at-bats in a five-year stint with the Boston Braves, "Bedford" Bill Rariden brought big league experience to the catching position. Five years later, he played alongside Edd in the Black Sox series. One of three native Hoosiers on the team, Rariden was born and raised in the town of Bedford, located about 60 miles south of Indy as the crow flies. Hence the nickname, "Bedford Bill." Then there was Bill McKechnie, a Pittsburgh Pirate utility infielder who changed course to play third base in Indianapolis. There he met Roush, who would become a lifelong friend. Long after their Indianapolis days ended, fate continued putting them in the same dugout before Bill found his true calling as a manager. They also traveled similar paths in their private lives, with both men retiring to the same Florida town.

Though depicted as labor anarchists, the Feds proclaimed themselves champions of contractual sanctity. Accusing the majors of stealing players with binding Fed agreements, league president J.A. Gilmore sent a menacing warning through the press on March 4. "If the American and National Leagues ignore our contracts and fail to appreciate the spirit of sportsmanship we have shown, we will start the biggest of baseball wars. When it is over, the Federal League will have the stars of the old leagues and will be the strongest in the game."[5] With an arsenal of wealthy owners to back him up, Gilmore threatened to unleash the hounds of currency. He claimed unlimited financial reserves and promised that Fed owners could hold their own in any bidding war.

Sports pages provided extensive coverage of the Hoofeds' spring training in Wichita Falls, Texas, which proved difficult because there wasn't much to cover. Practices frequently were cancelled due to cold, blustery weather, leaving players with time to kill. On one such occasion, Edd joined Benny Kauff and Biddy Dolan for a jackrabbit hunt. Claiming they would eat what they shot, the trio must have looked like rubes; locals never put the varmints on their dinner table. Some players passed time at the moving pictures and others hobnobbed with boys from the Kansas City Packers, another Fed club that trained nearby. As cold weather continued to interrupt practice schedules,

Packers manager George Stovall took advantage of the downtime to attempt a roster upgrade. Lacking quality outfielders, he met with Indy's boss and proposed a trade.

The *Indianapolis Star* reported, "He is particularly taken with young Roush, who, according to all reports, has been showing a lot of form at the bat, on the bases and in the field. Manager Phillips turned a deaf ear to the Stovall entreaty, however."[6] Bill Phillips knew what he had.

A March 24 off-day found the team waking up early, piling into 24 cars and traveling 25 miles for a lavish barbecue at a genuine Texas ranch. Along with the Kansas City squad, they were guests of honor for the event, sponsored by a local rancher and the Wichita Falls Chamber of Commerce. The athletes worked up an appetite during their two-hour trip across wind-swept prairies, and camp cooks waited with fresh beef, broiled on open fires. Putting the cowboy lifestyle on display for their visitors, ranch hands conducted a roundup and rode atop wild broncos. McKechnie gave it a try but cut his ride short after getting bounced too high for comfort.

When the team returned to practice, an accompanying *Star* reporter uncovered something major and his editors gave it big play. "Ed Rousch" was ambidextrous. During an otherwise uneventful workout, he surprised teammates and observers by throwing equally well with the right arm.

Ready or not, the Hoosiers broke camp on April 8 and left Wichita Falls. In 29 days, they'd conducted only 17 workouts, which wasn't enough to approach peak preparation. Still, the team certainly looked better than when it arrived and Phillips saw enough to form some opinions.

Back home, folks were talking about the Indianapolis 500, though it lay more than a month away. But with all due respect to the growing subculture of racing fanatics, baseball remained king of spring and opening day the coronation. Excitement was palpable in the nation's newspapers as the days counted down toward a shotgun start to several different leagues, including the American, National, Federal and the American Association minors. Indy fielded entries in the two latter circuits.

With its wholesale roster changes, the Federal League was tough to predict. The *Star* wouldn't even hazard a guess, leaving prognostication to newspapers from rival cities. A *Brooklyn Eagle* sportswriter anointed four contenders — St. Louis, Chicago, Brooklyn and Baltimore — and envisioned a low finish for Indy. "Indianapolis has two good pitchers and a fair (catcher), an indifferent infield and an experimental outfield as first-class teams go."

The *Kansas City Star* picked those same four challengers while also knocking the Hoosiers: "...[W]e'll dig down in the family stocking and produce a worn and frazzled dime to bet that Bill Phillips will not be one, two, three when the final reckoning is tabulated."

Today, Indianapolis has been out of the loop so long that nobody connects it to the major leagues. Yet back in 1914 many still remembered the city's role as an early baseball pioneer, fielding National League entries in 1876, 1887, 1888 and 1889. Hoofed officials said big-time baseball was back and emphasized the point by constructing a brand new stadium. Similar building projects took place all across the league. In Chicago, the Whales (or Chifeds) plopped a new park on the north side that later became known as Wrigley Field.

The Federal League opened with fanfare on April 13, as a crowd of 25,000-plus filled Baltimore's Terrapin Park and watched a 3–2 hometown victory over Buffalo. Grandstand fans could see the diamond of another ballpark in the distance, this one belonging to the minor league Baltimore Orioles. Babe Ruth was pitching over there, facing John McGraw's New York Giants in a big exhibition game. Few witnessed it, as the mostly empty stadium held about 1,000 people that day. Seduced by a Fed siren call, Baltimore baseball fans deserted their Orioles and jumped on a bandwagon that promised major-league level baseball.

On the eve of their own April 16 debut at St. Louis, the Hoosiers had health problems. Vin Campbell nursed bum ankles and fellow outfielder Al Kaiser had fainted, supposedly from acute indigestion. That still wasn't enough to get Edd in the lineup.

7

Hoosier Hysteria

*Why, thunder, I was fast! Heck, I could run. I could run with any
of them when I was playin' ball and I was fast in the outfield and when
that ball was hit, I knew where it was goin'.*[1]

Approximately 23,000 fans attended Indy's opener in St. Louis, including Missouri Governor Elliot W. Major and the local mayor, a pitcher-catcher combo for the ceremonial first pitch. They repeated the process three more times and provided some unintentional comedy along the way. The portly pair looked out of place to start with, then Governor Major fired one way high and another way low. The mayor took over court jester duties on pitch three, inducing riotous laughter when he fell on his protruding gut while reaching for a wide throw. Dignity returned on the final toss and the battery executed flawlessly. Competency returned when the professionals took the field.

The moment had finally arrived. Two more Fed babies were about to be born, though one could've used more time in the womb. Illness, injury and spring training interruptus combined to form a cloud of doubt about Hoosier readiness. But a funny thing happened on the way to the gallows. Cy Falkenberg hurled eight scoreless innings, Biddy Dolan belted a three-run homer and Indianapolis took a 7–3 decision. Edd watched from the bench as his team lost its next three games, and then got a start on April 20. Filling in at left field, he went 2-for-4, scored once, and stole a base during a 7–2 win at Kansas City. He started again the following day, held hitless in a 6–2 victory.

All eyes now focused on the Hoosiers upcoming home opener, with plans for a spectacle every bit as lavish as the ones in St. Louis and other Fed cities. Laborers worked feverishly to put the finishing touches on the still-incomplete Kentucky Avenue facility. When the countdown reached one day, Federal Park became a beehive of last-minute activity and team officials bopped around the grounds to supervise. A steam-roller chugged away in right field, packing the newly laid sod while two men operated a large hand roller on the base paths. Hordes of workmen occupied the stands, performing odd jobs until day's end when a separate group went through the stands to hose down dirt and dust.

On Thursday, April 23, Indianapolis met its new team at the even newer ballpark, but not before a boisterous public welcome that rivaled receptions for returning war heroes. Led by the Indianapolis Military Band, a parade moved through the city's business sector for more than an hour before heading toward the ballpark. The route was thronged with cheering fans, hungry for another big-time team to call their own. As time wound down toward the 3:30 P.M. start time, a stream of motorcars chugged toward

Edd's Cracker Jack rookie card, manufactured during his Federal League stint with the Indiana Hoosiers in 1914 (Roush Family Collection).

Federal Park. Also heading in that direction were streetcars, packed so tight with passengers that even the running boards were full.

But most of all, there was foot traffic, with thousands of people walking under sunny skies to a common destination. More than 15,000 passed through the shiny turnstiles at Federal Park, many arriving early enough to give a hearty cheer when players first trickled onto the field around 2:45 P.M. More and more athletes emerged until the diamond swarmed with Brownies and Hoosiers. They went through their motions for 40 minutes or so, and then surrendered the field to a couple notable democrats — Indiana Governor Samuel M. Ralston and Indianapolis Mayor Joseph E. Bell. It was time for another ceremonial pitch and catch. Dressed in a frock coat and square-top derby hat, the honorable Ralston threw like someone wearing too many clothes, delivering four low ones in the general vicinity of the mayor and home plate. Bell couldn't corral his governor's mistakes; there had to be a clever political parallel in there somewhere.

Insiders expected Edd Roush to start this game in left field, or at least that's what the *Star* conveyed when it listed his name among probable position players. Benny Kauff got the call instead and delivered two hits in four tries. Despite a 3–0 deficit, Indy fans stayed in their seats during the bottom of the ninth and rooted for a rally. It didn't happen.

Though they lost a battle, the Hoosiers seemed to win the war — one for credibility and hometown support. Excitement still rode high at the end of the St. Louis series, as another healthy crowd turned out for the Sunday finale and watched the Roush-less Hoosiers prevail, 5–3. A day later, Edd made the finest catch of his life, one so inspiring that it demanded annual tribute. On April 27 he married Essie Mae Swallow in Indianapolis. No longer a baseball vagabond, he had the paycheck to support a wife now.

Edd continued to play sparingly while the Hoofeds finished May in fourth place, six games behind league-leading Baltimore. On June 3, Phillips found a way to work him into the starting lineup without disrupting the team's formidable outfield rotation; Edd manned first base and went 2-for-5 in a 9–6 win at St. Louis. His triple capped a first-inning, four-run uprising that put the Hoosiers in charge. Performing even better the following day, Edd rapped three hits in a 7–6 triumph.

Roush was rewarded for his recent play with a demotion back to pinch-hitter. Prospects for a starting spot became even slimmer with the arrival of Charlie Carr, an aging first baseman, seven seasons removed from a mediocre major league career. Carr smacked a triple and a single during his June 9 debut for the Hoosiers, while Edd went 0-for-1 in another pinch-hitting appearance. He was further out of the loop than ever.

Trying to make the most out of limited opportunities, Edd struck gold on June 11 while lashing a pinch-hit RBI double, and then scoring the winning run in a 6–5 triumph. He began to create a niche for himself in the Hoosier attack. Between the brief plate appearances and spot starts, young Roush generally outshone older teammates; his .333 average put him third on a team of hard hitters. Would the youngster perform as well if he played full time? Could he hold up under the daily rigors? There was only one way to find out.

A mid–June game found Edd starting in center field and contributing to a 4–1 victory over Buffalo. It was Indy's seventh straight success and the streak soon stretched to nine. Nipping at the heels of league-leading Chicago, the Hoosiers welcomed Brooklyn's Tip-Tops to town for a Saturday double-header. Two come-from-behind wins later, a crowd of 5,500 went crazy when their favorite sons moved into first place.

A 13th consecutive win followed, then 14, and then 15. It finally ended in a 5–3 loss to Kansas City, but what a wonderful ride for the Hoofeds. Bottom-feeders a few weeks earlier, they led the Federal League, though not by much. Playing some winning ball of its own, Joe Tinker's Chicago club pulled within a few percentage points of first. In the midst of it all, Indy management announced a 25-cent decrease in ticket prices, down to 50 cents in the grandstands and 75 cents for box seats. About the same time Indianapolis residents read that piece of good news, Serbians assassinated an Austro-Hungarian Archduke in Bosnia. The fuse was lit on powder-keg Europe.

Separated by an ocean and committed to neutrality, the United States could still enjoy her games for awhile longer. The "Chifeds" slipped past Indy in early July, setting up an important mid-month series at Chicago. With a lot on the line, Edd found himself in the starting lineup July 11 and delivered two hits. Indy took the game, 3–2, on "German Day" at Weeghman Park. Though it soon became unfashionable to salute German heritage, folks did it with pride on this day.

When the Hoosiers left town, they trailed Chicago by three games. As the team plodded along, Roush plugged away — starting occasionally, pinch-hitting regularly, and often making no appearance at all. The highlight came in Pittsburgh on July 24 when he produced three hits, stole two bases, caught six fly balls and threw out a couple base runners during an extra-inning loss. Twenty-four hours later, he went hitless in both ends of a doubleheader, prompting another demotion to part-time duty.

The big winning streak became a dim memory while Indianapolis dropped into fourth place, six games out of first. But the Hoofeds had another run in them, and so did Roush. He belted a series of clutch pinch-hits during their second charge toward the top. An explosive offense led the resurgence, with seven players batting .300 or better and McKechnie just a few points shy from making it eight. Sparking a winning rally against Brooklyn ace Tom Season, Edd received glowing praise in the *Indianapolis Star*. "Things were not going so bad for Seaton until Phillips sent Ed Rousch, his champion pinch hitter to the plate. Ed slammed a long single just to keep up his handsome pinch-hit batting average. Then the carnage was on full-blast."[2] Indy scored seven runs in that eighth-inning uprising and finished with a 12–6 triumph.

The cameo kid continued hitting and his team kept winning. World news trumpeted allied defeats on Belgian battlefields and a Russian advance toward German territory, but life was warm and fuzzy at the ball diamond, where the Hoosiers now held a three-game cushion over Chicago. Edd's average climbed to .333, second best on the club and sixth in the league. It was time for a promotion.

Around mid–September, he finally received his chance. With the season winding down and Indy embroiled in a tight pennant race, boss Phillips put the youngster on center stage. Not that his offense really needed much help; the Hoosiers led the league in hits and team batting average. For all their vaunted stick work, however, they couldn't shake those pesky Chifeds. Maybe it was because of porous defense or a lack of pitching depth. Another big bat wouldn't solve those problems, but a team can't have too many clutch hitters.

After losing an exhibition game in Atlantic City, the Hoosiers won five straight at Brooklyn, all with Edd in left field. He hit .429 over that stretch and scored six times. Chicago kept pace, however, and when the Hoosiers dropped a 4–3 decision to Buffalo, it was all tied up at 77 wins apiece with 10 games to go. Every contest seemed crucial now, every at-bat magnified. On September 20, a big crowd turned out at Federal Park to watch Indy take a 3–2 decision over Buffalo. Scoring the winning run in the bottom of the 10th was a fellow named Edd Roush — or "Ed Rousch" according to press reports. After a promising start, Indianapolis became like every other misspelling town. Whoever that guy was, the crowd exploded with joy when he slid home in a cloud of dust.

"For five minutes, the air was alive with sailing pads, and hats were knocked helter-skelter," wrote one sportswriter. "The field was stormed by the gladdened crowd and Hoosier players were forced to shake more hands in a few minutes than they had thought existed in the crowd."[3]

Thrills, adulation and a healthy paycheck to boot, life just got better and better for Mr. Roush-Rousch-Rausch. The victory put Indy's heroes in sole possession of first place, though just by a few percentage points. They quickly created a little breathing room by winning their next game, 9–1, while Chicago fell to Baltimore. Then the Hoosier bats went silent at the worst possible time, producing 11 hits and one run over the next three games, all losses, and the Chifeds took over first.

Momentum had shifted and Indy needed a jolt. Enter Edd J. Roush. In his most acclaimed performance yet, Edd's name and likeness rode the top of the *Star*'s Sunday sports section: "ROUSCH IS STAR IN HOOSIER VICTORY OVER REBELS" screamed the headline. He did it with defense, making a series of tough catches in left field. Rolling to an 8–4 win over Pittsburgh, the Hoofeds righted their ship and rejoined the chase.

With three games left in the season, Indianapolis had to beat cellar-dwelling St. Louis more than Chicago beat Kansas City. Both pennant-chasers owned the home field advantage, both boasted more talent than their opponents, and neither had ever felt such pressure. The Hoofeds handled it gracefully on October 6, jumping out to an early 3–0 lead at Federal Park and finishing with a 7–4 triumph. Then came joyous news out of Illinois. Those beautiful Kansas City Packers — Indy's spring training neighbors and Texas barbecue buddies — sent a wonderful gift to their old pals. They beat the mighty Chifeds not once, but twice, a doubleheader sweep by the league's sixth-place team. With the season nearly complete, Indianapolis moved back in first, needing only one more win to clinch. Phillips went with his ace, putting Cy Falkenberg on the mound, and St. Louis countered with Dave Davenport, a mediocre rookie with enough potential to excel the following season.

From the very start, it seemed fate wore a Hoosier uniform. Leading off the bottom of the first, Vin Campbell circled the bases on a bunt and a comedy of errors. An infielder threw wild into the outfield, an outfielder threw wild to the infield, and Campbell kept running throughout. Indy tallied another unusual run when Kauff scored from second on an infield single. While Hoosier hitters were winning ugly, Falkenberg constructed a mound masterpiece. He threw a one-hitter through eight innings, surrendered a couple harmless singles in the ninth, and finished with eight strikeouts in a 4–0 shutout. When Bedford Bill Rariden camped under a foul fly for the final out, hundreds of fans swarmed the field in celebration. Indianapolis was champion of the Federal League ... again.

One more game remained on the schedule but nobody was taking it seriously. With pre-game running and throwing contests, the Thursday finale seemed more like a company picnic. One particular event, however, became Edd's stage for a jaw-dropping achievement. The *Star* raved, "Ed Rousch sprang the surprise of the day when he got to first on the bunt-and-run event in :03 1–5 (seconds), which is said to equal the world's record."

Even from the left side of the batter's box, that is a staggering time, if accurate. The guy who built his forearms milking cows must have developed a couple calves along the way. Before his knees went bad, switch-hitting Mickey Mantle was freakishly fast. His best recorded time is commonly reported at 3.1 seconds, only slightly faster than Roush's mark.

When game time rolled around, Edd kept right on running, going 3-for-3 in a 4–2 victory. It wrapped up a wonderful afternoon for the Oakland City farm boy, not to mention a season of growth. He'd spent much of it sitting on the bench and learning from his manager, and then put the lessons to good use. A late surge carried him to the upper echelon of league hitters, where he tied for fourth with a mark of .333. It took a lot for a batter to get noticed on the league's top hitting team, and young Roush pulled it off. Yet he still stood in the giant shadow of diminutive superstar Benny Kauff. Everybody seemed light-deprived around this man, who became known as the Ty Cobb of the Federal League. Not only did Kauff lead his circuit with a smoking .370 mark, he also took top honors in runs (120), hits (211), doubles (44) and stolen bases (75).

Indy finished at 88–65, 1½ games better than Chicago (87–67) and 4½ up on Baltimore (84–70). The Hoosiers celebrated their title with a banquet at the Washington Hotel, attended by players, press, team officials and community leaders. Among the various tributes was a telegram addressed to boss Phillips from American League president Ban Johnson. "I congratulate you upon your great victory and am working diligently to get together a team that can compete with you. I am for you and always have been."[4] The message was a prank and everybody knew it. Johnson wouldn't spit on a Federal League team if it were on fire.

But the movement for a post–World Series showdown was very real. Sometime around mid–September, the Fed president mailed a letter of challenge to major league leaders. Nobody bit on that; they were probably laughing too hard to respond. Another appeal came at season's end, this time from the Indy franchise itself. A cocky-toned telegram went to presidents of the A.L., N.L., and both World Series teams, leaving Woodrow Wilson as the only excluded executive. Wrote James A. Ross, secretary of the Federal Baseball Club of Indianapolis:

> I hereby challenge the winners of the present so-called World Series to a contest for the world's championship in baseball, the schedule and terms for such a contest to be arranged by representatives of the competing teams. I hereby declare that failure upon the part of the winners of said so-called world series to accept this challenge precludes any right upon their part to lay claim either to the title of "World's champions" or to the name of true sportsmen.[5]

Could the majors be baited into a three-tier series for the championship of the world? Of course not. Without official sanction, however, the matter was mulled over on a franchise-to-franchise basis. Teams liked to make a buck and this kind of exhibition sounded profitable. Indianapolis newspapers reported that several Athletics, including legends Eddie Plank, Chief Bender and Home Run Baker, favored the proposal.

But first, there was the small matter of winning the World Series — a foregone conclusion by all accounts. No offense to the N.L. champion Boston Braves, but they weren't in the same class as the mighty Athletics. It seemed a terrible mismatch. Flash forward nine decades and it's hard to find any reference to the "Braves" of 1914; they're forever known as the "*Miracle* Braves." Not only did Boston's underdogs beat the unbeatable Athletics, they swept the series in four games. Beantown hadn't seen this big an upset since George Washington chased the British out to sea. A Philly-Indy series was out of the question and there would be no match-up with the Braves, either. Manager Johnny Evers flatly refused the offer, saying he couldn't be swayed by any amount of money.

Word soon circulated that John McGraw was trying to lure three Hoosiers to the Giants — McKechnie, Campbell and Roush. Contacted by boss Phillips, the first two said they wanted to remain Hoosiers. Edd, however, was incommunicado. Kauff reportedly heard an offer from the mighty Athletics but planned to honor his three-year contract with Indianapolis.

Would there even be a team to return to? Despite denials from the front office, rumors ran rampant that the champs were leaving town. A new home in a bigger city would better serve the Federal League's interests, or so the theory went. Hoofed officials assured their fans that the Hoosiers would be back in 1915.

All assurances meant nothing.

8

Jersey Boys

This Hoofed outfit boasts of the greatest collection of sluggers in base-ball and one of the strongest pitching staffs in the country. Its catching staff is almost over-balanced with talent, and in speed there are few teams that can equal this gang here. —Newark Evening News[1]

In March of 1915, the Federal League bought Indy's franchise, the first step in a transfer to Newark. What a catch for northeast New Jersey, reeling in a defending champion that was primed for a repeat. Taking over franchise ownership reins were P.T. Powers and oil magnate Harry Sinclair, the latter becoming famous as a central figure in the Teapot Dome scandal of 1923.

The city would have to wait before welcoming its new baseball sons, now called the "Peppers" or "Peps." They were busy with spring training in Valdosta, Georgia, first as Hoosiers, now as Newarkers. After entering the pre-season under a cloud of uncertainty, they must have felt relieved to know where home was and who'd be signing those paychecks. The news wasn't all good, however, because league officials approved a disputed, pre-existing deal that sent Benny Kauff to the Brooklyn Tip-Tops. The opening bell hadn't even rung and Newark already wheezed from a strong body blow. But things could've been worse. Just ask Indianapolis, the lone city to lose its Fed franchise. Relocation made good business sense, though, with the team moving to more densely populated territory. In addition to the greater Newark region, organizers believed they could draw fans from New York, too.

The league's financial profile reached new heights with the arrival of super-wealthy Sinclair, an Oklahoma oil baron whose worth was estimated at $10 million by the *Boston Post*. Other reputed multi-millionaires included ice magnate Phil Ball in St. Louis and Brooklyn's baked goods moguls, the Ward brothers. Fed money induced a couple monumental defections in 1915, with Eddie Plank going to St. Louis and Chief Bender latching on at Baltimore. Long-time veterans of the Philadelphia Athletics, Plank and Bender remained elite pitchers, not like the has-beens who came out of the wood-work a year earlier.

Forget the five World Series appearances and three championships, Bender didn't need to pull out a dusty resume. He went 17–3 in 1914, posting the highest winning percentage of his legendary career. Meanwhile, the equally illustrious Plank compiled a 15–7 mark while inching closer to the exclusive 300-win club. Unwilling to pay escalating salaries, owner Connie Mack decided to start from scratch and sold high-priced veterans; others, he simply let go. Mack preferred losing games to losing money and he got his wish in 1915, with the Athletics nose-diving to a 43–109 mark.

Slowly upgrading its reputation, the Federal League also landed a few other moderately talented big leaguers. Of course, detractors would still see the new circuit as a graveyard for the has-been, never-was and middling minor-leaguer. Their claim had a lot of truth to it, but at least the Feds seemed headed in the right direction.

Builders worked frantically to have Newark's new baseball field ready for the April 16 home opener. Fifty additional carpenters joined an already large construction crew and the workday increased by three hours. Freight cars began arriving, packed with chairs for the grandstand, and landscapers prepared field sod. It was the same last-second model that Indianapolis followed the previous year. Fortunately, the team opened both seasons on the road.

Catching an early-morning train on the Atlantic Coast Line, the Peppers left Valdosta on April 8. Two days later, they debuted with a 7–5 win at Baltimore. Accompanying the *Newark Evening News* game story was an Edd Roush feature, describing him as the Federal League's fastest man who once set a record of three seconds flat in getting to first base on a bunt. Did this allude to the day when Edd recorded a "world record" time of 3.15 seconds in Indianapolis? Or had the Hoosier become even faster in the eastern time zone? Roush's reputation was reaching comic book proportions.

After sweeping the three-game series in Baltimore, the Peppers finally got acquainted with their new home. To most of these former Hoofeds, Newark was no less foreign than the Maryland city they just left. Nestled near the mouth of the Passaic River, it rested just 10 miles from world-famous neighbor New York City. A short train ride east could open a whole new universe of cultural and entertainment possibilities. More importantly, the return route could tap into a huge pool of potential customers.

New Jersey bubbled with history, a common condition for former colonies that lived every moment of our nation's existence. The Newark area had its share too — a few miles east lay the site where Aaron Burr shot Alexander Hamilton in their famously formal duel of 1804. Of more pertinence to the Peppers was an 1846 event in nearby Hoboken, the site of the first organized baseball game. Then there was the living history of Thomas Edison, a prolific inventor who'd spent four decades in eastern Jersey and created some of his earliest work at a Newark office. Before the turn of the century, he filmed primitive footage of baseball games at a local diamond. Shot entirely from behind the first baseline, his minute-long moving picture, *The Ball Game,* was released in 1898. The old genius was still alive in 1915, still in New Jersey and still inventing. He owned a sprawling laboratory, just a few miles outside the city.

Newark hosted plenty of baseball through the years but nothing at the major league level. Excited about the arrival of big-time sport, local fans embraced their new team and fearless leader. Bill Phillips was portrayed as a strong, fatherly figure, without peer in developing young players. An *Evening News* sketch artist drew a respectful portrait of the manager, dressed in formal wear and a corncob pipe hanging from his mouth.

Excitement spread over the city as opening day approached and thousands lined the streets for a welcoming celebration, the greatest event of its kind ever arranged, according to local press. Peppered with marching bands, Boy Scouts and youth ballplayers, the mile-long parade traveled by city hall and received official review by Mayor Thomas Raymond. Eight mounted policemen headed a procession of dignitaries in automobiles, one with league President Gilmore sitting next to P.T. Powers. Noticeably absent was Harry Sinclair, who'd been "unavoidably detained," a familiar theme for the moneyman who usually worked behind the scenes while Powers provided a face to the organization.

Peps players held a position of honor in the proceedings, as did their Baltimore opponents. One Terrapin reportedly stood up in his car, waved a hand wildly and yelled out to Mayor Raymond, "Hello, Tom! How's the boy? Welcome to the big league." The mayor smiled.

Newark went down to defeat in its April 16 home debut, yet the day was deemed a rousing success. Setting a Federal League record for attendance, 26,032 fans paid to see the action, not to mention the thousands of paraders who got in for free, pushing the total to about 32,000. President Gilmore was one of those stadium-packed sardines, and he couldn't have been happier about it. At the end of an eventful day, he still sounded giddy. "Newark is a big league city in every sense of the word and will be one of the best cities in the Federal League. I am simply delighted with the opening and right now I want to declare that the fans in this vicinity are the livest wires I have seen anywhere."[2] Afterward, he headed to Pittsburgh for another opener.

Bedford Bill Rariden became part of the game's most memorable play that involved two runners sliding into the same base from different directions. Albert Scheer had entertained thoughts of scoring from first on Rariden's fifth-inning drive to center but changed his mind after rounding third. Meanwhile, Rariden chugged around second and kept running when the relay throw went to home plate. Both men slid into third base — one advancing, one retreating. The season was off to a colorful start.

A Benny Kauff firestorm soon eclipsed all other baseball news. Deserting his Brookfed team, he joined the New York Giants and appeared in uniform for an N.L. game against the Boston Braves. Not so fast, said Braves President Jim Gaffney, who refused to let his team take the field if the ineligible Kauff remained in New York's lineup. With only one squad willing to participate, the Giants were awarded a forfeit victory before the two teams played an exhibition without Benny non grata. Contacted by telephone, National League President John Tener confirmed the Fed defector's ineligibility. It was quite a mess.

Sinclair became furious about the desertion, his face growing even redder than when he lost Kauff to the Brookfeds. If the National League could swoop in and steal players under contract, every Federal League team was at risk. Fed magnates quickly gathered at New York's Waldorf-Astoria Hotel and began planning their response. No official statement could be released until President Gilmore arrived, but Sinclair seemed anxious to unburden himself to the press. He fired salvos in every direction:

> Kauff is under a binding contract with the Brooklyn Federal League club. There is no question about that fact. McGraw is trying to regain lost prestige. The success of the New York Americans and the miserable showing of the Giants even after he was given his pick of the men he believed to be the best players in the National League has caused New York fans to look toward Bill Donovan (as McGraw's replacement). Well, the Federal League is ready for war, I am ready to go to bat and the fact that I am in New York right in the midst of the fight pleases me immensely.[3]

It hadn't been long since Sinclair fought to keep Kauff on the Newark roster; now it looked like he got the better end of the deal. For his part, Kauff claimed he never signed a binding contract with the Brookfeds and was free to play where he wanted. McGraw had few allies in this fight; the Feds saw him as a thief, National League opponents resented his acquisition of the defector, and nobody wanted to see a war where signed contracts were ignored. On April 30, Kauff was banned from the National League. President Tener also overruled the forfeit decision and made the exhibition an official game, thus giving victory to Boston. Kauff quickly applied for reinstatement and was predictably refused by the three-man National Baseball Commission. In their eyes he represented one of the lowest forms of human beings — a contract jumper. When his Brooklyn pact was shown to Giants officials, they relinquished all claims to him. Hostile feelings eased and the two clubs concluded that Kauff was the culprit; he'd misrepresented his status to John McGraw and abandoned obligations to his true employer.

Newark was holding its own in a tight five-team pennant race. Through May 18 the Peps trailed first-place Pittsburgh by 1½ games and led third-place Chicago by a half game. Edd then turned in a virtuoso performance during a May 19 win over the league leaders. He doubled and tripled, scored three times, knocked in three runs and grabbed four hard-hit flies while patrolling center field. In another scrapbook moment, the local newspaper ran a large, two-column head shot of Edd with the caption, "Ed Roush, Star of Yesterday's Game." Consistency proved elusive, however, and his .270-ish batting average ranked toward the bottom of the league. At the top was a reborn Benny Kauff, hitting over .400.

Baseball retreated to the background on May 31 when the city paid homage to its war veterans with a Memorial Day parade. Crowd estimates reached 50,000, an impressive gathering for a city of about 350,000, especially with so many residents leaving town on holiday vacations. Of the approximately 250 Civil War vets who participated in the parade, a hundred or so were still spry enough to walk the route. Others rode. Of course, foot travel proved no obstacle for those young bucks of the Spanish-American War.

Edd made headlines again on June 2, this time lauded for scoring the winning run on a textbook fall-away slide. Vin Campbell's game-clinching hit was almost an afterthought on the next day's sports pages. Playing mediocre ball throughout the spring, the Peps dropped to the bottom half of the standings, more commonly known as the "second division." Suddenly, their venerated mastermind didn't know how to run a baseball team. After all, this was basically the same group that took championship honors the year before. A June swoon was the final straw for Peps management and Phillips received his walking papers after a five-game losing streak culminated in a 12–2 blowout by St Louis.

Bill McKechnie took over the reins and met his life's calling in the process. It marked the first step in a marathon managing career, although nobody knew that in 1915. Back

Bill McKechnie was a middling major leaguer before becoming a great manager. He also became a lifelong friend to Roush (Library of Congress).

then, he was just an average third baseman thrust into management of a fading team. Under his rule, the Peps won four of six against Pittsburgh, then lost a close one to Kansas City's Packers. When they returned to action on June 25, the game played second fiddle to one of the hot issues of the era — women's voting rights, or lack thereof.

Ladies Day turned into a suffrage rally at the ballpark, complete with energetic proponents, inspirational speeches and an exhibition game that pitted an experienced women's team against local high school boys. The brightly gowned feminists caused a stir on their way to the ballpark, and industry came to a near-standstill as factory workers stopped to watch the colorful parade. The *Evening News* reported:

> A census of opinion among the employers of the neighborhood would undoubtedly indicate that woman's place is in the home. Among the wage-earning classes, however, there was great enthusiasm for the cause, and every factory window was filled with honest, manly faces, eager to get a look at a genuine live suffragette.[4]

All oratory stopped once the exhibition game commenced, not so much because of sports-obsessed men but due to loud cheering from a female faction. They roared when "Minnie Pearl's College Nine" took the field, kept yelling as the fairer sex beat the foul, and stuck around to cheer the Peppers too. All throughout, suffrage banners waved in the wind while promotional balloons bobbed in the stands. The "Suffs" wore sashes of green, white and violet, bearing the phrase "Votes for Women."

It was a good day for the cause, though one writer couldn't resist connecting the female hurler to a sexist, yet amusing, double entendre: "...[B]aseball has never known a pitcher with such curves. Even the Pennsylvania locomotive engineers can see those curves from the railroad yonder."[5]

By the end of June, the Peppers still hovered at .500 and resided in the second division. At least Edd showed signs of life; he raised his batting average over .300 while moving closer to the league leaders. Ranking second on the team, he trailed only the .340 average of Vin Campbell.

Newark got hot in July, winning six of seven games at one point. But an ugly rumor became bigger news: the Peppers were moving to another city before the close of the present season. After a glorious opening day of high praise and packed stands, attendance had become sparse, especially at weekday games. Published in both the *Evening News* and *New York Times*, this tale had a ring of truth. When the team returned from a road trip for a brief homestand, some thought it the last chance for Newark fans to watch their Peppers. Two games were scheduled for the weekend of July 10–11, and if turnout didn't improve, the franchise was as good as gone.

Newfed Nation did not rise to the challenge, as only 1,000 people turned out for the Saturday contest and 3,000 on Sunday. Then again, it wasn't really Newark's team. The ballpark sat in nearby Harrison, a location that provided easier train access to New York fans but made local passage difficult. No trolley lines traveled near the park's entrance and other forms of public transportation seemed inadequate.

"There is a choice of but two routes, either walk or motor," said one frustrated fan. "What is needed most is a corps of trained wisk broom artists to brush off the dust and cinders and remove the grease spots from the clothes of the patrons due to walking railroad tracks and climbing over freight cars to reach the grounds."[6]

Leaving on a road trip the following Monday, Peppers players weren't sure they'd return. With his team still mired in mediocrity toward the end of July, McKechnie rearranged the batting order and saw immediate results. The Peps put together a five-game winning streak, then took three of four in Chicago and knocked the Whales out of first. Sitting just 3½ games behind the new league leaders — Kansas City — the Newfeds were suddenly contenders again.

Just as suddenly came great news from the home front, stating that Sinclair and Powers would keep the franchise in Newark permanently. They also announced a reduction in ticket prices. Meanwhile, Essex and Hudson county officials voted to permit a railway company to lay tracks over the Jackson Street Bridge, making the stadium more accessible from all parts of Newark.

Fans got their money's worth and more on August 7, as a near-riot broke out after Newark's thrilling 4–3 triumph. While Kansas City's second baseman held the ball and argued for a runner's interference call, Edd snuck home from third with the winning run in the bottom of the 13th inning. This just made the visitors angrier, and their catcher soon took a swing at an umpire.

Winning 13 of 14 games, the red-hot Peppers improved to 56–44 and pulled within percentage points of the top. Thus began a logjam pennant drive that saw four teams flowing neck-and-neck. On August 16, a doubleheader sweep put them in a first-place tie with Chicago. What a turnaround for a squad that recently looked hopeless, and it coincided with a change of leadership. Bill McKechnie could have run for mayor.

Down the stretch went Pittsburgh, Chicago, Kansas City, and Newark, and the order could change on a daily basis. Just when it looked like things couldn't get any more crowded, St. Louis joined the hunt too. On August 22, Edd launched another sweep, this one against visiting Pittsburgh. His two-out, 10th-inning homer clinched game one and set off an eclectic celebration. "Little 'Red' Finkelstein, mascot in chief, was the first of the reception committee at the dugout to greet Roush," wrote the *Evening News.* "The grandstand and bleachers roared. Moran was all smiles. Germany Schaefer was repulsed after inflicting his customary punishment. He hugged Roush, (and) John Kennedy, the ground-keeper, did a clog dance...."[7]

A game two victory put Newark back in first place ... barely. Kansas City stood second by one measly percentage point (.563-.562), while Pittsburgh and Chicago were 1½ games behind. As August turned to September, Chicago edged into first and the Peps faded. Nobody could forecast how things would turn out in the Federal League pennant race, but President Gilmore knew one thing for sure: he wanted his eventual champion to take on organized baseball's best in the World Series. Undaunted by rejection of a similar entreaty the previous year, he sent a letter to baseball's National Commission. It was met with icy silence.

The Fed pennant race came down to the season's final game, the second half of a doubleheader between Steel Town and the Windy City. After losing the opener, Chicago came back to win the finale and take the pennant. To say it was a close finish would be the understatement of the Progressive Era. Since none of the contenders played the same number of games, mathematicians sorted it out through winning percentages. At 86–66, the Whales finished with the highest fraction: .565723. Pittsburgh's 86–67 mark came out to .562091, extraordinarily close but not even good enough for second place. The runner-up spot went to St. Louis with a record of 87–67 and .564935. A tighter pennant chase had never been witnessed.

The offseason would see sweeping conjecture about the league's collapse or an imminent settlement with organized baseball. Newark's P.T. Powers called it "bosh" and similar denials came from every direction.

President Gilmore: "The story is absurd."

National League president John Tener: "The story is another pipe dream."

New York Giants executive John Foster: "Absolutely, it is the wildest of all wild stories ever printed."

All of which left only one logical conclusion. A deal was in the works, and the Federal League was history.

9

Edd Roush vs. John McGraw

*I bought Roush because nobody else would take him at that time.
He was not considered a star. I paid $6,000 for him.—John McGraw*[1]

The Federal League came and went like a flash of lightning. Now, more than 200 players sat in the dark, wondering if they'd made the mistakes of their lives. For the cream of the crop, there was little to worry about; banishment proved an empty threat and the majors took them back. Nothing gooses attendance like a quick talent upgrade, so all those scarlet letters magically transformed into crimson dollar signs.

Picking over Newark remains, the New York Giants scooped up Bill McKechnie, Bedford Bill Rariden and Edd Roush. The Yankees supposedly coveted Roush, as did Boston Braves manager George Stallings, who considered him the Federal League's best outfielder. John McGraw brought home the bacon, however, buying three strong prospects from Jersey. But they all paled beside his big prize from Brooklyn: Benny Kauff. He led the Fed in hitting (.342), stolen bases (55), and played a mean center field to boot. What's more, Kauff carried himself like a star both on and off the field. In his 1952 book on Giants history, author Frank Graham wrote, "Kauff's arrival (in 1916) created a mild sensation. He wore a derby hat, a fur-collared overcoat, a gray suit, a glaring striped silk shirt, and patent leather shoes, and was liberally sprinkled with diamonds. His wardrobe, which included seventy-five silk shirts, was contained in four trunks and three bags. Roush, looking like the farm boy he was, had two suits and enough shirts to hold him until his laundry came back."[2]

McGraw paid either $35,000 (per *The Baseball Encyclopedia*) or $25,000 (per his autobiography) for the little man with big ability; the addition couldn't have come at a better time. As Harry Sinclair heatedly pointed out, those legendary Giants were falling from grace. After a stirring streak of three pennants and one runner-up finish, they'd finished dead last in 1915. The Fed injection provided hope for instant success.

Of course, Kauff couldn't turn things around by himself but he didn't have to. Some considered Rariden the best Fed catcher, and McKechnie wore a winning aura after leading his Peps into contention as player-manager. The Roush kid? McGraw denigrated him a throw-in, someone to use as trade bait in some future transaction. He only paid the six grand (*The Baseball Encyclopedia* says $7,500) because it was a bargain price.[3] Edd finished the second Fed season with a strong .298 average, but how far would his numbers dip against big league pitching? Joining a squad of veterans, the youngster might not even get an opportunity to find out.

Despite their miserable 1915 showing, the Giants had some worthwhile players returning. Second baseman Larry Doyle hit .320 while leading the N.L. in hits and doubles, Fred Merkle was serviceable at first base, and the outfield had a couple solid cogs in Dave Robertson and George Burns. Owners of the league's worst earned run average, Giants pitchers were the problem. Their weak staff had a headline name in Christy Mathewson, but he'd become old and increasingly ineffective. Looking to upgrade, McGraw cast a Federal League line toward Niagara Falls and reeled in Buffalo's 19-game winner Fred Anderson.

In-team competition was brutal among outfielders — Kauff, Robertson, Burns and Roush for starters. Also taking a shot was the world's greatest athlete, Jim Thorpe, winner of decathlon and pentathlon gold medals at the 1912 Olympics. Before that, the Sac-and-Fox Indian was best known for running over the country's best football teams as an All-American at tiny Carlisle Indian Industrial School. A physical freak of nature, he could do just about anything and do it exceptionally well. History says Thorpe could not hit a curveball and failed at baseball, which is not an inaccurate assessment but not entirely fair either. He did, after all, play six years of major league ball in what was, at most, his third-best sport. Thorpe had his moments on the diamond but didn't deliver consistently. Far more frequent were the moments of mediocrity and bench time. Astonishing athleticism only takes a player so far in baseball.

Some Giants teammates tested their speed against the world-class sprinter and lost ballpark races by wide margins. Count Edd Roush among those left in the dust. "Jim, anybody in those Olympic games ever make you run your best," he once asked. "Never saw anybody I couldn't look back at," Thorpe replied. Another account has Edd and others trying their luck at wrestling Big Jim.[4] They were a playful bunch, to be sure, but Thorpe had a well-documented dark side. He drank heavily and his quick temper could turn dangerously violent.

The Giants opened training camp at Marlin, Texas, in March of 1916. The gathering marked the beginning of another annual event — the Edd Roush contract squabble. At issue was the supposed transfer of his Fed contract to the Giants. Sinclair had an option on his services, which was purchased by McGraw. Edd said his Peppers agreement expired the previous fall and he wouldn't agree to new terms. This no-show didn't last long; by March 17 word arrived that both sides were in agreement and Edd soon came to Marlin. Kauff held out, too, though both men joined the lineup in plenty of time for a spring training tour of Texas.

McGraw's crew would eventually return to the Northeast and play exhibitions with the Yankees in New York, Yale University in Connecticut and the Newark Indians at New Jersey. Returning to his former Fed home, Edd knocked in the game-winning run against Newark's minor leaguers. He made a strong enough impression that spring to earn the ultimate reward: on opening day, Roush started in right field for John McGraw and the New York Giants. Will and Laura's little boy had come a long way from the dairy farm.

The Big Apple was newly ripening when Edd arrived. A couple decades earlier, the five boroughs united to form greater New York. Baseball had a firm foothold in magnificent Manhattan, the original New York City and center for all things glittery and grandiose. It was home to Carnegie Hall, where Tchaikovsky once appeared as guest conductor. Forever unfinished but still functional, the mammoth St. John's Cathedral served as bishop's throne at its Upper West Side locale, and another opulent landmark — the 17-story Waldorf-Astoria Hotel — offered about 1,000 rooms to a well-heeled clientele. Connecting Manhattan to a neighbor borough was a marvel of 1880s engineering known as the Brooklyn Bridge.

More recent civic milestones proved just as impressive, such as the arrival of subways and completion of underground train tunnels beneath the Hudson River. Then there was the awesome sight of Pennsylvania Station, a sprawling train center designed with classic Rome in mind. It became a monument of architecture and a symbol of the city, much like that tall, torch-bearing lady out in New York Harbor. By 1913, she shared thin air with the Woolworth Building, also known as the world's

After the Fed League folded in 1915, Edd Roush went to work for John McGraw and the New York Giants (Roush Family Collection).

tallest skyscraper. Legendary newspapers called midtown Manhattan home, including the *Times, Sun* and Joseph Pulitzer's *New York World.* Beneath and beyond these shimmering landmarks lay a 13-mile strip of everything — theatre, financial and garment districts, teeming ports, immigrant colonies and upper-crust hideaways.

This was the borough Edd Roush worked in.

New York must have seemed the epicenter of the universe. Even if it was also home to slums, crime, corruption and messy sanitation. Tucked away toward the top of Manhattan lay the Polo Grounds, home field for the Giants and Yankees. It was the original time-share, with the American Leaguers becoming tenants after their lease ran out on nearby Hilltop Park. Like the city around them, the Giants became fabulously famous. Everything took on added significance in the megalopolis and even small things seemed big under the scrutiny of 10 million pairs of eyes. In that kind of spotlight a baseball uniform could be mistaken for shining armor, or a bat for Excalibur.

Though the Giants had not won many jousts lately, they took five pennants under the leadership of their enlightened despot, John J. McGraw. Beginning his baseball career a year before Edd was born, McGraw first gained notoriety as part of a Baltimore Orioles dynasty that won three straight N.L. pennants in the 1890s. After a brief stint as manager of Baltimore's new American League franchise, he took the Giants' reins in 1902. Quick tempered, acid-tongued and tough as crusty leather, this legend became Edd's earliest foil. It seemed such a mismatch, the apprentice versus the master.

Edd's new chapter began on a chilly Wednesday, April 12, in Philadelphia, opening day of the 1916 season with the Giants facing the defending National League champions. On the mound for the home team was Grover Cleveland Alexander, beginning the sixth season of his long Hall of Fame career. He would retire with 373 victories, tied for most in N.L. history. Roush faced him four times that day and delivered two singles, making for a wonderful debut at the plate.

Things didn't go so well on the base paths, however. First, Edd left too early on a steal attempt and Alexander cut him down at second, and then he ran into an out while trying to stretch a single into a double. The Giants lost in disheartening fashion, as Philly scored the winning run on a walk, stolen base, passed ball and wild pitch. Philadelphia 5, New York 4. One game down, 153 to go.

Edd also made a splash at New York's first home game, poking three hits at the Polo Grounds while 25,000 watched. Benny Kauff rapped three safe ones, too, but the Fed connection couldn't prevent a 7–6 loss to Philadelphia. No matter, this ranked as another Edd Roush milestone — his first game at the Manhattan ballpark, and he arrived with a bang. But the detonation dispersed and he soon dropped from the starting lineup. Relegated to pinch-hitting duty, he sat while hard-hitting Dave Robertson took over right field. Other outfield spots were set in stone, with Kauff batting .300 and George Burns a dependable run producer. None of it seemed to matter, though, as the dreadful Giants dropped 13 of their first 15 games.

The *New York Times* reported, "There is no good to be gained by beating around the bush, so every one might as well know at the start that the Giants were beaten again yesterday. This condition has become chronic."[5]

It looked like the makings of another hopeless cellar dweller before McGraw's boys took a 180-degree turn. Suddenly, they couldn't lose. Mathewson pitched liked his old self, other hurlers followed suit, and Giants batsmen knocked the covers off baseballs. When the dust cleared, they had 17 consecutive wins, all on the road. A few weeks earlier, McGraw's team sat in last place, given up for dead. Now they owned second place and a 19–13 record, just 1½ games behind the Dodgers.

Edd saw little action during the big streak, appearing only once between wins five and 17. When the team returned home, he finally got back into right field, his long-awaited appearance coinciding with another suffrage promotion. It was the same drill, featuring colorful silk banners waving in the wind while "Suffs" talked up their cause. They also presented chocolate cakes as a reward for anyone who hit a home run. Maybe that's why Edd was thrown out trying to stretch a triple into a four-bagger.

Quickly falling from favor, Roush appeared frequently in pinch-hitting roles and infrequently as a spot starter. Somewhere along the line he had his oft-repeated conflict with John McGraw. Old man Roush would tell the story over and over, changing details here and there but always remaining true to the theme. McGraw jumps his case, saying his bat is too heavy; he lashes back and defends his choice of weapon; McGraw presses; Edd insists his heavy bats have produced .300 batting averages in every league he's ever played in. What's more, he would do it in the N.L., if given the chance to play regularly. McGraw is unimpressed.

The Giants came back to earth after the improbable win streak. They'd never be as bad as they were earlier, nor as good as they seemed lately. Edd remained buried on the bench through late June while Dave Robertson raised his average to a sizzling .340. George Burns kept his mark in the mid–.270s, which amounted to nothing special but he had a knack for crossing home plate. Benny Kauff was the next Ty Cobb and nobody benches Cobb. No greenhorn was going to crack this outfield rotation.

By mid–July the Giants were hovering around .500, a non-factor in the pennant race. Then came an amazing story that stunned all of New York: Christy Mathewson was going to be traded. Why not trade Manhattan back to the Indians while they were at it? Tall, handsome and historically heroic, Matty was the soul of the Giants, which explains why one local sports column read like an obituary. "The severest shock that New York baseball fans have had in many a day in the announcement of the passing of Christy Mathewson. For 16 years, the big boxman has been the idol of not only Manhattan enthusiasts but of baseball fans the country over."[6]

No such tributes flowed for other Giants included in the exchange — Bill McKechnie and Edd J. Roush. It was simply the "Matty trade." In return, the Giants received player-manager Buck Herzog and outfielder Wade Killefer. Though not yet official, it seemed a done deal: Zeus for a bag of peanuts. Then came a last-minute stay of execution from the baseball gods. There was a hitch in the deal. Offering more of a loan than trade, the Giants wanted an option on Mathewson, allowing them to reclaim him after two years. Cincinnati's side saw it as an unacceptable provision and McGraw wouldn't proceed without it. The Reds would still entertain offers for Herzog, but the Matty deal was dead.

Cincinnati folks seemed thrilled to have Christy Mathewson at the helm of the Reds ship (*Cincinnati Enquirer*).

It soon became clear how the Giants could part with the beloved veteran. They were sending their kid to college, and then bringing him home to run the family business. Cincinnati folk would've chosen a different analogy, something along the lines of a married man having a fling with their daughter.

The Giants eventually agreed to a proper wedding, without strings. Reds president Garry Herrmann secured a drawing card for his last-place team and McGraw upgraded his infield with versatile Herzog, a shortstop in Cincinnati but a third baseman during previous years. In Killefer, New York gained only a mediocre player whose career was almost done.

If Giants fans weren't tempted to burn down the Polo Grounds, it was probably because of the benevolent motivation for the trade. Matty wanted to manage and the Reds gave him an immediate opportunity. Herzog was

Cincinnati's player-manager, so the exchange created an immediate opening. No such opening existed at the Polo Grounds. The deal would go down as an important milestone, but not because of a fading legend and his administrative aspirations. It became the launching point for Edd Roush's career.

To the casual observer, it must have seemed a depressing downgrade. Cincinnati was no New York and the Reds certainly couldn't hold a candle to the Giants. But Edd's life revolved around baseball, not Broadway, and he would rather be a good player on a bad team than a benchwarmer on a good one. Besides, it wasn't like he'd been shipped out to Siberia. Cincinnati was Midwest royalty; if not a king or queen, then a plain-talking prince who'd helped carve a kingdom out of the woods. Once a rollicking river town and pit stop on the Underground Railroad, the city had matured considerably by 1916. The 1880s saw the arrival of a nationally renowned zoo, art institutions, a music hall and symphony orchestra. Included among the newer arrivals were Redland Field, a couple of downtown skyscrapers and Cincinnati Motor Speedway. Perched in a picturesque pose high above the city was the University of Cincinnati's McMicken Hall.

Once upon a time, civic leaders looked down from those heights and envisioned the growth of a world-class metropolis. Using the Ohio River and national canals as commerce routes, Cincinnati looked like the next big thing during the early decades of the 1800s. Industry grew rapidly and slaughterhouses popped up all over the city. With hog products as a chief source of trade, it earned the nickname "Porkopolis." For a time, it seemed Cincinnati would become a pearl of the Midwest, even if it meant casting them before swine. But river trade diminished when railroads took over, and municipal growth subsided along with dreams of a bigger-than-life megalopolis.

Like the city they represented, the Reds never quite achieved equal footing with the New Yorks, Chicagos or Bostons. But what an amazing pedigree — Cincinnati fielded history's first professional baseball team in 1869. Traveling from coast to coast, the "Red Stockings" went 57–0, were declared national champions, and accepted a mid-season invitation to the White House as guests of President Ulysses S. Grant. In 1870, they compiled a mark of 67-6-1. Six years later, Cincinnati became a charter member of the National League.

Precious little success followed in the wake of those illustrious beginnings. The Reds produced one championship over the next four decades and that came in the American Association, a watered-down version of major league ball. Still, there was honor in being a Red. Beyond its role as birthplace of pay for play, the franchise ambitiously blazed trails for promotion, grounds keeping and night baseball. The road to pastime history passed through Cincinnati. With President Herrmann serving as the swing vote on baseball's National Commission, the franchise also owned disproportionate influence on the present and future.

This was the tradition Edd entered during the summer of 1916.

Cincinnati proved similar to the Big Apple in some ways. Like New York, it had a class structure with geographic dividing lines. Affluent hillside neighborhoods looked down on the riverfront factories, railroads and slums of "the basin." In the category of political corruption, New York's Tammany Hall had nothing on George "Boss" Cox, the former city councilman turned influence peddler and vote trader. His

Reds president Garry Herrmann landed a hidden gem when he made the trade that brought Edd Roush to Cincinnati (Library of Congress).

three-decade reign as Republican godfather petered out by the early years of the 1900s and he died a couple months before the big trade. But a reminder of that former power remained at Redland, where Herrmann owed his position to the Cox machine influence.

Give Mathewson some credit: One of his first moves as Reds boss was to make Edd his starting center fielder. McGraw deserves a little recognition, too, for he told his pal that Roush would become a good player — even though the youngster left New York with a .188 batting average. Making his managerial debut on Friday, July 21, Mathewson was greeted with a thunderous ovation from fans at Redland Field. He signed a three-year contract earlier in the day, committing to the team through 1918. Rainy weather diminished the turnout for Matty's welcome, but 2,500 was actually a decent weekday figure by local standards. At 35–50, Cincinnati had a solid hold on last place, which is never good for attendance.

The new boss conducted typical pre-game routines, hitting fly balls and grounders to his players. Hearty cheers arose when Mathewson first appeared on the field and he smiled in acknowledgement. The biggest roar came later, as he approached the umpires and presented his lineup card. Penciled second in the batting order was Edd Roush.

Sixty-four years later, old Edd revisited that day, saying, "We was two runs behind and there was two on and I got a three-base hit. Goddammit, in the tenth inning we beat 'em. So they thought I was a hell of a ball player in the league."

Actually, the Reds *lost* in the 10th but Mr. Roush got everything else right. Facing Philadelphia's formidable hurler Eppa Rixey, he blasted a two-run triple that tied the game at 4–4 in the bottom of the ninth. Edd kept running and was thrown out at the plate. How could he resist going for a game-ending homer in his Cincinnati debut? Also knocking a couple of singles, he finished 3-for-5 in the 6–4 loss. Despite the defeat, Reds nation glowed with hope. "There was zip and aggressiveness and optimism about the work of the team which has been absent for a long time," wrote the *Cincinnati Enquirer*. "It is evident right from the start that the players are anxious to win for Matty, who has the good will of them all as well as their respect."

Edd built local goodwill with that big 48-ounce bat, drilling another triple in his second Reds game and pounding two more against Grover Alexander during a July 23 contest. Three days later, Mathewson returned to the Polo Grounds in a Reds uniform and received a royal welcome, complete with pre-game ceremonies at home plate. He'd requested a ban on flowers but admirers couldn't resist and sent a clothes basket full of them. Most of the 12,000-plus fans switched allegiances and cheered Matty's charges to a 4–2

What a sight to see: Giants legend Christy Mathewson in a Reds uniform, managing against New York. Pictured, from left, are John McGraw, Buck Herzog and Mathewson (Library of Congress).

victory. As a visiting player, Edd patrolled the outfield patch that McGraw rarely let him touch. McKechnie received his first start at third base — perhaps a gift from Matty for the homecoming — and came through with three hits.

The team struggled in those early days of Mathewson's reign, but he still had Cincinnati's support. Nobody expected the rebuilding to happen overnight. Though his playing days were over, Matty took the mound one last time on September 4 at Chicago's Wrigley Field. There, he matched up against fellow graybeard Three Finger Brown in a contrived showdown between former superstars. Facing each other for the first time since 1912, they surrendered a combined 34 hits and 18 runs. The legends couldn't even get each other out — Mathewson went 3-for-5 and Brown was 2-for-4. But attendance hit a season-high that day and most fans were there only to pay affectionate tribute.

Roush hit .287 as a Cincinnati starter and the Reds finished their season in the National League basement with the St. Louis Cardinals, both posting marks of 60–93. Hal Chase provided the biggest highlight, winning the league batting crown with a mark of .335, and a grateful *Enquirer* sang his praises: "Chase has been a real man for the Reds and there is many a manager today who wishes that he had got ahead of the Cincinnati club in signing him. He is the important ball player and the quickest thinker in the National League today. He is a model for the young ball player to emulate because he is a real artist in his profession."[7]

With the benefit of historical hindsight, we now know Chase was quite the opposite. Though a supremely talented first baseman, he might have made more money from throwing games than catching throws. A few folks probably knew that in 1916, as well.

10

Signs of Greatness

Roush wasn't present when the Reds opened their 1917 training camp in Shreveport, Louisiana. That fact provided little cause for alarm because nobody expected perfect attendance during those early March days. Then came a bombshell that complicated matters. Edd didn't want to play baseball anymore, not in the big show anyhow. Major leagues meant major cities and Edd preferred quieter environs.

"It is not simply a question of salary with Eddie, but he likes his work on the farm and does not want to leave it," Jack Ryder wrote in the *Enquirer*. "He says that he dislikes traveling and hates living in the big cities. He stated that if he had been retained by New York he would never have considered playing ball again, but he is fond of Cincinnati and a great admirer of Manager Mathewson, which may influence him to continue in the game for a least one more year."[2]

If he had played the overwhelmed country boy a few years later, it would have seemed nothing more than a bargaining ploy, but President Herrmann believed him sincere and said so publicly. Edd mulled over his options and decided to play, though he never did make it south for the Shreveport experience. Still unsigned on March 29, he appeared in uniform for a Reds exhibition at Louisville. Now, it was just a matter of time until "Roush" appeared on the dotted line.

Mathewson received a surprising telegram from Ty Cobb on April 2, asking permission to train with the Reds. He gave no explanation, but the baseball world knew all about his fistfight with Buck Herzog, the recent Red and current Giant. It happened while the Giants and Detroit Tigers paired for an exhibition tour in Texas. Cobb won the brawl and feuded with John McGraw, leading some New Yorkers to grumble about retaliation. Cobb was not safe from them and they probably weren't entirely safe from Cobb. Mathewson welcomed the ornery one with open arms, saying his players could learn much from watching him. It proved a brief stay, though long enough to serve its purpose.

As the regular season inched closer, Reds nation prepared for an inauspicious April 11 debut against the St. Louis Cardinals. On the surface it looked like a dull affair between two duds that tied for last in 1916; now they were tied for first at 0–0. Such is the annual rebirth of all teams, standing bare next to a pile of robes and rags.

With America declaring war near the end of spring training, the pastime entered uncharted territory in 1917. Would anybody even care about games while the globe soaked in unprecedented bloodshed? As it turned out, baseball and war proved quite compatible. Some of the most impassioned displays of patriotism took place at ballparks, which also proved fertile ground for fundraising drives. When 25,000 fans crowded Redland Field on a raucous opening day, many carried American flags and waved them at every opportunity. A pre-game concert brought thunderous cheers while the band performed such standards as "Yankee Doodle" and the "Star Spangled Banner." Army buglers periodically played reveille and other assorted calls from a station near the Reds bench.

Cincinnati prevailed that day, riding Pete Schneider's four-hitter to a 3–1 triumph. Edd produced nothing with the bat but made a couple tough catches in center field. When he went 2-for-3 the next day in another Reds win, it marked the start of something special — his first of many two-hit games during the opening week and a half. Through April 22, Edd owned a .429 batting average. Here was the player Matty envisioned, though it's unclear if he expected it so soon. For Roush, it proved what he had always known: all he ever needed was a chance.

If it seemed too good to be true, it was. The red-hot Hoosier injured his ankle while sliding into second base at Chicago. Carried off the field by teammates, he was diagnosed with a bad sprain. Now short-handed in their outfield, the Reds went back to a favorite trading partner for help. In return for an undisclosed sum of cash, the New York Giants sent Jim Thorpe to Cincinnati.

Sparsely used in his first three seasons, Thorpe missed all of 1916, and Edd was at least partially to blame. With promising prospects like Roush and Kauff in tow, the Giants cut Thorpe during the preseason and sent him to

Milwaukee of the American Association. Most followers thought it signaled the end of his baseball career and the super-achiever reportedly told friends he would quit if he couldn't make the big leagues. Some thought him a human publicity stunt from day one, and only an iron-clad, multi-year contract kept him around this long.

Thorpe remained Giants property in 1917 and Edd's misfortune became his opportunity. The Reds moved rookie Greasy Neale into center field and put big Jim in right. Answering naysayers everywhere, he delivered four hits in his first 10 at-bats — a small sample, but Thorpe would prove an adequate replacement and remained in the starting lineup long after Edd's return. Cincinnati's record stood at 6–6 when Roush went down and four under .500 when he returned. Picking up where he left off, his average stood at .360 on May 25, good for third in the league.

An early June showdown saw Cincinnati take three of four against the visiting Giants. The results knocked New York out of first and put its entire team in an angry mood. Punches flew during one game, with at least one landing on the nose of umpire Bill Byron. McGraw delivered the blow, claiming he was provoked and not because of the frequent bad calls. An insult apparently set him off. In the manager's version of things, Byron slandered him by saying he'd been run out of Baltimore. That apparently qualified as fighting words, so the little Napoleon felt justified for what followed.

Improving to 21–27, the Reds were still a second-division team with little hope of significant advancement. For one series, however, they made an impact on the pennant race and for a few minutes played supporting roles in a notorious McGraw meltdown. History makes note of the nose knock but not of Roush's punch at the plate. He delivered two hits and a sacrifice fly.

Edd stood second in the batting race on June 20 and moved into the top spot a week later, posting a .356 mark. Meanwhile, Ty Cobb led the other league at .369. Cobb and Roush — the two best hitters in baseball. But Cincinnati wasn't entirely a one-man show. Fred Toney had the spotlight on July 1 and made it shine twice as bright when he tossed three-hitters in both games of the home doubleheader against Pittsburgh. Even in an era of rubber-armed hurlers, this achievement stood out.

It was actually a bit inconsiderate because the Reds went to a lot of trouble making the day a tribute to a loveable Pirates legend. With the shortstop's remarkable career winding down to its final season, Cincinnati arranged a "Honus Wagner Day" at Redland Field. Applauded at every plate appearance, Wagner seemed genuinely touched by the tribute.

Supplementing the Cincinnati faithful was a group of fans who traveled from Louisville, Kentucky. That's where Wagner began his major league career in 1897, three years before the franchise moved to Pittsburgh. Over the next

21 years, he won eight batting titles and set the standard for shortstop defense. If Ty Cobb and Babe Ruth are carved into baseball's Mount Rushmore, Wagner is sculpted in Roman marble.

Pirate bats produced few hits that day and the guest of honor cracked two of them. Still, by the end of the afternoon it became "Fred Toney Day." Young Roush rapped four hits on the day, twice as many as the great Wagner, but this was a time to honor his elder.

The Reds started making noise in early July, winning seven of eight. On July 12 they swept two at the Polo Grounds, improved to 45–39, and pulled within a game of second-place Philadelphia. Cincinnati wasn't irrelevant anymore, and Matty drew widespread praise for giving hope to a historically inept franchise. Finishing that road series with three wins in five games, the Reds made New York their home away from home. To punctuate the point, they proceeded to sweep five straight at Brooklyn and moved into sole possession of second. The Giants led by only one in the win column but had far fewer losses. Owing to inclement weather, and lack thereof in Cincinnati, they'd played 15 fewer games.

Returning home in late July, the Reds beat Philadelphia twice, stretched their latest win streak to seven, and moved 11 games over .500. While the team soared, Jim Thorpe descended toward oblivion. For the better part of two months he had hung onto a starting job before diminishing returns led to a change and Tommy Griffith took over right field on June 20. Thorpe spent the rest of his Reds tenure platooning in left with Neale. Both were destined for the Hall of Fame but not the one in Cooperstown. They are enshrined at pro football's Valhalla, in Canton, Ohio. Thorpe became a pioneering pigskin professional and Neale coached the Philadelphia Eagles to two NFL titles during the late 1940s. In 1917, however, baseball remained the only sport that paid a decent wage and two future gridiron greats plugged away on the ball diamond.

The Reds eventually settled on one left fielder, and their Olympian proved too fragile at the plate. He could turn the fastball around but never looked comfortable with breaking balls, especially ones from right-handers. By August, Thorpe found himself back in New York. Finishing his Cincinnati stint with a .247 batting average, he didn't fit the long-range plans of Mathewson's resurgent Reds. After winning their seventh straight on July 27, they had to be excited about what lay ahead: two more home games with Philadelphia, and then a couple of series against the Dodgers and Giants at Redland Field. Excitement turned to despair, however, as they proceeded to drop 10 of their next 11 games. The unexplainable free-fall put them in fourth place at 55–53.

With all pennant hopes crushed, Cincinnati turned its attention to the

Smooth-faced Roush became a young star in 1917, winning his first batting title (Roush Family Collection).

The Roush follow-through is shown here (Roush Family Collection).

lone remaining drama — Edd Roush's quest for a batting title. After jockeying for the top spot with Walton Cruise of St Louis, he went in front and stayed there awhile. By early August, Cruise had dropped 23 points behind Edd's .341 and his St. Louis teammate moved into second. That fellow Cardinal was Rogers Hornsby, the man destined to become the greatest right-handed hitter of all time. For the moment, however, he remained just a promising 21-year-old who trailed Roush by 16 points.

Suddenly, Benny Kauff leapfrogged into second, and if past history was any indicator, he'd soon overshadow the Hoosier. Edd didn't blink, keeping his average around .350 while the pretenders mirrored a winter weather report by dipping into the teens and rising to the upper 20s. It soon became a two-horse race between Roush and Hornsby.

In the midst of everything, life interrupted. During a road trip to New York, a Western Union telegram arrived for Edd at the Ansonia Hotel. Dated August 18, it came from Oakland City and announced that he was the father of a nine-pound baby girl. They named her Mary. Even though he went hitless at Brooklyn that afternoon, it was a good day for the Roush clan. Things didn't go so well the following day at the Polo Grounds — not for Matty and John McGraw, anyhow. Both were arrested for violating a "blue law" that forbade Sunday baseball. The game went on as scheduled, however, and Edd delivered two hits in a 5–0 Reds victory.

End of the month statistics showed Roush at .346 and Hornsby at .330. With only four weeks left in the season, time was on Edd's side, but he didn't coast to the finish line. On September 22 he blistered a three-run homer during a 4–2 win over Brooklyn. Coming against veteran pitcher Rube Marquard, the game-turning swat inspired quite a tribute from the *New York Times*: "Never was baseball fiction penned in which the lordly home run did not cap the climax and make of some young man a hero. In the reality staged at Redland Field today between the Reds and the Dodgers, this time honored swat took its toll of interest, with Ed Roush the hero and astounded Brooklynites the beaten."[3] A day later, he went 3-for-6 in a doubleheader split, and then disappeared from the lineup for the final week of the season. Was it a ploy to assure a batting championship? No, he hurt his leg during the second half of that September 23 twin bill and left in the third inning. Hornsby never made another serious run at the crown.

Edd finished at .341, taking the title by a comfortable margin of 14 points. He had become a genuine superstar. Benny Kauff enjoyed a nice year, too, placing fourth in the N.L. with a .308 mark. But he was no Roush.

Cincinnati ended up fourth at 78–76, 20 games behind pennant-winning New York. So the Giants didn't feel *too* bad about letting Roush go. They had bigger things to worry about, like preparing for the World Series. Transforming a doormat into pennant winners in two short years, John McGraw was a genius again. His team went on to lose the series in six games, falling to a Chicago White Sox team comprised of most of the same players who later appeared in the Black Sox series.

But that's a story for another chapter.

11

A Batting Battle and
Wartime Baseball

Both of us hope that you give question of retiring from game most serious consideration.... You should at least give us your service during coming season, thus affording us an opportunity to secure someone later on if you decide to retire from game.... Join us this request.— March 12 telegram co-signed by Christy Mathewson and Garry Herrmann

There is no good to be gained by beating around the bush, so everyone might as well know at the start that the Reds did not win the pennant in 1918. The details are as follows: third place, a 68–80 record, 15½ games out of first.

But it made for two consecutive years in the first division and that spelled progress. The roster underwent change, most significantly with the April 28 trade for Yankees second baseman Lee Magee — another name that became associated with dirty doings. Hod Eller came back strong after a promising rookie year that saw him go 10–5 and make headlines by striking out three Giants batters on nine pitches. In 1918, he posted a team-high 16 wins and team-low 2.36 ERA.

Born north of Indianapolis in Muncie, Eller was another native Hoosier who reached the pastime big time. He made his mark with the "shine ball," a doctored pitch that broke sharply and unpredictably. By rubbing or polishing the ball smooth on one side, it created uneven air resistance. Eller was known to apply paraffin. Other Cincinnati hurlers faded into mediocrity. Fred Toney went 6–10 before getting traded to the Giants, and Pete Schneider saw his ERA balloon from 1.97 to 3.51.

Meanwhile, Edd Roush proved he was no flash in the pan by chasing another batting title. Yet it all rang hollow compared to what was happening on European battlefields. With a year's worth of dead doughboys on the ledger, America's national pastime became less relevant. War intruded into its very dugouts and turned athletes into soldiers. The provost marshal announced a "work or fight" order that commanded all draft-age men to join the military or work for essential war-related industry. Failing to win exemption, baseball was classified as non-essential and had to end its season by Labor Day, about a month earlier than usual.

Christy Mathewson enlisted in late August, became a captain in the army's Chemical Warfare Service, inhaled mustard gas and never managed another game. Popular theory says a training exercise damaged his lungs and dealt a slow-moving death sentence. Some believe he simply contracted tuberculosis and the disease was unrelated to his war experiences. Whatever the cause, Matty lived in ill health until his death in 1925.

War became a sobering backdrop to the season. Of course, that shadow loomed since 1914, when the great conflict first started. But those were other people's sons and fathers dying during the early years. The United States officially entered the fray on April 6, 1917, spending most of the year in parade mode while mobilizing her military. The mood changed in 1918, as U.S. soldiers arrived in force and fought bloody battles along the Western Front.

Predictably, the year saw a wave of anti–German hysteria sweep the country and, despite its long, proud link to the fatherland, Cincinnati proved no different. Even before the declaration of war, education officials announced that German school books would be sold as junk. *Literary Digest* released a national poll that showed the German language suffering serious decline, both locally and nationally. In nearly every Ohio city, it dropped from curriculums or died a natural death from lack of student interest. When Cincinnati officials voted to change German street names, it was front-page, big-headline news in the April 3 edition of the *Cincinnati Post*: "Thus, Bremen-st must go and also Bismarck-st, and Berlin-st, and Hapsburg-st, and Hamburg-st, and Hanover-st and Wilhelm-st — just as The Post has been urging during the past three weeks while Council hesitated."

Uncle Sam left Roush and Hornsby alone, giving them a chance to reprise their duel for the N.L. batting crown. Also avoiding the service were Reds third baseman Heinie Groh and Brooklyn's Zack Wheat, which meant four of the top five hitters returned from 1917. Kauff was the only one who traded his bat for a rifle, playing 67 games before bidding adieu.

Edd's pursuit of a second title proved fraught with potholes. In 1917 he never fell far from the top and spent most of the season as a front-runner, but 1918 saw him eating dust from beginning to end. Magee looked like Cincinnati's best batter in the early stages when he exploded for five hits in his second game as a Red, then followed with a couple 2-for-4 efforts. Nobody could maintain that pace, not even Cobb, but Magee remained a Redleg revelation. Near the end of May, Edd was hitting around .300, a nice enough average but not top 10 worthy.

June saw the arrival of Roush as a writer, his byline accompanying a *Baseball Magazine* article titled "How I Won the Batting Crown. A Few Comments on My Best Season — So Far." It didn't exactly provide a blueprint for successful swinging. Calling himself a natural hitter, Edd said there are no particular rules for the "curious study, this batting." No particular pitch or pitcher affected him significantly more than another, though he admitted an aversion to southpaws. Good hitting came in unpredictable streaks and slumps were just as mysterious. One day, a player can hit anything a pitcher offers and the next, he couldn't hit a watermelon with the side of a house — Edd's exact words, or those of a ghost writer.

He told of his youth, playing ball as a righty and making the difficult transition back to a southpaw. Edd also informed readers that he was married and had a daughter, which put him in class 4 of the military draft. Message to the sports world: Roush is no slacker; he's just a family man and an unlikely candidate for conscription.

Another declaration would become a renewable mantra — he disliked spring training and believed farm work provided ample conditioning. The article concluded with a self-affirming goal for the current season: "I surely want to prove that my good showing last year wasn't any flash in the pan and that I am not one of those mushroom phenoms who flare up one season and flivver all the rest." He accomplished that and much more. Nobody could ever call Edd Roush a mushroom flivverer.

Nothing came easy, however. After maintaining a solid batting average through mid–June, he sprained his right ankle in Brooklyn and sat out the next two weeks. During his absence the Reds lost eight of nine and, upon his return, that weighty war club generated only five hits in 24 plate appearances. Groh picked up the slack, knocking 10 hits over six games and raising his average to a league-leading .350.

The Hoosier hitman would soon leap among National League leaders, and it all started during a

The grip that launched a thousand rips (National Baseball Hall of Fame Library, Cooperstown, New York).

July 10 doubleheader sweep of the Brooklyn Dodgers. He went 2-for-4 in the opener, and then followed with a 3-for-4 effort against future Hall of Famer Burleigh Grimes. The streak continued through the next three games: 2-for-5, 1-for-4, 3-for-5, and all in winning efforts. Then came a four-hit explosion against New York's Al Demaree, a better-than-average hurler. After six contests, 15 hits and 27 plate appearances, Roush rejoined the "first division." When the latest top 10 averages came out on July 14, Groh topped the list comfortably at .352 and Edd stood 50 points back in eighth place.

Cincinnati fans could take great pride from three different Reds winning successive batting titles — Hal Chase in 1916, Roush in 1917, and now Groh. Edd didn't mind surrendering his crown to a teammate, but Groh fell into a horrible slump over the next few weeks and Zack Wheat shot past him into first place. Somewhere along the way, Edd told his fading comrade that he'd better get going or the Roush train would resume at full speed toward title town. Groh admitted he had run out of steam and urged Edd to leave the station without him ... words to that effect, anyhow.

In the middle of a sizzling batting chase, baseball's dark side emerged during a July 25 doubleheader at Boston. Edd won the first game with a two-run homer in the top of the 13th inning, a remarkable feat considering that two teammates were trying to throw the game. The details emerged a couple years later at trial. Hal Chase supposedly brought Lee Magee in on a deal to lose game one of the twin bill and told his gambling connection that starting pitcher Pete Schneider was tanking, too. After the Reds took a 4–2 decision, Magee reportedly offered to make up for it by throwing other games but the "connection" wasn't interested. He demanded restitution.

Those were the dirty particulars that few people knew at the time. Many grew suspicious, however. Though Chase drew no negative attention to himself, Magee stood out like an un-opposing thumb. He committed an unthinkable ninth-inning error that tied things at 2–2, throwing wild to the wrong base when an easy toss to first would have ended the game. Hitless in five plate appearances, Magee seemed an unlikely rally-starter when he came to the plate with two outs in the 13th, but the baseball gods insisted on pulling this scoundrel down a heroic path.

In his 1964 interview with author Lawrence Ritter, Edd described what happened next:

> He hit a ball and it took a bad hop, hit Johnny Rawlings in the nose at shortstop, broke his nose. Of course, (Magee) got to first base. Matty said to me, "I'm gonna send Lee on the first pitch, then if you get a base hit, maybe we'll win the ball game."... Well, whoever was catching threw it out into center field. He had Magee throwed out half-way to second ... saw the ball go out to center field and he rounded second and was going to third base and the (ball)

had him thrown out half way over *there*.... Jack Smith (was) the third baseman and the ball took a bad hop and hit him on the knee.... The left fielder came in and played (short) and I hit the next pitch over his head for a home run, see."[1]

It was a comedy of the absurd, success forced upon a quest for failure. A routine grounder turns into an unavoidable single and a half-hearted steal attempt puts Magee on third base. He simply could not make that third out. A couple weeks later, the Reds suspended Chase for the rest of the season.

As a senior citizen, Edd still had vivid memories of the dark prince. He said all Reds knew Chase was crooked but Mathewson wouldn't do anything about it. (Not without proof, anyhow.) They also knew there were none better at first base when he played to win. If a loss would benefit Chase better, however, he might cover the bag late. He could also deliver two or three hits and still subtly lead his team to defeat. The man was talented.

"Hell, he hit in front of me and drove in runs every game," Roush told the *Hamilton (Ohio) Journal-News* in 1974. "It was hard to tell. But Heinie (Groh) and the other fellows on the infield would throw the ball over to first and he wasn't there to get it. He'd make it look like it was a bad throw to the fans. Groh was after him all the time. He'd say, 'Well Chase, how are you betting today? I want to know how many errors I'm going to have before the game starts.' Of course, some time he was betting on us. He didn't always bet against us."

By August 7, Wheat led the league with a .336 mark, followed by Groh's .332. Edd seemed out touch at .304, but with time running out on the war-shortened season, he finally made his move. First came a 3-for-4 effort at Pittsburgh, then a five-hit explosion the following day against St. Louis. Included in that quintet was a game-winning knock in the bottom of the ninth.

Edd sizzled during a nine-game stretch in mid-to-late August, belting 16 hits in 31 tries. They weren't a bunch of harmless singles either; many went for extra bases. Highlighting the power trip was a grand slam off Rube Marquard in an 8–4 win over Brooklyn. Not coincidentally, Cincinnati won eight of nine contests and improved to 57–55. As Edd Roush went, so went the Reds.

On August 24, it was Wheat .343, Roush .328. Edd remained red-hot, smacking four hits against seldom-used Gary Fortune of the Phillies, and then following with eight knocks in his next 17 plate appearances. By August 28, the margin between first and second had shrunk to a wafer-thin margin: .341 to .338. Groh rejoined the hunt, too, pushing his average to .333, but those carefree title-chasing days came to a sudden halt. Named as Cincinnati's new manager, Groh inherited the burden of leadership from army-bound Christy Mathewson

Also making war-related news was a newly commissioned officer named

Ty Cobb. Owning an insurmountable lead in the American League batting race, he left the game to become a captain in the Chemical Warfare Service — a common destination for baseball players of note. Matty would join him there.

With both pennants and one batting crown settled, the eyes of the baseball world centered on Zach Wheat and Edd J. Roush. Two Cubs twirlers held Edd to one hit in an August 29 doubleheader, but there were six games to go and that Roush bat still smelled of burnt horsehide. He never took another swing. Informed that his father was seriously injured in a fall from a telephone pole, Edd quickly left Chicago and headed home.

In addition to running the farm, William Roush had also worked regular jobs. He came in on the ground floor of a young industry, becoming local manager of the Independent Telephone Company. Pole climbing was considered part of the job and falling a risk of the trade. He had plunged before and lived to tell the tale, then avoided further risk by settling back into full-time farming. Returning to the phone company in 1918, William had only been on the job a few days when a problem arose on Oakland City's east side. Called in to "adjust some trouble with the lines," he entered a backyard and climbed to the top of a pole. Nobody saw what happened next but several people heard the impact. Neighbors ran to the scene and saw William lying unconscious on the ground, an arm broken and his head badly injured.

Carried to his home, the Roush patron never regained consciousness and couldn't have noticed when his famous son arrived for a bedside vigil. William died on Sept. 5, almost a week to the day since tumbling earthward. He was 50 years old.

Listing survivors in the obituary, the *Oakland City Journal* spelled Edd's name with one "D" but at least it didn't refer to him as "Edward." William would have appreciated that. In addition to a stunned family, he left behind eight Holstein cows, two heifers, a couple of mules, three $500 Liberty bonds and an estate worth about $2,500.[2]

At this point in time, a batting battle must have seemed trifling to the Roush clan, but the baseball nation reveled in a race too close to call. At season's end, some numbers crunchers had Wheat edging Edd by a point or less, others said the Red won by similar margins, and a few unofficial statisticians proclaimed it a tie. The sporting world had to wait until winter for official word, when the league office released its final figures and proclaimed Wheat champion. He trimmed Roush by two points, .335–.333.

Back at Cincinnati, the *Enquirer* claimed Wheat was fading at the end and took the crown because he sat out a season-ending doubleheader. It's true he went cold, producing three hits in his last 15 plate appearances, but Edd went 4-for-15 before departing town and leaving his batting average in stasis for the final six games. It seems only fair that Wheat did the same for one day, even if it was the last day of the season.

The Dodger veteran probably felt due for a title. Nine long seasons had passed since he had made his major league debut in Brooklyn and started that steady climb toward elite status. A batting crown seemed like the next natural step for the Wheat resume, but 1918 started with a holdout at his Missouri farm. He threatened retirement rather than submit to a salary reduction that club officials justified as an unavoidable wartime measure. Management eventually gave in but not before its slugger missed all of April. From that tempestuous beginning sprang the ultimate hitting honor, one that could have just as easily gone to Roush.

What would have happened if he'd been around for those final few contests? The answer was always simple for Edd: He wins the 1918 title, case closed. But maybe he won it anyhow — a two-hit performance was wiped from the record books, thanks to the St. Louis Cardinals' protest of their April 29 loss. Edd went 1-for-4 when the game was replayed in August, and that made all the difference. Some labeled the overrule an unjust usurpation of on-field authority.

Fittingly enough, the controversy centered on a play by Roush. It happened with one out and a runner on third base. Operating in a rain-soaked outfield, he slipped while chasing a fly and deflected the ball upward. From a seated position, he reached out and caught it before it hit the ground. The base runner apparently tagged up and took off at first contact between the ball and outfielder. After catching the deflection, Edd fired to third and was awarded a double play. Officials said the runner left too early, but the Cardinals insisted he didn't have to wait around until the ball finally settled into Roush's glove. After umpire Hank O'Day rejected their argument, they appealed to N.L. president John Heydler and won.

The game was wiped from the record books, along with Edd's 2-for-3 showing at the plate. The rematch saw St. Louis triumph, 5–3, but that proved a trifling matter. Another victory would not have improved Cincinnati's third-place finish. The true significance couldn't be measured until season's end, when statisticians pored over numbers of individual players. They discovered that without the do-over, Edd successfully defends his title, .336 to .335. Second place was certainly honorable, however, and it secured his place among National League royalty.

The baseball world wondered aloud why John McGraw ever let Roush go. Tired of the criticism, the Giants skipper fired back in a *Baseball Magazine* article. "It is true I let Cincinnati have a grand good player but why didn't some of the other owners get after Roush when he was on the market? I didn't pay very much for him, as prices go, when I secured him from the

Federal League. No other owners seemed to want him until I had him.... As it was I had no immediate use for Roush, while Cincinnati wanted him as a regular outfielder. So I let him go and do not consider that I used bad judgment when I made the transfer."[3]

12

A Year to Remember

I led the league in '17, got beat out by two points in '18 (and) they sent me a contract in 1919 for $4,500—a $500 cut. That's the way they did things back in those days. If they would have sent me a contract for $7,000 or $8,000 I would have signed it. But they made me mad and I said, "If you can't beat $10,000, I won't be there."[1]

The planet whirled at a dizzying pace in 1919, packing an endless array of historical highlights and lowlights into one 12-month period. With the passage of suffrage and prohibition legislation, Congress backed a woman's right to vote and denied a nation's right to consume alcohol. A deadly flu epidemic still raged across the globe, killing more people than World War I, and diplomats arranged a harsh peace treaty between the war's victors and vanquished. Internal discord bubbled over in a wave of race riots that spread through U.S. cities, while a "Red Scare" saw government crackdowns on suspected Communists. Labor battles popped up everywhere, with millions of workers involved in thousands of strikes. In sports, Jack Dempsey became heavyweight champion of the world, Man O' War launched the greatest career in horse racing history, and Babe Ruth reinvented baseball.

Everything happened that year, hence the title of William Klingaman's book, *1919: The Year Our World Began.* High on the roster of signature events was the fixed World Series. It took names like Cicotte, Shoeless Joe, and Roush, and put them on the same front pages that trumpeted cultural revolution. There could not be an ordinary Fall Classic at this stage of history, not in 1919. Something spectacular had to happen, such as a huge underdog upsetting one of baseball's all-time great teams.

Reds fans harbored hope for the upcoming season, which wasn't the same as raising expectations in New York, Chicago or Boston. Those cities knew what a championship felt like. Though the old Red Stockings invented the wheel in 1869, Cincinnati remained a unicycle town for the next half-century. Success was long overdue and current players seemed talented enough to make a run at the pennant. Management also pulled off some addition-by-subtraction moves that made the roster more dependable.

During the previous winter, Hal Chase was traded to the Giants for Bedford Bill Rariden. On paper, it looked like a lopsided swap — the light-hitting, part-time catcher in exchange for a .300 hitter with elite defensive skills. The Reds, however, were just glad to be rid of the con artist formerly known as Prince Hal. Lee Magee was sent packing, too, his .290 bat traded to Brooklyn for cash. One crooked moment caused an ignoble ending for a man who should have had the city eating out of his hand. After all, he was born in Cincinnati.

Replacing Magee at second base was Morrie Rath, a former White Sox infielder who hadn't played big league ball since 1913. He spent most of the lost years on a long minor league tour, with stops at Kansas City, Toronto and Salt Lake City. The team landed a strong replacement for Chase, trading outfielder Tommy Griffith for Brooklyn's two-time batting champion Jake Daubert. Granted, the veteran stood five years removed from his last crown, but he still came off a solid .308 season.

Serving as interim first baseman during Chase's 1918 suspension, Sherry Magee now moved to the outfield. Then there was tough-guy Greasy Neale, the ordinary but dependable fixture in left field. Heinie Groh reprised his role as slugging third baseman after leading the league in runs and doubles, while Ivey Wingo brought a reputation as one of baseball's best defensive catchers. Second base looked shaky, but overall the daily lineup seemed strong.

Now the Reds had to get that Roush guy into camp. With the season opener only days away, Edd remained steadfast in his latest holdout and folks prepared themselves for the worst. "Roush's holdout is calm, persistent, unshakeable," the *Sporting News* wrote. "He firmly believes that he is worth a $10,000 salary and no argument has moved him." Shortstop Larry Kopf also refused to report, though few seemed to notice. He had missed the previous season while serving in the military and hit only .255 in 1917.

Both men reached terms just in the nick of time, with Edd predictably fit and trim. On April 20, he joined the starting lineup for Cincinnati's final pre-season tune-up at Redland Field. One report had the stubborn Roush calmly capitulating after management showed him proof of the franchise's shaky finances. Some sixty years later, elderly Edd remembered setting a price of $10,000 and getting it. Either way, Reds fans had cause to celebrate.

How did the two sides finally come together? Partial credit went to Jimmy Widmeyer, owner of a Cincinnati newspaper stand at Fifth and Walnut streets. Serving as a go-between, Edd's friend journeyed to Oakland City and tried to pry open the lines of communication. They returned to the big city together, completing a 19-hour drive in the Roush "touring car." A shadowy though mostly harmless figure with low-level connections to the city's criminal underworld, Widmeyer would later feed inside information to Edd about the Black Sox fix.

Ironically, the opponents for Roush's first, and Cincinnati's last, pre-season game were the Chicago White Sox. They came in as 8–5 favorites to win the meaningless road contest, proving that even when games didn't count, gamblers could find action in a baseball town. The still-clean Sox took a 5–3 decision in front of seven thousand fans, a Redland attendance record for exhibitions.

When games *did* count, nobody knew quite what to expect from Cincinnati's pitching staff. Hod Eller returned with his shine ball but was the only Reds hurler to crack double figures in wins the previous season. Once-promising Pete Schneider was jettisoned to the Yankees for cash and Cincy replaced his rotation spot by trading for aging Giants hurler Slim Sallee. Coming off an 8–8 season, the 11-year veteran seemed on the downswing but his 2.25 ERA ranked best among New York starters. At the opposite end of the spectrum rested Cuban import Adolfo Luque — heavy on potential and light on track record. Returning from military service was Dutch Ruether, a young Californian who'd get his first shot at a full season in 1919. Picked off the waiver scrap heap after missing all of 1918, former Yankee Ray Fisher rounded out the starting staff.

The biggest off-season mystery revolved around Christy Mathewson. With the war over, most had expected him to come back to Cincinnati and resume managerial duties. But nobody could make contact with him in Europe and that made Garry Herrmann nervous. Unaware that Matty was convalescing in a French hospital, he hired Pat Moran as manager on January 30. A highly respected skipper, the new field boss was fresh off a four-year stint with the Phillies, where he delivered a pennant in 1915. Still, it hurt to lose Mathewson, the white knight who was supposed to take the Reds to new heights.

Moran had his work cut out for him. Though he had made a habit of exceeding expectations, Cincinnati expected more than usual. Coming off a distant yet unusually lofty third-place finish, the next logical step was serious contention — maybe second place or even first. Did Cincinnati have the roster to compete with defending N.L. champ Chicago? No other team came close to the Cubs' league-leading ERA and now their staff looked even stronger with the return of sergeant Grover Cleveland Alexander. Then there were the New York Giants, perpetual contenders who always finished ahead of Cincinnati.

The Windy City also had a fast horse in the American League race, as Comiskey's White Sox lineup looked nearly identical to the one that captured the 1917 World Series. If not for the war, that group might have made it two in a row. Now the pieces were back in place, with a few left over. Of course, the Sox could expect plenty of competition from defending world champion Boston, where Babe Ruth continued his personal ascension.

April 23, Redland Field, Reds versus Cardinals. The first post-war game was a no-frills affair, played in front of a sizeable and orderly crowd of 22,000. No wild-eyed revelers with annoying noisemakers and none of the typical lunacy brought on by opening day celebrations. Instead, there were only composed displays of polite enthusiasm. "The ball game was the thing and it occupied the attention of the huge throng to the exclusion of all other interests," the *Cincinnati Enquirer* explained. "Most of the tiresome preliminary ceremonies were wisely omitted.... But all hands were cheerful when Umpire Bill Byron called 'Play ball' and the rooters realized that the national pastime had returned to its lofty pinnacle of popular esteem."

Ruether pitched seven strong innings and the Reds prevailed, 6–2. Fisher tossed a six-hitter the following day, leading the home team to a 3–1 victory, then Eller went the distance in a 5–1 triumph. Cincinnati made it a clean sweep when Luque scattered nine hits in another 5–1 decision. Led by their dominant moundsmen, the Reds won their first seven games before tasting defeat. Two more victories followed, courtesy of a couple more pitching gems, then Slim Sallee crafted a three-hitter in his franchise debut — an 8–1 triumph over the visiting Cubs.

Ten games into the season the Reds were 9–1 and the Queen City finally had a true-blue contender. Meanwhile, Edd J. Roush was removing all mystery from the batting race, and not in a good way. He got off to a horrible start, going hitless in 18 at-bats, and his batting average stood at .048 through six games. The Reds barely noticed, however. With such magnificent pitching, they could afford to be patient.

It would make for quicker reading to say Cincinnati rode its great start to the finish line, without worry or challenge. The real story, however, takes some twists and turns. That early success didn't create any breathing room in the pennant race because Brooklyn proved just as hot. When the Reds lost a 12-inning struggle to the Cubs and "fell" to 9–2, it put them in second place, behind the 7–1 Dodgers. Nobody would run away with this flag.

On May 9, Grover Alexander faced the Reds in his first game since returning from war. He held them to one run on six hits, but Ray Fisher performed just a tad better by blanking Chicago on four knocks. Fisher the castoff beating Alexander the Great — something special was brewing in Redland. Two days later, Eller twirled a no-hitter against the Cardinals.

John McGraw's Giants soon surged to the top, their 12–4 record slightly better than Brooklyn (11–5) and Cincinnati (13–6). Next up was a first versus third showdown at the Polo Grounds, where New York took the opener,

5–0, in front of 35,000 fans. The hometown *Times* devoted most of its game story to denigrating the visiting Reds, writing particularly harsh assessments of certain Big Apple expatriates. Jake Daubert was a has-been who'd left his best days in Brooklyn. The same went for Slim Sallee, except his glory years were spent in a Giants uniform. Bill Rariden didn't have much talent, so it was a good thing he and Sallee had farms to fall back on.

Pat Moran earned praise as a good manager but, boy, did he ever have a mess on his hands. Only one-and-a-half games out of first on May 18, yet the Reds weren't any good. The pennant pursuit was apparently a two-horse, one-city race.

Cincinnati evened up the series with a 6–4 win, Edd scoring the go-ahead run in the top of the 10th. Opening that frame with a double, he eventually came home on a bases-loaded squeeze bunt. It was a disappointing end for the large contingent of wounded soldiers who attended as guests of the Giants, but at least they saw plenty of action, and not all of it between the lines. Thinking Fisher had thrown at him, New York slugger Heinie Zimmerman challenged the Reds pitcher to a fight in the back lot and both parties headed that direction before teammates blocked their paths. New York came back to win the rubber game, 7–5.

Edd recovered from his early slump, hit .403 in May, and burst into the N.L.'s top 10 on June 4, his .333 average tying for fifth. Leading the league with an impossibly high .450 was Philadelphia slugger Gavvy Cravath. Wingo stood second at .373, a surprising mark from the light-hitting Reds veteran, and Rariden hit .324, giving Cincinnati the best catcher combo in baseball.

By late June, it was shaping into a four-team race — the Reds hot on New York's trail, Pittsburgh on the Reds' heels, and Chicago pushing Pittsburgh. Edd led his team to an important win over the Pirates on June 27, going 4-for-5 with a double, triple and two runs. He also shined defensively, making two "clever" catches and taking a home run away from Casey Stengel.

In the batting title battle, Jim Thorpe emerged as an unlikely frontrunner during early July. Appearing in only 22 games, he was hitting .411 for the Boston Braves, and some said he'd overcome his former fatal flaw of whiffing at curveballs. Cravath held a .376 mark, built in 52 games, and Edd owned a somewhat-modest .310 average. He would have to cover a lot of ground to even come close to the top or wait for the field to come back to him.

A team crown remained priority number one, however, and the Reds still stood locked in a tight battle with the Giants. By early July, it had become a two-team race again. Cincinnati's six-game winning streak created a virtual dead heat for first, while Chicago and Pittsburgh dropped several lengths behind. Nobody seemed worried in New York, where pundits believed their team superior to the upstart Ohioans. Owners of the league's most explosive offense, the Giants certainly seemed better on paper. The only thing keeping it close was mystifying inconsistency among their talented pitchers, which wouldn't last forever.

On July 6 the Reds swept a home doubleheader from Pittsburgh and moved into sole possession of first. They led, 2–0, when the second game ended after six innings; it was getting late and the team needed to catch a 6:00 P.M. train to Boston. The Pirates acquiesced to the abrupt stoppage but John McGraw filed a protest, insisting that the Reds earn every inch of ground on the pennant battlefield. Unaffected by Mac's maneuver, Cincinnatians remained giddy over a rare moment in city history — the calendar said "July" and their team sat in first place. Reported the *Enquirer*:

> Not since the days when the late "Buck" Ewing was piloting the team back in 1896 have they ever had such glowing prospects of landing a National League pennant. Even in those days they aspired to second place, for the leaders were out in front so far they were hardly approachable. Second place at that time meant that they would play in the Temple Cup series and participate in the receipts.[2]

At Boston the Reds took four of five and in the process witnessed how Thorpe maintained his average; he hardly ever played. Still hovering around the .400 mark, he totaled three at-bats for the entire series. Cincinnati's heroes triumphed again in an opener at Philadelphia, running their current win streak to five, but New York swooped into first when the Reds lost their next contest.

The Giants could even win without playing. That's what happened when officials upheld McGraw's protest and expunged the Reds' six-inning triumph from July 6. But it went back into the victory column a few weeks later when the final three innings were completed.

A New York–Cincinnati showdown series was slated for late July but rain ruined the drama. They completed just one lonely game on July 23, a strange day that saw Polo Grounds faithful cheering for the enemy. It was supposed to be a doubleheader, but when fans showed up they discovered game one was cancelled. What's more, they had to wait two hours for game two to begin. The field looked a watery mess and officials wanted to let it dry out awhile — all perfectly logical, but spectators were in no mood for logic. Greeted with jeers when he first approached the field, John McGraw became the first to feel their wrath. Next, the mob turned on its own players. What better way to get back at Giants management than to root against the home team?

New York triumphed, 6–1, and its fans eventually embraced a home team victory as a good thing. It was consecutive win number five for McGraw's crew and the streak didn't stop there; they stretched it to seven, lost on July

26, and then strung together three more successes. One day after the Polo Grounds mud bath, the Reds launched an impressive charge of their own. With their deep pitching staff leading the way, they won seven straight and 10 of 11.

The Giants barely budged. They had already deposited their own 10 of 11 streak in the pennant bank. It all led to a pivotal three-game series at Redland Field and another ugly weather forecast. Rain came pouring down as Cincinnati broke on top in the fourth inning of game one and Roush knocked in both runs with a soggy single. At one point, bleacher spectators ran across the field to take shelter under the grandstand. Victimizing former teammate Fred Toney, the Reds added two more runs in the fifth and gave the same treatment to a reliever in the sixth, when Ivey Wingo belted a two-run triple. Never seriously challenged, Cincinnati moved into first place with a 6–2 win. Day two saw another lopsided result, as Sallee tossed a five-hit shutout in a 6–0 success.

Abuzz with pennant fever, the whole city seemed to covet a spot at Redland Field for the series finale on Sunday. Though game time was scheduled for 3:00 P.M. and the gates wouldn't open until 12:30, fans still packed morning streetcars that traveled toward the ballpark. By 1:00 P.M., every seat was filled except for those in reserved sections. At 2:00 P.M., President Herrmann ordered his crew to stop selling tickets and close the gates. Strained beyond capacity, his stadium couldn't accommodate so many bodies.

Anticipating an attendance surge, the club augmented accommodations by circling the playing field with long rows of benches. Beginning in an area behind home plate, the seats extended down both foul lines, all the way to the outfield fences, and curled behind fair ground in left and right field. Yet even with all that overflow space, many fans were turned away.

Paid attendance registered at a Redland-record 32,000, and the figure didn't include folks who received free admission through the pass gate or the illegal arrivals that scaled outfield fences. Add them to the total and it probably exceeded 33,000. It wasn't worth the climb. Armed with a swift fastball and mesmerizing curve, Jess Barnes tossed a five-hit shutout in a 4–0 New York win. After escaping a first-inning jam, he allowed only one man to reach third base the rest of the way — that man being Edd Roush, who drilled a triple in the sixth.

Numerically speaking, the Reds remained in first place, but for all practical purposes it was another dead heat. At the moment, Cincinnati ranked first with an impressive 61–29 record and .678 success rate while New York owned corresponding marks of 57–28 and .671. Things weren't nearly so tight in the A.L. race, where the 58–34 White Sox had a 6½-game lead over Cleveland. Chicago had moved into first on July 10 and never left.

Rebounding from their Barnes beat-down, the Reds won five of the next six games, all at Redland Field. Everything clicked during that stretch, their offense averaging more than six runs a game and the pitchers holding opponents to two or fewer runs in all five triumphs. Heading the opposite direction, New York lost two of three to last-place St. Louis, and then scored one lonely run during a three-game implosion at Chicago. No need to calculate percentages now, the records told the story: Cincinnati 66–30, New York 58–33. As of August 11, one team had finally blinked in the long stare-down.

Unhappy with their underachieving pitching staff, the Giants traded for Braves ace Art Nehf at mid-month. "Ace" was a relative term; he went 15–15 the year before, yet still had the staff's best record. Now he owned an 8–9 mark, which wasn't bad considering the team he played for, but his high ERA provided cause for concern. As things turned out, a change of scenery did wonders for Nehf, who did wonders for New York by going 9–2 and posting a 1.50 ERA over the final six weeks of the season. Would it be enough?

The Giants soon saw a great opportunity to pull close again with three consecutive doubleheaders against Cincy and all within comfy home confines. It was the talk of the town, with New Yorkers descending on their stadium in overwhelming numbers. "Before 12 o'clock the crowd started to come and every vacant lot within many blocks of the grounds was jammed with automobiles," wrote the *Times*. "The subway at 157th Street poured forth thousands and the elevated and surface lines were jammed to overflowing. In the crush at the gates men lost their hats and wiggled their way in only after their coats had been almost torn from their backs."[3]

The word "sellout" didn't do this throng justice. A standing-room crowd went five-to-six deep behind the lower grandstand seats and many more stood in the upper reaches. Attendance was estimated at 38,000, an enormous figure for that era. Hundreds more die-hards watched for free from Coogan's Bluff. Even during yesteryear World Series, there had never been so many folks on that famous hillside above the stadium.

Inside and out, they all left disappointed. Nehf took a beating in his Polo Grounds debut, surrendering four runs through seven innings. It looked as though New York's offense might bail him out when Hal Chase belted an RBI triple that cut the deficit to one. Responding to that eighth-inning rally, the crowd went berserk, throwing straw hats onto the field and creating a confetti storm of torn newspapers. They yelled themselves hoarse but to no avail. After a delay to clear the debris, Kauff hit a routine grounder and Chase was cut down at the plate. Cincinnati held on for a 4–3 win.

Also making a home debut, Phil Douglas threw well for the Giants in the second game but a former Giant pitched better. Slim Sallee crafted a three-hitter in Cincinnati's 2–1 triumph. Douglas was another quick fix, brought in from Chicago to beef up McGraw's staff. He put zeroes on the scoreboard for eight of nine innings, but was undone by shoddy fielding in the fourth.

It was a crushing afternoon for the home team, yet tomorrow was another day and another doubleheader. The teams battled through 13 long innings in the August 14 opener before New York emerged with a 2–1 win. No such drama presented itself in the second game, as Cincinnati surrendered eight runs in the first three innings and dropped a 9–3 decision.

New York had struck back — tit for tat and sweep for sweep. Given new hope, Giants fans swarmed into Harlem for the final twin bill on Friday, August 15. It was similar to the first day, only more hectic and congested. More than 10,000 people were turned away from the park; the sea of humanity became so great at an Eighth Avenue turnstile that police couldn't hold them back and stopped trying. Hundreds jumped the gates.

At another entrance, five men were taken to St. Lawrence Hospital after an iron railing collapsed under a mob's weight. Some zealots even scaled the fence beyond center field and dropped 20 feet down to the bleachers. Giants president Charles Stoneham pleaded with fans to fall back into orderly lines and take their turns at the ticket windows. They continued to storm the turnstiles.

Club officials estimated paid attendance at 38,000, but nobody knew how many more invaded for free. Once again, they all went home disappointed. Eller starred in the opening 4–3 victory, pitching a six-hitter and belting a three-run homer into the left-field bleachers, before Ray Fisher blanked the home team in a 4–0 triumph. Beating the Giants in four of six games, the Reds stretched their N.L. lead to 6½ games and New York was never the same. Not that McGraw's men folded up and quit; they won eight of their next 10. Cincinnati, however, reeled off 10 straight in a one-week stretch, from August 19–26.

It started with a 1–0 win and then the offense went super nova, ringing up run totals of 6, 10, 7, 7, 8, 6, 7, 4 and 8. Groh hit .439 during that stretch, Rath .405 and Roush .395. Before going 0-for-10 in the last two games, Edd blistered the ball at a .535 clip. Even Reds pitchers got involved, delivering 10 hits in 30 at-bats for a nice .300 average.

With 12 more wins and six fewer losses than the Giants, Cincinnati had things wrapped up. One more compelling cliffhanger remained, however, as Roush took another shot at a batting title. Coinciding with the Reds high tide, he surged into a second-place tie with Thorpe, both owning .326 averages and trailing Cravath by 14 points.

Edd's stretch drive started inauspiciously. He went 1-for-5 against Pittsburgh's Babe Adams on August 30 and produced only two hits in the next four games. Prospects didn't look any brighter on September 3 when Cincinnati faced Grover Alexander in Chicago, but Edd reached the great one for three hits. Witnessing that fine performance were several White Sox, using an off-day to scout their likely World Series opponent.

It was back to mediocrity after the brief outburst, as Edd managed only three safeties in a four-game series at St. Louis. A respectable 4-for-12 stretch followed, and then he went 4-for-4 against Boston on September 14 and delivered two more hits the following day.

That's how his last month went — long dry spells alleviated by the occasional cloudburst. The Reds removed Roush's final distraction on September 16 when they clinched the N.L. pennant with a win over New York. Eight days later, Chicago secured the A.L. flag.

Edd looked ordinary down the stretch, but that proved more than sufficient to outlast fading contenders. One notable exception was Rogers Hornsby, the Cardinals infielder whose hot September propelled him past Ross Youngs, Larry Doyle, Milt Stock, Heinie Groh and Irish Meusel. By mid-month only Edd Roush remained in the Texan's path. It was an uphill path, however, with a steady gap of 20 points separating the men.

Hornsby sizzled over the final couple weeks, beginning with 11 hits in a five-game home series against Boston. On September 25, reports had Roush leading Hornsby, .322 to .317. Edd's bat went limp at the worst possible time: 1-for-7 in a September 26 doubleheader and 0-for-2 the following day. Hornsby maintained a blistering pace, cranking three hits and scoring twice in a 12-inning triumph over Pittsburgh. On Sunday, September 27, he went 2-for-4 and belted a grand slam against 19-game winner Wilbur Cooper.

The season ended a day later, and on September 30, the *New York Times* published a top five list that showed Hornsby edging Roush, .322 to .320. The next day's edition featured comprehensive league statistics that gave Edd a slim advantage, but that same report crowned Gavvy Cravath champion. A few days later the *St. Louis Post Dispatch* reported Roush as the winner, trimming Hornsby, .320 to .316. In a November syndicated column, *Sporting News* pioneer Al Spink said a review of the season's box scores proved Hornsby took first by the slimmest of margins, .317 to .316.

Like the previous year, nobody would know for sure until the N.L. office released official figures in December. Edd got the early Christmas present, officially declared king by a margin of three points. The record book shows Roush with 162 hits, 504 at-bats and a .321 batting average, while Hornsby's corresponding stats register at 163, 512 and .318. Work backward from those numbers and a picture emerges of dramatic season finales in both cities. Edd led by four percentage points (.321 to .317) but another bad outing could open the door for his hard-charging challenger. Hornsby would move into first if he went 3-for-5 (or better), combined with an 0-for-3 (or worse) from Roush. Both scenarios seemed distinct possibilities, as Edd posted three hitless showings in his last four games and Hornsby batted .500 over the previous couple weeks.

On September 28, the Reds hosted Chicago and Grover Alexander got the start for the Cubbies. Over in St. Louis, Hornsby faced an ordinary Erskine Mayer of the Pirates. "Old Pete" looked like his old self that day, throwing a shutout and allowing only one Red to reach second base. Maybe the N.L. champs were tired from their previous day's pennant celebration, which included a parade through the streets of downtown Cincinnati. But Alexander surrendered six hits and Edd Roush shared in the bounty, delivering two singles that proved more than enough to secure the crown. Hornsby went 2-for-4, as well.

Cravath finished with a .341 mark but recorded only 214 at-bats, while Thorpe hit .327 in 169 attempts. Add both their plate appearance totals together and it still fell well short of Edd's 504. Though reported as league leaders throughout most the season, Cravath and Thorpe were really just children playing on a throne. When it came time for a coronation, N.L. officials sent them back to the nursery.

With two batting titles and one runner-up finish in his first three full seasons, Edd was a legend in the making. Since 1900, only three players had won more crowns — Nap Lajoie (4), Honus Wagner (8) and Ty Cobb (11). Of that trio, only Cobb remained active and the 1919 title would be his last. At the tender age of 26, Edd became a model for the next generation of baseball stardom.

Over in the American League, Babe Ruth broke the mold by finishing with a staggering record of 29 home runs. It nearly tripled his nearest competition and eclipsed the total of four entire teams. The Boston bomber also led his league in runs and RBIs, yet still found time to post an 8–5 record on the pitcher's mound. He was a revelation, but the Babe was also just another guy on a fourth-place team. When the season ended, his spotlight went dark and all attention shifted to the battle of league champions.

With only a slight shift in the winds of fate, Edd Roush could have landed in the opposite dugout for the 1919 World Series. Though Chicago's roster inspired rave reviews that year, pickings were decidedly slimmer when he was White Sox property, and it doesn't take a vivid imagination to picture him getting a call-up in 1914. Chicago outfielders hit woefully during the previous season, with Ping Bodie's .264 average the highest of the bunch. Shano Collins batted .239 and the third spot was divided between a couple ne'er-do-wells who produced even worse marks.

In a different scenario, Edd could have returned to Lincoln, met his potential and earned another look from Comiskey. That way he would have a good shot at cracking the weak White Sox outfield of 1914. The "no vacancy" sign went up a couple years later after they brought in Shoeless Joe Jackson and Happy Felsch, but things looked wide open as young Roush searched for his first big break. Destiny delivered him to Cincinnati instead and it seemed for the best when his Reds soon won a National League pennant. Nothing could diminish that accomplishment, not even the inevitable beating that awaited them in the Fall Classic.

13

The Real Tale of the Tape

We had a goddamned good ball club back then. The writers come along and everything was Chicago, we didn't have a chance ... all Chicago. So what?[1]

Historians tend to paint the 1919 match-up in broad, simplistic strokes. The White Sox were a team for the ages, the Reds a spunky but overmatched pretender. It makes for a quick, tidy assessment and prevents brain fatigue, but truth doesn't fit into narrow sound bites or catch phrases. It spills over the landscape and runs in streams next to hyperbole. Were the White Sox so much better than the Reds? The answer is an emphatic "yes" in the Bazooka Joe gum-wrapper guide to history, but a thorough treatment reveals a question not so simple, an explanation far more complicated.

Briefly put, Chicago owned the better everyday lineup and Cincinnati fielded a far deeper pitching staff. So why are the Black Sox portrayed as master swordsmen and the Reds as damsels in distress? Baseball authors don't deserve all the blame; they simply write the same things that pundits were saying in 1919. With a notable exception here and there, most experts picked Chicago as a clear-cut favorite. People said a *lot* of things that proved incorrect: Negro leaguers weren't good enough to play with whites, Prohibition would uplift our nation's morals, Germany was finished as a world power, the Reds had no shot at winning the Series.

Yes, the Sox were loaded, but Cincinnati didn't win 96 games by default. That lofty victory total came in a shortened season, as baseball experimented with a 140-game schedule—14 fewer than usual. Adjust for deflation and it comes out to a 106-win pace. The Reds were simply magnificent in 1919, recording baseball's best winning percentage (.686) in seven years and the National League's best in a decade. They led the senior circuit in fielding percentage and shutouts, committed the fewest errors, surrendered the least runs, tied for second in batting, and came within a whisker of the team ERA title.

Orchestrating it all was a not-so-secret weapon in the dugout — Moran the mastermind. He vaulted into managerial prominence by generating 268 wins and one pennant during a three-year stretch with the overachieving Philadelphia Phillies. A bad 1918 season ended his tenure there but barely dented a growing reputation among baseball insiders. When the Reds took off under his direction, it became one more feather in a cap of brilliance. A catcher during his playing days, Moran spent decades analyzing pitchers before guiding baseball's best staff in Ohio.

With ample pitching, hitting, defense and leadership, one question begs answering: Where were the weaknesses that made this squad incapable of competing against the vaunted Sox? A position-by-position analysis shows how the two teams really matched up. For obvious reasons, it's appropriate to start in the middle garden.

Fast and skilled, Roush had all the tools of a great outfielder. He also made a study of hitters and knew their tendencies (National Baseball Hall of Fame Library, Cooperstown, New York).

Center Field: Happy Felsch shouldn't be sold short. He burst into White Sox prominence during the 1917 title march, batting .308 and knocking in 102 runs. That put him in some rare air as the league's second-leading RBI man and fifth-best hitter. Though hitting only .275 in 1919, his run production still ranked ahead of such stars as Tris Speaker and Sam Rice. But Edd J. Roush wins the matchup by a Hoosier country mile.

First Base: Cincinnati's Jake Daubert prevails on pedigree alone. A two-time batting champ with Brooklyn, the veteran provided leadership and a dangerous stick. Though hitting an ordinary .276 in 1919, his 79 runs tied for the team lead. Chick Gandil was on the downswing of a so-so career that included a long stay with the Washington Senators and a short one on the Cleveland Indians. He scored 25 fewer runs than Daubert, drove in more, hit .290, and committed only three errors in 115 games. Gandil was no slouch.

Second Base: No contest for Chicago veteran Eddie Collins, one of the best infielders in history. True, his best days lay behind him, but he still outclassed all other second sackers. A .319 batting average was just the start, for not only did he dominate his counterparts in every major hitting category, but he also posted the most putouts and double plays. His .974 fielding percentage fell a scant .001 off the A.L. lead.

As part of the famous "$100,000 infield," Collins won three World Series with the Philadelphia Athletics. But the boss was a bottom-line businessman, and when winning got too expensive, he unloaded high-priced talent. Hence the 1914 clearance sale that saw Collins sold to the Sox for $50,000. His batting average had suffered steady decline since then, but 1919 proved a resurgent season. On Cincinnati's side of the ledger was Morrie Rath with his .264 average. He scored 77 runs, fourth-best in the National League.

Third Base: Buck Weaver had more runs and RBIs but the scale tips slightly toward Cincinnati's Heinie Groh. His .310 average stood 14 points higher, he had a better fielding percentage, and the run-production numbers would have been comparable if he hadn't missed most of September with an injured finger. What's more, Groh established an elite reputation over several years, while Weaver was a late-bloomer who broke out with a career year in 1919.

Shortstop: Neither candidate was any prize, though Cincinnati's Larry Kopf had better numbers. Swede Risberg proved slightly less error-prone.

Catcher: Ray Schalk's stats seem ordinary, but his .282 average ranked third among A.L. catchers and he scored the most runs. On defense, none surpassed his combination of skill and intensity. Everything unfolds in front of the masked man; he's a pitching coach, defensive coordinator and barroom bouncer all wrapped into one. Few teams could claim a better renaissance man than the Chicago White Sox.

Cincinnati's two-catcher rotation had advantages over the singular Sox setup. On offense, Moran could start left-handed hitting Ivey Wingo against right-handed hurlers or use Bedford Bill Rariden's righty bat against southpaws. Even 90 years ago, baseball men were crunching those numbers and knew the path to statistical success. Defensively, the Reds tag-team approach probably maintained fresher legs.

Still, Chicago's future Hall of Famer gets the checkmark.

Left Field: Shoeless Joe Jackson was one of baseball's all-time great hitters, and though his star lost some luster from the Cleveland days, it still lit up Chicago's skyline. He hit .351 in 1919, which was pretty close to his career average. Babe Ruth called Jackson "the most natural hitter who ever lived."

No such praise was forthcoming for Cincinnati left fielder Pat Duncan. A graduate of the Central League, he hit .244 in 31 games after making a late return from military service. Duncan cracked the outfield by default when Sherry Magee and Manuel Cueto washed out.

Right Field: Chicago also had a native Hoosier in the outfield. Born near the Ohio border in the northeast Indiana town of Butler, Nemo Leibold would make his major league debut in Cleveland. He spent two-and-a-half nondescript seasons with the Indians, joined the Sox in 1915 and did nothing noteworthy at Comiskey Park until 1919. His .302 average was third-best on baseball's best offense and 60 points higher than Greasy Neale's floundering .242.

The choice, however, is not automatic. Leibold committed 19 errors, by far the highest total for right fielders of either league and tied for worst among all outfielders. Leibold scored many more runs (81 to 57); Neale enjoyed a decided edge in RBIs (54–26) and stolen bases (28–17). During the Series, the left-handed hitting Leibold split time with righty Shano Collins, a less-accomplished batter but more reliable defender. Advantage to the White Sox.

The unofficial tally for everyday positions was Chicago 4, Cincinnati 4. The Reds outhit their counterparts at three positions, outscored them at three, and had a better run–RBI combo in four. It's certainly not a scientific repudiation of the mismatch theory. The Sox, after all, owned baseball's best team batting average and scored 90 more runs than the Reds. One through eight, Chicago probably had more talent, but the chasm is greatly exaggerated.

Meanwhile, the pitching gap goes largely unreported. Cincinnati was loaded with quality starters, all overshadowed by that super Sox tandem of Eddie Cicotte and Lefty Williams. The Reds could pick from four hurlers with ERAs under 2.30, plus another one at 2.40. Adolfo Luque posted a 9–3 record and 2.63 ERA, yet ranked sixth on the team depth chart.

The Reds spread innings around, with nobody accumulating more than 248. Meanwhile, Cicotte's right arm carried 307 innings of wear and Williams had nearly as much mileage on his left. Granted, both appeared to hold up well — especially Cicotte, who recorded one of history's great seasons by compiling a 29–7 record and 1.82 ERA. But heading into the Series, there was talk of a tired arm. Red Faber, a hero of the 1917 title run, would sit out the postseason because of injury. Unproductive in 1919, he seemed unlikely to make a big impact anyhow, but the Sox could've used another post-season veteran.

Dickie Kerr stepped into the Sox void, bringing with him a 2.89 ERA that rang mediocre by standards of the day. Blindfolded and swinging a fake donkey tail, Pat Moran could find a better-qualified candidate in the Cincinnati bullpen. Sallee, Eller, Ruether, Fisher, Ring, Luque ... winners, every one of them. Their combined 2.23 ERA stood out like rippling stomach muscle compared to the Sox 3.04 bulge, and they produced a 23–14 edge in shutouts.

Were those numbers relevant to the Fall Classic and its short-series format? After all, baseball history is peppered with examples of teams riding *one* elite pitcher to the title: Christy Mathewson in 1905, Jack Coombs 1910, Bob Gibson 1964. Chicago could hitch its wagon to *two*.

Though few seemed to notice, the Reds owned dominant tossers, as well. Sallee, Eller and Ruether were a one-two-three punch capable of decking any offense, and four-five-six could raise welts, too. Does the surplus pitching compensate for Sox advantages in other departments? At the very least, it makes it a horse race. Even if Chicago gets the overall nod, it's just a slight north-south flinch and not a bobblehead whiplash.

Finishing with eight fewer wins than the Reds, the 88–52 White Sox could only be crowned superior if they played in a superior circuit. And the American League made a strong case for supremacy; it had won four straight World Series and eight of the last nine. Most were lopsided affairs. All fair points, but the pendulum has to swing back eventually.

By virtue of a coin flip, the Reds hosted the first two World Series games, which, however briefly, made Cincinnati the center of the universe. It wasn't just a time to boast about beloved ballplayers, though there would be plenty of that, but a golden opportunity to promote the city. What better time to publicize it as a growing metropolis, led by men of vision? If visitors enjoyed their stay, they might sing Cincinnati's praises back home, and then return with friends to spend more money.

As if the bustling baseball pilgrimage wasn't enough, a bunch of auto racing folk also arrived for an upcoming event at Cincinnati Speedway. Hotels sold out quickly and the chamber of commerce reported more than 1,000 visitors were paying for rooms in private homes. Some stayed in sleeper cars at the railroad yard. Those who couldn't put any kind of roof over their head were allowed to sleep on park benches while police patrols protected them from thieves.

On the eve of Game One, downtown streets and sidewalks became packed with pedestrians, particularly around hotel lobbies, the sites for many a wager. It reminded some of the bustling old days when Cincinnati earned its nickname, "Queen City of the West."

Not all Red rooters believed their team would win. In some circles, cynics expected something bad to happen and realists acknowledged the Sox as a better team. Their spirit came from a different place, one that suggested they celebrate now because they may never experience this again. A popular refrain went something like this: "Fifty years since the Reds won anything and it might be another 50 before they do it again."

Most out-of-towners gave the Reds little chance. Talk of "chances" turned into talk of "odds," then out came the cash. The Hotel Gibson forbade its clerks and bellboys from holding bets, fearing it might interfere with their job duties. Chicago had been strong favorites for a long time, their odds of winning posted at 10–7. But as the days went by, more money came in on the Reds. The line dropped to 6–5 by game time, with some reports of even-money stakes.

Today, it seems obvious — gamblers had inside information of the fix, bet heavily on the underdogs and thus influenced the odds. But few red flags were raised at the time because it could all be explained by a rumor that Eddie Cicotte had a sore arm. Reading between the lines of a *Cincinnati Enquirer* article, either scenario sounds plausible. "In the (Chicago) Stock Yards district a lot of money was (placed) on the Reds. According to a well-known gambler the tip went out through the yards that Cicotte was not in his best form."[2]

Cicotte saw limited action in the regular season's final month, pitching only 11 innings over the last 25 days of September. Did that signify something was amiss, or were the Sox just keeping their ace fresh for the Series? Historical hindsight says the old pitching wing held up fine. Besides, it didn't take a whole lot of arm strength to throw a knuckle ball, his bread-and-butter pitch. Cicotte was also known as grandfather of the illegal-substance shine ball. He denied that charge following the 1917 World Series, saying the shiner was a myth, but two years later accusations continued unabated. One author tried to lay it to rest while writing a preview for the latest Series: "Ball after ball has been taken out of the game and brought to the headquarters of the league for examination, and there never has been found any foreign substance on the sphere."[3]

Game day saw several businesses giving employees a day off to attend the opener. Of course, most had no chance of getting in, but they could watch the results unfold on makeshift scoreboards in theaters, meeting halls and outside newspaper offices. With more demand than supply, Reds officials arranged a lottery for admission tickets. If that failed, the unlucky still had one avenue left by paying scalper prices.

Lines began forming in the early-morning darkness of Tuesday, October 1, as faithful fans stood in front of gateways leading to the bleachers and pavilions. Those sections had open seating. As daylight arrived around 6:35 A.M., the thin lines turned into stout columns that protected hard-earned high ground from later arrivals. Policemen arrived with the sun and by 8:00 A.M. the night fog had burned away to reveal a scene of thousands surrounding the ballpark. Gates opened at 10:00 A.M.

A big brassy band provided pre-game entertainment. Dressed in a navy lieutenant's uniform, an elderly guest conductor took over for one song and led the musicians through "Stars and Stripes Forever." His name was John Phillip Sousa, the man who wrote the tune. Adding treble to the bass was a spirited two-year-old named Mary Roush. Sitting with her mother in the

Edd holds his toddler daughter in 1919. She had a prime seat for the World Series opener and frequently yelled out to her father (Roush Family Collection).

players' family section behind home plate, she chattered away in high-pitched tones. Every Roush at-bat was accompanied by cries of "Dad! Dad!" and she also expressed interest in joining him on the center field grass.

Paid attendance registered at 30,511, a figure far higher than the Game One turnout in 1918. It was comparable to other Series openers of yesteryear and superior from a population percentage angle. For professional people-watchers, the cosmopolitan crowd proved nearly as fascinating as the game itself. The *Cincinnati Enquirer* noted:

> There were wide sombreros worn by cattle kings from Texas, planters from Georgia, sporting men from "little ol'" New York, correctly attired scholars from cultured Boston, lumbermen from Michigan and Wisconsin and miners from the far West. And practically all of these visitors from the four corners of the nation cheered for the Cincinnati Reds quite as enthusiastically as if they lived on Walnut Hills and Mt. Auburn.

About 15 cameras pointed at home plate when umpires, opposing managers and captains met for their pre-game conference. Fans cheered the final picture — a posed shot of Moran shaking hands with Sox skipper Kid Gleason. Elsewhere, the city's financial district stood at a virtual standstill as moneychangers focused instead on the price of admission. A day earlier, Waldo Stein broke the track record over at the Cincinnati Speedway, reaching 125 miles an hour during a practice session. Now the course lay mute as a graveyard, its drivers gone to the ballpark. The city merged into one collective heartbeat on October 1, and every artery led to Redland Field.

14

The 1919 World Series

Three on base and Eddie Roush up, and a moving van has to get in my way.— Unidentified fan, watching scoreboard updates in New York's Times Square.[1]

Any amateur historian knows how the dirty business began — Game One, bottom of the first inning, and Eddie Cicotte plunks the leadoff hitter in his back. This was the secret signal between fixers and fixed; drill that first batter to show everybody's on the same page. To most people, that's where the story begins. But there was a top of the first inning, too, and it ended on a great catch by Edd Roush, who chased down Buck Weaver's long fly in front of the temporary stands in left-center. A shining moment by a young baseball knight and nobody remembers it. What followed was too dark, too devious.

Opening the home half of the first, Morrie Rath took the first pitch for a strike, and then Cicotte lost control and strayed from the middle of the plate to the middle of the spine. Awarded first base, Rath later raced to third on a Jake Daubert single and scored courtesy of Heinie Groh's sacrifice fly to deep left. That brought the clean-up hitter to the plate, a proud Hoosier by the name of Roush. The former farmer had reached the clouds. No trace remained of the Henderson Hen, Evansville Yankee or Indianapolis Hoofed. He certainly bore no resemblance to the reticent kid who had to be prodded into his first game with the Oakland City Walk-Overs. In all his glory this was the National League batting champion, the best player on a pennant-winning team and the toast of Cincinnati.

Cicotte let loose with a pitch, then all eyes focused on Edd. Hundreds of sportswriters waited to record his reaction, and telegraph operators sat poised to relay the results across the country. His movements also fell under the knowing gaze of other major leaguers, dressed in civilian clothes and wishing they could trade places. The great composer George M. Cohan was watching, as were governors, congressmen and lesser politicians.

Ball one. Another ball followed, then a strike. Daubert took off on the next pitch — a ball — and Ray Schalk cut him down on a strong throw to second. Remaining patient, Edd earned a walk. He stayed put for the next two pitches, then stole second. Pat Duncan grounded out to end the inning but the Reds had drawn first blood.

One hit, one run, two walks, no errors. It didn't look like a fix yet. Chicago tied the game with an unearned run in the second after Shoeless Joe Jackson reached by error. He eventually scored from third on a Chick Gandil looper that barely avoided Edd's glove. Two batters later, Roush caught a fly for the third out.

The score remained tied until the bottom of the fourth, when the first sign of silent surrender emerged. Buried in the *New York Times* play-by-play account is this golden nugget: "Cicotte seemed apprehensive as he took the mound for this frame. He scanned the field minutely and gave the outfielders particular attention."

Two-thirds of that outfield wore a "Crooked Ranch" brand, just like Cicotte. Edd led off the inning, smacking the first pitch to deep left-center and Happy Felsch sprinted after the ball with a wonderful opportunity to earn his blood money. Chasing a long drive with his back to the infield, he didn't have to make a bad play, just avoid a good one. But for the moment, at least, Cicotte stood all alone on the diving board. Felsch made a nice running grab, thus relegating Edd to bystander status for the infamous events that followed.

Cicotte surrendered a single to Duncan, then Larry Kopf hit back to the mound. Standing in front of that grounder was a veteran who had turned countless 1-6-3 double plays.

The biggest catch for Black Sox bribers, Eddie Cicotte demanded $10,000 up front and got it (Library of Congress).

The Sox got a force out at second but Kopf beat the relay to first — that much is a matter of record. Other details are presented differently by a variety of sources. It's a routine ground ball in some accounts, a hard-hit smash in others. According to *Chicago Tribune* writer I.E. Sanborn, Kopf "slammed a fast one back at Cicotte, who scooped it and forced Duncan at second. Risberg, who pivoted in the play, caught the ball low, then had to straighten up before the relay. He paused too long and let Kopf beat the play to first by a toenail."

When scandal came to light a year later, the *Trib* published a different tune. Kopf tapped an easy grounder up the middle, Cicotte fielded and inexplicably hesitated before finally throwing offline to second. (A different writer probably penned this un-bylined account.)

Some point to the play as partial proof of Cicotte's complicity, saying he intentionally upset the timing. Others claim the problem rested with Swede Risberg's relay throw, adversely affected by a conspicuous stumble over the bag. Up in the press box, Christy Mathewson and noted Chicago sportswriter Hugh Fullerton were on the lookout for suspicious misplays and this one went down on both their lists.[2]

Still, with two outs and a runner on first, it seemed small cause for alarm. Then things went downhill for the visitors. Sparked by the bottom half of their lineup, the Reds hit and hit and hit. Even the pitcher got involved, as Dutch Ruether blasted a two-run triple to the fence in center. By inning's end, Cincy held a commanding 6–1 lead. By game's end, it was a 9–1 blowout.

Sitting amongst the ecstatic masses were three aged veterans of the 1869 Redlegs, baseball's first professional team, which was roughly equivalent to the Wright brothers attending an air show. George Wright (no relation), Cal McVey and "Oak" Taylor were the last surviving members of that 57–0 national champion. They happily proclaimed that history was repeating itself and the Reds would soon reign again as world champions.

Roush went hitless on the day, but what a stunning demonstration of defense in center field. His quick feet carried him to eight catches, some falling into the category of "jaw-dropping." Unfortunately, this game would not be remembered for spurts of excellence. It is encased in time as a foul-smelling opening act to a rancid play.

Much has been written about the power broker powwows that followed at the Sinton Hotel — manager Kid Gleason expressing doubts to team owner Charles Comiskey, Comiskey voicing strong suspicions to N.L president John Heydler, then the latter two taking the matter to A.L. president Ban Johnson. The higher the official, the less likely he was to attach credence. "Fix" rumors were nothing new in baseball, especially at World Series time. Even before talk radio, conspiracy theories cost a dime a dozen.

Cincinnati celebrated its opening win like it already clinched the Series.

Throngs of giddy fans melded into the largest downtown gathering since the Armistice was signed, and a group of youngsters carried a stretcher bearing an effigy of Cicotte. Preceded by a trumpeter, they marched up and down streets, in and out of hotel lobbies.

One blowout and the Reds suddenly became betting favorites to beat the unbeatable. That's how quick a sure thing could change. But baseball pundits did not give up on the mighty Sox.

"The White Sox will show up better tomorrow and the fans will realize that it is a powerful team. Their heavy hitters did not do much today but they are liable to break loose at any time," wrote Henry P. Edwards in the *Cleveland Plain-Dealer.*

"They'll come back for the White Sox always have come back strong. You can't keep them down," reported Joe Jackson in the *Detroit Free Press.*

"Their record in the American League and the way they beat off the opposition proved that they have the ability. One game does not make a series," added George Robbins in the *Chicago Daily News.*

Maybe so, but this particular game prompted New York's gambling fraternity to make the Reds 10–7 favorites.[3] Now it was Sox bettors who bargained for friendly odds on underdog wagers.

Game Two

> *There is a beautiful tale about St. George and how he stabbed the terrible dragon, which is purely allegorical. But the real story, the story which will be told in Cincinnati ... which will be listened to by children yet unborn, is that of how St. Edward stabbed Felsch's murderous fly at Redland Field; which is absolutely, beautifully true.* —Cincinnati Enquirer[4]

After a day of glory and a night of celebration, fans woke early the following morning for round two. Once again, lines began forming in the pre-dawn hours and the park was surrounded by opening time. When the initial rush subsided, however, Redland Field filled at a slower pace than the day before. Still, the end result was another packed house, right to the last step of standing room. Heat returned, too, hitting a sweltering high of 90 degrees. According to the *Enquirer,* Thursday's crowd seemed different than the one lured by the pageantry of Game One: "The real fans were out in force. Thousands attended the opening contest because it was something they had never seen before. Many came to be seen, and still others were present because they had to take friends from distant places. Yesterday it was different. Apparently every person present knew and appreciated baseball inside stuff."[5]

The game pitted Sox southpaw Lefty Williams against Cincinnati's Slim

Sallee, one of few Reds with World Series experience. He'd pitched for the Giants when they lost the 1917 Fall Classic to these same Chicagoans. Cheers erupted as Edd walked to the plate, the fans remembering his opening-game glove work. Bending into that fidgety crouched stance, he stared out at another popular pitcher who became far more famous in disgrace. Two pitches sailed wide of the strike zone, prompting a mound visit from catcher Ray Schalk. When play resumed, Williams fired another ball, then a strike, and then a ball. Edd went to first with a walk. Breaking for second on a hit-and-run, he got doubled up when Duncan lined out to second base.

Cincinnati went on the attack in the home half of the fourth, as Rath took a leadoff walk and went to second on a sacrifice. After Groh walked, Edd made his second plate appearance of the day. Williams missed the target twice more, prompting another conference with his catcher. It produced results this time, as the hurler responded with a strike that brought the count to 2–1. Edd smashed the next offering into center field, sending Rath home with the game's first run. It marked the first hit of the young series for Cincinnati's batting king. He was thrown out on a steal attempt but the rally continued and Kopf later blasted a two-run triple. The home crowd let loose with a deafening roar as their boys stretched the lead to 3–0.

Chicago put a runner on third with two outs in the sixth inning, then Happy Felsch launched a missile to center and Edd sprinted back for a leaping grab. Bleacher bums got the best view of it and they went nuts. So did the non-paying customers on a hillside beyond the outfield, some celebrating with an impromptu "snake dance."

Between innings, an airplane flew low over the diamond and dropped a body from the cockpit. The figure plummeted onto the field near third base, its descent accompanied by screams of horror from some female fans. But this was the World Series and play would quickly continue after someone removed the corpse. Of course, it helped that the skydiver wasn't real, only a dummy and an unconvincing one at that. Clad in overalls, it did, however, fool a few people on the way to terra firma. A policeman disposed of the body.

Was it some menacing, secret

He didn't contribute much with the bat but Roush earned widespread accolades for his fantastic defense (*Cincinnati Enquirer*).

sign from powerful gamblers? Unlikely. Prior to the previous day's game, that same aircraft swooped by and dropped advertising circulars on the ballpark, much to the dismay of the grounds crew.[6]

Trailing 4–0, the Sox finally showed a pulse in the top of the seventh and scored twice. It would get no closer, however. The underdog Reds now led the World Series, two games to none. Edd had a productive day the plate, producing one hit, a couple walks, a run and an RBI. But it was his defense that made headlines and inspired a hometown salute by legendary scribe Damon Runyon:

> Turn the spotlight on Oakland City, Ind.—preferably and appropriately a big red light. A citizen of Oakland has the center of the sporting stage and his name is Edward Roush. His occupation is center fielding for the Cincinnati Reds. He pursued that occupation to such effect in the second game of the series that the Reds took the contest from the Chicago White Sox by a score of 4 to 2. Wherefore is Oakland City, Ind., now a sort of little sister to the proud old Queen city of Ohio, linked by the bond of the baseball greatness of their favorite son.[7]

Outhit 10–4, the Reds seemed fortunate to take Game Two. Six walks certainly helped their cause and Sallee issued only one pass to Chicago. Though reaching double figures in hits surrendered, the Cincinnati hurler persevered with help from his defense. Kid Gleason dismissed the Reds as lucky, though he expressed great admiration for one particular opponent: "Fielding that happens only once in a lifetime robbed us of enough runs to win," the Sox manager explained. "Roush is a marvel in the outfield and my players all give him credit for his work."[8]

Lucky or not, the Reds trumped Chicago's two aces. Facing an 0–2 deficit, the Sox needed a lift and went looking for one in that shallow pitching well. Gleason talked about putting Cicotte back on the mound but it seemed a poor option. If he couldn't get anybody out with a fresh arm, what chance did he have on a tired one? In the space of a couple days the Reds went from underdogs to "White Fang" and a chorus of "I told you so's" erupted from Cincinnati faithful. Back in the Windy City, critics bemoaned their team's effort after it clinched the pennant. A late regular-season skid seemed to have carried over to the World Series—a preventable malady if they'd taken those last games seriously.

Cincinnati's victory celebration seemed less wild after Game Two. Crowds still lined the downtown streets and some carried about an effigy of Lefty Williams, but fewer people turned out and most stayed off the streets. Though overtly joyous, the overall mood was tempered with restraint. Game One had already provided the revelation and what followed required only a hearty "Amen!"

Now it was time to take the revival north. While the Reds waited in front of their hotel for cabs to the train station, Edd's shady friend approached him with some juicy information about dirty Sox players taking a dive, then vowing to break their agreement with deadbeat fixers. Jimmy Widmeyer supposedly heard about it while eavesdropping on them from an adjacent hotel room.

"Did you hear about the squabble last night after the first ball game?" he asked Roush.

"No, what's the matter?" Edd replied.

"They were supposed to get so much money after the first ball game in Cincinnati (and a player) said, 'We didn't get the goddamned money.'"[9]

The fix was off.

Game Three

> *(Kerr) could have pegged a ball through a six-inch hole any time during the afternoon. Sometimes he bent them over with his deceptive cork screw curve. Sometimes he shot a fast one past the batter and sometimes he handed 'em up with nothing on them but the grass stain.—* Chicago Tribune[10]

The Series now moved to festive Chicago, where Sox fanatics seemed undaunted by the 0–2 hole. Excitement filled the air around Comiskey Park, and it had to be a refreshing change from the aroma of those livestock killing fields that shared the south side.

"White Sox can boast of being the only team in either league to fly a pennant with a smoked ham flavor, as the ball pasture is only a few short sniffs from the stockyards," wrote syndicated columnist/cartoonist Gene Ahern. "Chance there to fatten the player's purse if they cop the world's championship bunting by selling both flags at 79 cents a pound."[11]

Some fans spent the night outside the stadium, waiting for their chance to buy admission tickets. Many more arrived in the pre-dawn hours, and by 9:00 A.M., about 5,000 stood outside the bleacher gates. All morning long, special trains brought rabid Red rooters into Chicago. Waving team flags and prancing down Michigan Boulevard, they made their foreign loyalty as conspicuous as possible. As the day wore on, more and more fans poured into Comiskey Park, but not enough for a sellout. Official attendance figures reached 29,126, approximately 5,000 short of capacity.

Heavyweight champ Jack Dempsey made an appearance, sitting in an upper tier box before leaving in the early innings. Down behind third base, a singing trio performed with musical accompaniment while players took batting practice. Edd scorched a liner through the ensemble, barely missing a megaphone-toting crooner.

It would take more than a wounded warbler to dim this crowd's fun. Optimism abounded, for no apparent reason other than blind devotion. They hung their hopes on a sawed-off rookie southpaw who could almost pass for a batboy. All that stood between the Sox and an 0–3 cavern was a 150-pound control pitcher named Dickie Kerr. Reds fans cheered when his name was announced. Posing for a pre-game picture of starting hurlers, Kerr was dwarfed by Cincinnati's sturdy six-footer Ray Fisher. Red-hot over the last two months, Fisher had won seven straight starts with an ERA under 1.00.

Though the forecast called for nighttime showers, it proved a beautiful baseball afternoon — warm and sunny with refreshing, cool breezes drifting in from Lake Michigan — a good day for a new beginning. After stroking a two-run single in the bottom of the second, Chick Gandil later loafed into a force-out at third base. Still, he *did* plate the go-ahead scores.

The way Kerr was hitting his spots, Chicago could've stopped batting after the first run crossed. Finishing with a three-hitter, he proved especially dominant down the stretch — retiring the last 15 batters in order. With no Red even making it to third base, the Sox coasted to a 3–0 shutout. Gleason gushed over his team's newfound fortitude, pointing to three verbal confrontations that almost turned physical: Eddie Collins versus mouthy bench-warmer Jimmy Smith, Joe Jackson taking exception to Ray Fisher's brushback pitch, and Nemo Leibold walking toward Henie Groh at third base before an umpire interceded. "I tell you, it's spirit like that makes a ball team win," Gleason said. "The gang has that spirit now and they're going to win sure."[12]

Game Four

I have never allowed our boys to become overconfident but I have been very sure all along that we would win the series and win it rather easily.... How are they going to beat pitching like Ring displayed this afternoon? Not a chance in the world. — Reds manager Pat Moran[13]

Chicago rejoiced at the revival of its hometown heroes. Pulling within two games to one, the Sox had finally shown their mettle. Now it was Cicotte's turn for redemption. His opponent was Jimmy Ring, a solid but unintimidating Reds hurler whose resume paled in comparison to that of the A.L. ace. What were the chances that Cicotte would pitch poorly in two consecutive starts? Then again, rumors continued to circulate about the demise of his right arm.

Unlike the day before, there were no unsightly empty seats at Comiskey on October 4. A huge crowd of 34,363 packed the stadium, giving Chicago one of the highest attendance marks in World Series history. Two brass bands filled the air with music, one from each city. Denied admittance the previous day, Cincinnati's ensemble found some tickets this time and marched into the park with trumpets blaring. Its musical tastes leaned toward the old standards, while the hometown band focused more on modern jazz.

Vocalists performed every few minutes, singing all sorts of songs through long, cardboard megaphones. Some went solo, others joined in duets, trios or quartets. After narrowly avoiding injury the previous day, a green-suited chap held his voice projector in one hand and wore a baseball glove on the other. He continued crooning while keeping a wary eye out for line drives from batting practice.

Lovely weather accompanied the frivolity but both would disappear shortly before the first pitch. A cold lake breeze swept in and temperatures dropped 10 degrees, causing the lightly garbed spectators to reach for coats. The thermometer continued a downward dip through the game, falling another three or four degrees. At one point, heavy winds tore gravel roofing off the grandstand and tossed it at box seat occupants.

Cicotte seemed unaffected by it all, bending wicked curveballs past baffled Reds hitters. After surrendering a leadoff single in the first inning, he retired 10 of the next 11 batters. Then came the infamous top of the fifth. It would be recreated in the *Eight Men Out* movie as irrefutable evidence of complicity. With shame in his eyes, a grim-faced Cicotte screws up so bad that there can be no doubt. And there was Edd Roush, leading off the inning that would go down in history. He grounded out and exited the ugliness before it began, which was probably for the best.

That brought up Pat Duncan, who bounced a grounder above the pitcher's mound. Cicotte leaped for the ball, which deflected off his glove toward the third base side. He chased it down and rushed a wild throw past first for a two-base error. Not an easy play, but that wasn't the error that damned him.

Larry Kopf followed with a single to left, where Shoeless Joe fielded and rifled a powerful throw toward home plate. Cicotte moved over to cut it off but only deflected the ball, sending it rolling to the grandstand behind home plate. By all accounts, Duncan showed no desire to test Joe's arm. It was only after the ball went into foul territory that he made a move, scampering across with the go-ahead score while Kopf settled on second.

This was the smoking gun for future conspiracy theories. How could a crafty veteran suddenly play like a clueless greenhorn? But there's plausible cause for his strategy, if not the execution. With Duncan anchored at third base, someone should have intercepted the throw to dissuade the other runner from advancing. They say Kopf never considered going, but that doesn't discredit the tactic.

What incriminated Cicotte was his bungled execution of a simple act — catching the baseball. He didn't drop or miss it. Those types of miscues probably wouldn't have cost a run. He knocked the ball into an area where no fielder could make a play, and this came from someone hailed as one of the game's best defensive pitchers.

"It was a careless bit of baseball," observed the hometown *Tribune.* "The ball hit Cicotte's uplifted gloved hand and it deflected off his hand, rolling wild to the backstop." Publishing a similar assessment, the *Cincinnati Enquirer* claimed "Cicotte foozled the ball badly, allowing it to bounce off his glove and roll to foul ground back of the plate so far that Duncan was able to tear home."

Neale came up next and belted a double over Shoeless Joe's head, scoring Kopf. Some sportswriters couldn't fathom why Jackson was playing shallow and said so in the next day's reports. However, at least one scribe explained that Joe did it to give himself a better chance at throwing a runner out at home. This, too, is standard strategy.

A couple more hard-hit balls were turned into outs, leaving the score at 2–0. The Reds never touched home plate again yet didn't need to, as Chicago's offense withered on Ring's vine. Firing hard fastballs and mixing in an effective curve, he finished with a three-hit shutout against those matchless stickmen of the American League.

On the surface, it looked like Cicotte pitched a whale of a game and his offense just let him down. After all, he finished with a five-hitter and dominated for eight of nine innings. But that reeking fifth frame implied that he would surrender as many runs as necessary.

A figurative rain on Chicago's parade turned literal that Saturday evening, falling steadily through the night and into the early morning. When the umpires arrived at Comiskey Park, they found a quagmire where the playing field used to be. The game was called on account of inclement weather.

With an entire day to kill, fans engaged in the only possible discussion: Which team benefits more from the rainout? "White Sox" was the popular answer. Their lean pitching staff could use the rest and red-hot Cincinnati was forced to cool its heels. Perhaps conversations turned outside baseball and into the White House, where Woodrow Wilson lay gravely ill from a paralytic stroke. He collapsed during an exhausting national tour to encourage acceptance of the revised peace treaty and its provision for a League of Nations. On rainout Sunday, headlines reflected one of the first hints of optimism. The president's condition had improved after a good night's sleep. It was a "fluctuating illness," however, and today's gain could be erased by tomorrow's loss.

The same could have been said of the Reds championship drive.

Game Five

> *The ball as it went whistling across the breasts of some of the greatest hitters in the American League, twisted and turned and dipped and dropped in uncanny fashion.... It was the "shine" ball which carried the Chicago White Sox to a couple of American League championships, coming home to roost, for they say Eller rubs the magic of his pitching into the baseball along the seam of his trousers after the manner of Eddie Cicotte.— Damon Runyon[14]*

With Lefty Williams back on the mound, Chicago folk liked their chances. Sure, he had walked too many in his previous outing, but this was the same guy who had ranked third in wins in the American League. He held the Reds to four hits a few days earlier and was sunk by bad breaks. Williams was due.

In the opposite dugout, Pat Moran reached into his bulging bag of pitchers and pulled out Hod Eller for the first time. Despite strong regular-season numbers (20–9, 2.40 ERA), the shine ball artist had yet to see any World Series action. But who could argue with the benching while Moran guided his team toward a lopsided romp? He plucked all the right strings like a banjo virtuoso and now it was time to strum the high "E" note, as in Eller.

Rath led off the first inning with a walk, prompting a collective "uh-oh" among fans fearing another Williams wild streak. Then he easily retired the next three batters. Eller walked his leadoff hitter in the bottom half of the inning, retired Eddie Collins, and surrendered an infield single to Buck Weaver. With one out, runners on first and third, Shoeless Joe Jackson was at the plate. Just a few minutes into the game, Chicago already threatened to break it open. Now it became crystal clear why Moran passed over Eller for earlier starts. He saw this coming, or at least suspected the man might fold in a pinch.

The danger quickly passed, however, with Jackson and Felsch retired on routine fly balls. Eller did not walk another batter and allowed just two more hits the rest of the way. During one particularly dominating stretch he struck out six consecutive batters — Gandil, Risberg, Schalk, Williams, Leibold, and Collins. "The boy is going good today," understated Hod's father, as he followed the results via telegraph in Muncie, Indiana.

After attending the first four contests, W.F. Eller bypassed Game Five when told his son wouldn't pitch. The Oklahoma resident decided to "transact a little business" in Muncie, his old stamping grounds where Hod was born and learned baseball. A local newspaper arranged for the elder Eller to follow the play-by-play while sitting next to a local telegraph operator. There had been some great pitching performances in the 1919 Series, but none so overwhelming as Eller's three-hit, nine-strikeout masterpiece. After awhile, even home fans began cheering their conqueror.

Hod Eller was the star of Game Five, striking out six consecutive White Sox at one point. Meanwhile, Eddie Cicotte lost his mystique thanks to two consecutive losses (*Cincinnati Enquirer*).

Held to one paltry hit through five innings, Reds batters didn't fare much better against Williams. Eller took things into his own hands in the sixth inning by belting a lead-off double to left-center and going to third on Happy Felsch's errant throw. Rath followed with a single to right, giving Cincinnati a 1–0 lead. Daubert laid down a sacrifice bunt, and then Groh walked on four pitches. That brought overdue Edd to the plate, looking to make an impact with his bat instead of the glove. Back in the fourth, he exchanged words with Williams when a pitch sailed close to his head. According to an eavesdropping Groh, Roush said, "Pitch the ball through here and I'll knock it down your throat."

Edd got his revenge, breaking the game open on an extra-base shot to deep center. Felsch misjudged the towering drive, getting a late jump before the ball glanced off his outstretched glove. He slipped, regained his feet, recovered the sphere, then threw back to the infield. That whole sequence looked so fishy that, after the game, co-conspirators warned Felsch to stop making it so obvious. A year later he told the *Chicago American*, "You can believe me or not, I was trying to catch that ball. I lost it in the sun and made a long run for it, and looked foolish when it fell quite a bit away from where it ought to be."[15]

Rath scored easily and Groh slid by Schalk's tag on a close play at the plate. Enraged by the safe call, Chicago's excitable catcher lunged at the umpire and made contact. Multiple media accounts had that contact coming from the knuckle side of a clinched fist. Schalk was ejected and Edd ended up on third, credited with a two-run triple. He came home on a short sacrifice fly when the backup catcher dropped Jackson's strong throw from left field. Snakebit once again, mighty Chicago trailed by a score of 4–0.

Eller permitted a base runner to reach third in the first inning and again in the ninth when the game was already decided. In between, nobody even got to second during Cincinnati's 5–0 triumph. Meanwhile, Williams held the Reds to four hits and two walks in eight innings of work but was victimized by bad defense. The Sox committed three official errors, which didn't include the suspicious misplay on Edd's three-bagger.

Williams is lumped in with the worst of the fixers, however. He would later admit to taking a $5,000 bribe on the eve of his Game Five outing. In a column on the latest contest, Hugh Fullerton hinted at the idea of scandal, without coming right out and saying it. "There is more bitter feeling among the fans and the players over this series than ever has been manifested before. The reason is, perhaps, the heavy gambling—the heaviest ever recorded—and the fierce resentment of the Sox.... Read carefully the details of this sixth inning for, unless I am much mistaken, it is going to be the most fertile cause of baseball argument in the next year or two."[16]

Game Six

There was probably not one fan in a hundred amidst the dense throng surrounding the playing field who would have wagered a burnt match against a ten dollar note that the White Sox could come through.—Jack Ryder, Cincinnati Enquirer[17]

Five games down and the former underdogs held a commanding 4–1 lead. In a traditional best-of-seven format, this Series would already be over. Still, with the venue shifting back to Redland Field, Cincinnati seemed to have it in the bag. After winning two of three in enemy territory, the Reds could close things out in front of a packed house that cheered their every move. Sox supporters fell off the bandwagon in droves, with far fewer booking travel for the second Cincinnati junket. Who could blame them? Even Kid Gleason had turned into a gloomy Gus: "I don't know what's the matter but I do know that something is wrong with my gang. The bunch I had fighting in August for the pennant would have trimmed this Cincinnati bunch without a struggle. The bunch I have now couldn't beat a high school team."[18]

Wagers were hard to come by now. Reds rooters might find even-money bets for the sixth game alone, but it seemed nobody would pick the Sox to win the Series at any odds. Smelling the kill, local fans arrived in droves for the Tuesday game and set two records—one for attendance, the other fueled by attendance. A crowd of 32,006 set the all-time mark at Redland Field, beating the standard set a couple months earlier when the Giants came to town for a Sunday showdown. Game Six also set a World Series record for single-game gate receipts, with Cincinnati pulling in $101,768, thanks to ticket prices that were the highest in Series history.

Dutch Ruether returned to the mound for the home team, while Chicago placed another anvil of pressure on Dickie Kerr's narrow back. Taking an 11-inning scoreless streak into the third, Kerr finally showed signs of vulnerability. He allowed a one-out single to Jake Daubert, struck out Groh, plunked Edd in the side, then surrendered a two-run double to Pat Duncan. When the Reds added a couple more runs in the fourth, victory seemed just a matter of time. Leading 4–0, they stood five innings away from glory.

Suddenly Ruether hit a wild stretch, walking the first two batters of the fifth inning. Kerr followed with a hard shot off the shortstop's glove that loaded the bases. Chicago plated its first run on an Eddie Collins sacrifice fly, but the bigger story was over on second base where two Sox stood at the same bag. For some unfathomable reason, Kerr tried to advance when Roush threw to third. Ray Schalk frantically waved back his teammate, but the oblivious Kerr kept coming and was tagged for an inning-ending double play. If anybody ever pondered whether Kerr was involved in throwing games, that play should have cleared up the mystery. Nobody makes it that comically obvious.

It was immediately recognized as one of the most significant blunders in pastime history, ranking with the "Merkle Boner" of 1908 and "Snodgrass Muff" of 1912. With hot-hitting Buck Weaver scheduled to bat next, Kerr's carelessness killed a golden opportunity. Inside the stadium and out, fans started a countdown toward the first World Series title in Cincinnati history.

Feeling a time crunch of their own, the Sox went back to work in the sixth, starting with Weaver's leadoff double, a pop fly that fell between left field and shortstop in a classic case of "I thought you had it." Jackson rapped an RBI single, and then scored on Felsch's double to cut the lead to 4–3. Boss Moran had seen enough and replaced Ruether with Jimmy Ring, winner of Game Four. Retiring the first two batters without incident, he then surrendered a game-tying single to Schalk. It was a brand new game.

In the seventh inning, Cincinnati put runners on first and second but the rally ended when Edd hit into a double play. He redeemed himself with the glove, however, making a shoestring grab that saved a run in the eighth. Never dreaming that the ball might be caught, Jackson took off from second and was easily nailed for another inning-ending double play. Roush had a hero's chance in the bottom of the ninth, coming up with two outs and a man on first base. His opportunity evaporated, however, when the runner was thrown out trying to steal.

That play sent the game to extra innings, where Chicago quickly went on the attack. Weaver led off the 10th with a looper that dropped safely in left field and took second when Pat Duncan overran the ball. Jackson dropped a bunt single, putting runners at the corners. Felsch then fanned and Chick Gandil smacked an RBI single to center.

When Kerr retired the Reds in order, Chicago savored a 5–4 win. On the verge of elimination, the White Sox had pulled off a dramatic comeback that shifted the Series momentum.

Game Seven

> *The war against the Bolsheviki, the conflict on the Adriatic, the race riots, the struggle between labor and capital, all fade into the background just now. The one topic of transcendent interest is the struggle now being fought out between the White Guards from that great city which certain of its own poets have hailed as "hog butcher to the universe" and the warlike Reds from the Metropolis of Malt.*—New York Times[19]

Reds and Whites, just like the two color-coded factions in Russia's raging civil war between Communists and Nationalists. The analogy was inevitable. Could Pat Moran prove as successful as Vladimir Lenin or would Gleason's old guard prevail?

On game day, surprisingly few Cincinnatians seemed to care. One win away from a championship and Redland Field resembled an oil town gone bust. It wasn't empty, but only 13,923 attended, less than half the previous day's total and about 10,000 fewer than the crowd that watched electronic scoreboard updates at Chicago's Grant Park. "Reds Fans Desert Cincinnati Team," read one headline.[20]

Several factors contributed to rows of empty seats. Topping the list was confusion about new ticket purchases. Fans bought a package deal to watch the first three home games but had to secure single-game tickets in a relatively brief period of time. Nobody was sure how to do it, and team officials seemed almost as confused as the rest of their city.

"It simply was impossible to distribute the tickets in the short time we had and take the precautions we adopted to prevent speculators from grabbing them," explained team president Garry Herrmann.[21]

Two other causes were fan disgust and the format change from best-of-seven to best-of-nine. Many rooters took it personally when their team choked in the latter innings of Tuesday's loss. Others saw the lengthened series as a calculated drain on their wallets. Then there was the conspiracy fringe, claiming Cincinnati lost intentionally in order to drag things out and increase gate receipts. Whatever the root of their discontent, Reds supporters had less than

24 hours to make Game Seven arrangements, and most stayed home. Meanwhile, White Sox folk provided an amusing spectacle, dashing through hotel lobbies and city streets in a fruitless search for scalpers. They eventually discovered a simpler and more effective method of walking to the stadium ticket box and buying premium seats for far less money.

Cicotte returned to the mound with two perfect opportunities — redemption in the eyes of Sox fans or induction into the fixers hall of fame. Already 0 and 2, he needed only one more loss for a hat trick of shame. Representing the Reds was Slim Sallee, the man who pitched so well in Game Two.

The visitors coasted to a 4–1 triumph, causing a sparse crowd to become even sparser in the latter innings. Cincinnati put two runners on base in the ninth but few remained to cheer the comeback or curse fate when Rath made the final out on a line shot to right field. It culminated a whale of an outing for Cicotte. His final statistics looked less than stellar — seven hits, three walks, four strikeouts — but the venerated one dominated when it mattered. Cicotte's pitches had that old movement again, prompting batters to wonder aloud about his methods. The officiating crew, however, saw no evidence of doctored baseballs. Roush's 0-for-4 outing certainly didn't count as evidence; if it did, every Sox pitcher would face charges. Edd entered Game Seven with only three hits to his name.

Lacking offensive input from its batting champ, Cincinnati still scored enough runs for early World Series dominance. Now the White Sox had turned the tide. With their backs to the wall, they won two straight in enemy territory and pulled within one game of tying things up. Even better, the venue was shifting back to comfy Comiskey Park.

Game Eight

> *The (team) has given us pep. We feel now there is nothing too big for us to do. When a community, like an individual, begins to feel that it amounts to something, there is no stopping that community. We are breathing today the life-giving atmosphere of success.* —Cincinnati Post editorial[22]

If Lefty Williams ever wore a smile of confidence, it disappeared when a gangster-type approached him on the eve of the eighth game in Chicago. The message was simple and succinct — lose tomorrow, or else. The thug's threat included Williams' wife.

With Hod Eller manning the mound for Cincinnati, the contest would be a rematch between Game Five starters. Nearly 33,000 fans turned out, a vast majority of them cheering for what seemed an inevitable outcome, a Series-tying triumph. All the famous analysts told them so.

Rain clouds hung over Chicago in the morning before a strong breeze chased them away, but the wind still blew hard by afternoon. It created difficult fielding conditions, so the Sox prepared with a practice session that focused on high infield pop flies. Unpredictable flight paths weren't the only problem, as defenders also had to deal with diamond dust storms, fueled by a mixture of gusts and infield dirt.

A storm was brewing behind closed doors as well. While the Reds gathered for their pre-game meeting, Edd pulled his manager aside and told him of a disturbing rumor about gamblers, bribes and fixed games. It did not involve the Chicago White Sox. Earlier that morning, Roush's informant warned him about traitors in his own midst. As an old man, he recreated the ensuing clubhouse dialogue:

ROUSH: Pat, before you start this goddamned meeting I got something I want to say.

MANAGER PAT MORAN: Well, what is it?

ROUSH: Well, I've understood that the gamblers has got some of the players on our ball club. Damned if I'm going out there and trying to win a World Series if somebody else is losing the ball game.

MORAN: Daubert, I haven't heard anything from you.

JAKE DAUBERT: I don't know a damn thing. Only what I've heard.

MORAN: Hod, anybody offer you anything to throw today's ball game?

HOD ELLER: Yep.

MORAN: What did he offer you?

ELLER: Five thousand dollars if I lose today's ball game.

MORAN: What did you say?

ELLER: I told him if I ever saw him again, I'd knock....

MORAN: (*He looked at Hod for a long while.*) Hod, you're pitching today. If I see anything out of you that don't look right, you're coming right out of there.[23]

After Rath led off the game with a harmless infield fly, Daubert took Williams' first pitch for a strike, then shot a low liner into center. That was usually Felsch territory, but he'd been moved to right field the past couple games, probably because of earlier defensive struggles. Nemo Leibold became the center fielder de jour and he failed to make a shoestring catch. Groh singled to right, putting runners on first and second, then Edd doubled over first base, scoring Daubert and sending Groh to third. Duncan followed with a two-run double, pushing the lead to 3–0.

In an exceptionally early exit for one of baseball's best hurlers, Kid Gleason yanked Williams. His final stat line: one-third inning pitched, four hits, three earned runs and another soon to follow. Bedford Bill Rariden rapped an RBI single against reliever Bill James, extending the lead to 4–0.

The Sox fought back in their half of the first, putting runners on second and third with no outs. Just like his last outing, Eller faced early trouble while a relief pitcher warmed up in the wings. This time, the bribery mess put him on a much shorter leash. He fanned Weaver for the critical first out, got Jackson to pop up, and set Felsch down on strikes.

Edd belted another RBI double in the second inning — this one an opposite field blast that sailed past Jackson in left. Never mind that he got tagged out in a rundown between second and third. The run scored and Cincinnati led, 5–0. Roush also came through with a two-run single in the sixth, as the romping Reds stretched their lead to 9–1. They'd just salted away the game and the World Series. Even with umpires looking over his shoulder, nobody was going to make up eight runs on Hod Eller.

The *Chicago Tribune* reported, "The umps kept examining the ball to see whether Eller was fuzzing the horsehide for shine pitching.... Eller did more damage to the cover of the ball with his bat than with his pants."[24]

Leading off the eighth Edd got hit by a pitch, took second on a sacrifice bunt, and came home courtesy of a Hoosier hit by Bill Rariden. Now the score was 10–1. Chicago finally showed some grit in the bottom half of the inning, scoring four times on four hits and a couple fielding flubs. But Cincy still had five runs of separation heading into the ninth.

After the Sox lead-off batter reached first, Edd made a diving catch of a Leibold drive to deep right-center. Snagging the ball inches from the grass, he hit the ground hard, turned a somersault, then fired back to the infield before the runner could advance. Yet another gem in the Roush fielding clinic, it dealt the final blow to hopes of a home-team rally.

Eddie Collins followed with a single, which meant Edd's play probably saved two runs. It could have been 10–7, runner on first and no outs — still a long way from tying the game but close enough to send a shiver through Reds nation. Sticking the landing on a rare triple negative, the *St. Louis Post-Dispatch* wrote, "Had Roush *not* pulled Eller back to earth with the most remarkable catch of the game it is *not* such a sure thing the Chicagoans would *not* have driven 'Hod' from the box and possibly ridden on the crest of their batting wave to a miraculous victory."[25]

Deflated by Edd's thievery, Chicago bowed out quietly, the game ending on a meek grounder to second by Jackson. Jake Daubert squeezed Rath's throw at first base and the 1919 World Series was history. When that final out went into the books, the news soon spread through every corner of Cincinnati and crossed the Ohio River into bedroom Kentucky communities. From the waterfront to distant hilltops, fans formed a tidal wave of celebration.

Redleg emeritus Cal McVey heard congratulations from every direction, though he stood about a half-century removed from any connection to local baseball. The California native had endured tough times since 1906, when the great San Francisco earthquake killed his wife and ruined his finances. Now he embraced joy again, if only for a day.

Cincinnati officials proclaimed Friday a half-day holiday and encouraged residents to greet the Reds in a 10:00 A.M. gathering at Fountain Square. It seemed half the city was on hand when the team train arrived Friday morning at Central Union Railroad Station. Cheers started at first sight of the championship chariot, then exploded to ear-splitting decibels when players emerged with wide grins on their faces. Hats went flying through the air and women screamed just as hard as the men. The crowd called players by name, cheering them all individually, as well as collectively. Struggling through the mass of adoring worshipers, they eventually climbed into automobiles that carried them to an elaborate banquet, sponsored by the local Business Men's Club. As fans trailed on foot, an impromptu parade proceeded under a deafening din of church bells, fire engine sirens and automated whistles from factories, steamboats and locomotives.

The Fountain Square tribute got rained out, which was fine by the players. Most were anxious to get home. After the banquet, they headed for Redland Field to divide the spoils of victory. Presented a winners share check for $117,157.35, team captain Heinie Groh hurried to the bank and arranged for individual payments. It came to about $5,200 per player — by far the largest share in Series history. Sox players earned $3,250 apiece, the richest haul ever taken by a runner-up and more than most winners. For those double-dippers who also took bribe money, it became quite a profitable week.

The rumor mill worked overtime but most attributed it to sour grapes. Upsets happen and White Sox worshippers needed to accept that. So did the gamblers who lost money betting. Charles Comiskey pointed a finger at the latter group, saying those kinds of "sore heads" were notorious for concocting conspiracies. Wasting no time, he began damage control right after the Series ended. "Nobody has produced a thing to show that these rumors have any solid foundation," Comiskey told a *Post-Dispatch* correspondent. "If anybody has anything on any of my players I will give him $10,000 to show me proof that there was anything wrong. The players are entitled to the doubt and should not be accused without evidence."[26] Later that night, he upped the ante to $20,000.

Cincinnati's afterglow went undimmed by predictable gossip. Its glorious triumph transcended sports, effecting a rise to the ranks of other great American cities. Edd's remarkable defense drew high praise from the country's biggest newspapers and most famous sports commentators. Though hitting only .214 overall, he finally put his prowess on display in the deciding game, going 3-for-5, with two doubles, two runs, and five big RBIs. The batting king wore clothes that day, regal attire fit for a champion.

It had been an exciting Series that saw multiple momentum shifts before the underdogs finally closed things out. In the bigger picture it marked the end of an important season, with fans streaming back to ballparks after the war. Yet there was nothing to indicate that the 1919 Fall Classic would live on, long after its actors were dead and buried.

15

New Day Dawning

Back in 1920 they put a live ball in the league. Before that, we played with six balls. The umpire had six balls out there in that dang thing and we only used two of 'em. Hell! If the god-danged ball got soot on it he'd just take it, (rub) it off and throw it back in. Now that's the way it was back in those days. But in 1920, for Babe Ruth, they changed the whole god-danged thing around.[1]

Fame, family, money, two batting titles, one magnificent glove, a World Series championship ... Edd Roush had it all. And he was only 26 years old. The 1920s awaited him like virgin snow on an uncharted mountain.

It would be a decade remembered for prosperity, wild times and transcendent sports figures. Conveniently glossed over was the explosion in farm bankruptcies and a growing divide between the fabulously rich and wretchedly poor. A divide also existed in baseball — the Cincinnati Reds and everybody else. Basketball and football were small potatoes compared to the national pastime and to rule baseball was to walk among gods. Cobb, Hornsby, Speaker ... all shady silhouettes behind Technicolor Reds like Roush and Groh.

Cincinnati's Big Two seemed serious about defending their title — both arriving at the Miami training camp on March 13, just in time to lose an intrasquad game to a group of unproven hopefuls. It didn't matter. Pat Moran remained giddy about the relatively early appearance of his best players, which meant the team could focus on returning to championship form.

Of course, Edd believed his form developed better without protracted southern sojourns to the land of dangerously substandard diamonds. Speaking to the Cincinnati press, he described the perfect pre-season regimen: Stay on his farm, then report for duty about a week before the first official game. That's all the time he needed to hone his baseball skills, and physical conditioning was better left to the natural rhythms of rural life. Throw in a daily two-mile run and Roush was right as rain.

Yet who could fault a manager for wanting players in camp? Moran got his wish this time but the preseason proved brutal, with the Reds losing one exhibition game after another to American League teams. Their primary opponents were the Washington Senators and New York Yankees, which meant the champs would sharpen batting eyes against two elite pitchers in Walter Johnson and Bob Shawkey. Spring routine called for two teams to engage each other over and over, becoming traveling partners in a Southern road show.

In 1978, Edd reflected back on his days among the Senators. "I had to play six innings and Walter had to pitch one inning every day. That's a sight. Well, I was the star on the Cincinnati ball club and he was the star on the Washington club.... We'd come up with the Washington ball club and Walter had to pitch one inning and I had to play six innings every day, rain or shine."

When pairing with the Yankees, Cincinnati took its lumps from New York's latest and greatest tourist attraction, Babe Ruth. During the offseason, Boston Red Sox owner Harry Frazee sold the rising star for $100,000 and a huge loan, then used the cash flow to finance his first love — Broadway musicals. Frazee leaned more toward art than athletics.

The Reds lost a lot of spring games but looked like champions again when the regular season kicked off by cranking out 12 hits in a 7–3 home win over Grover Alexander and the Chicago Cubs. That just goes to prove what Frazee's people liked to say: bad dress rehearsal, good opening night. Nailing the role he was born to play, Edd hit a home run and caught five fly balls.

Over at Comiskey Park, Buck Weaver delivered four hits in an extra-inning victory against Detroit. So far, there seemed no reason to doubt a World Series rematch, as both rosters were nearly identical to the ones that captured pennants the previous season. Chick Gandil never returned, his big league career ending in a long holdout that failed to sway management, but Shano Collins proved an able replacement at first base. With a healthy Red Faber upgrading the rotation, Chicago's pitching staff looked better than ever.

The Reds won the following day, 4–3, then completed the sweep in an 11–6 slugfest. They lost the next three, reeled off six consecutive wins, lost three more, then moved into first with a May 4 victory. Ebbs and flows, charges and retreats — recurring themes for the 1920 season. Meanwhile, Edd got off to another slow start, recording six hits in his first 29 at-bats. It took awhile to rejoin the league's elite hitters, but he got there eventually, upping his average to .336 by early June.

A four-game series went bad in New York, with Cincy dropping three, and the June 8 opener would go down in Roush lore as the day he got ejected for falling asleep on the job. It happened when he grew bored by a lengthy on-field argument between a mob of Reds fielders and the officiating crew. A George Burns double should have been ruled foul, they said. Expressing that sentiment in cruder terms, the players formed an imposing and animated front. Catcher Ivey Wingo threw a glove skyward in disgust, then flung his chest protector in the same direction. Umpire Barry McCormick promptly threw him out of the game.

One account had the squabble lasting more than 15 minutes, way too long for Edd Roush to endure. So he discarded his glove and cap, lay down in center field and closed his eyes. When the combatants finally settled down and took their positions, Edd remained horizontal. Wake-up calls went unheeded, so Heinie Groh ran to the outfield and stirred Rip Van Roush, who then slowly rose to his feet. Unamused, McCormick ejected him. One of the few Reds who remained peaceful during the initial brouhaha, Edd became enraged and charged the ump. This caused another lengthy delay before teammates and Manager Moran could convince him to leave the field.

"I didn't get up quite soon enough to please the umpire so he put me out of the game and I drew an indefinite suspension on the grounds that I was trying to burlesque the game," Edd told *Baseball Magazine*. "It is my opinion that some of these umpires burlesque the game a good deal more than the players do."[2]

The Roush outburst was overshadowed two days later when newspapers carried a story of game-fixing, crooked players and a trial to sort it all out. None of it concerned the 1919 World Series. This lesser scandal centered on Lee Magee and his lawsuit against the Chicago Cubs, who dumped him after learning about his shady past with the Reds. Taking a turn on the witness stand, Magee admitted betting, denied taking a dive, and implicated Hal Chase as the real villain of a failed fix scheme in 1918.

On July 2, Cincinnati beat Chicago in extra innings and extended its N.L. lead to two games over Brooklyn. Late that night, big news echoed from the Polo Grounds that Benny Kauff had been traded. This didn't come as a huge surprise, because such talk had swirled for months. But nobody anticipated a deal that sent him out of the majors and into Canada. Nailing down an agreement over long-distance telephone, the Giants sent Kauff and cash to Toronto of the International League. In return, they received a hot prospect by the name of Vernon Spencer.

Thus ended the meteoric major league experience of Benjamin Michael Kauff. In the span of seven years, he had burst onto the scene as a Federal League superstar, played great for the Giants in 1917, belted two homers in the World Series, recorded three solid seasons, and hit the lively ball at a .274 clip before getting shipped north. He finished with a .287 career average. Spencer hit .200 in 140 at-bats and was never heard from again.

In the midst of an impressive stretch that eventually produced 16 wins in 18 games, Brooklyn's boys were back in first by July 11. Though fielding essentially the same lineup that finished fifth a year earlier, they bore little resemblance to that squad. Their pitching staff went six deep, spitballer Burleigh Grimes was enjoying a breakout season, Zach Wheat continued to pound N.L. pitching, and fellow outfielder Hy Myers hit at a nice clip, too.

The Dodgers came to Cincinnati for a four-game series and won the first two, then Adolfo Luque stopped the bleeding in front of 26,000 energetic Redland fans. His tourniquet — a six-hit, 4–1 triumph. The Reds took a 5–4 decision the following day, as former Dodger Jake Daubert scored the winning run in the bottom of the ninth. That pulled Cincy within a couple games of first, and by month's end it was a virtual dead heat.

Edd pumped out three hits in a July 31 win at the Polo Grounds, giving him 12 in his last 18 at-bats. Then Cincinnati dropped three straight to its hosts, the final defeat coming by an embarrassing 11–1 count. Complaining that the visitors played listlessly, the *New York Times* singled out Edd Roush as principal offender: "Once the Giants got out to a commanding lead Roush adopted the attitude of one who was in no way concerned about the outcome.... The tactics of the Red star did not set very well with a crowd of more than 18,000 fans, and he was jeered and hooted for his refusal to play ball. Roush glared into the stands as if to pick out some particular tormentor, but failed to single one out."[3]

Edd played hard enough to move into second place in the batting chase. It was the high-water mark of an amazing ascent, begun during those dark early-season days. Over the course of a six-month season, talent trumps bad starts or brief slumps. Unfortunately, Edd's uncommon ability was matched and surpassed by Rogers Hornsby, whose .372 outclassed the field. All drama centered on the race for runner-up, with Roush's .333 barely better than the next two contenders.

Cincinnati rebounded from the Polo Grounds fizzle and won nine of its next 13 games. Staying neck-and-neck through the rest of August, the frontrunners were soon joined by a third contender, the Giants. By sundown of August 30, three horses bobbed heads in unison: Cincinnati 67–52, Brooklyn 69–55, New York 67–55. One day later, the Dodgers seized first by .002 percentage points. A tight race captivated the American League too, where the White Sox held a half-game advantage over Cleveland and led the Yankees by a full game. Baseball fans looked forward to an exhilarating finish for both circuits.

Smelling the finish line, the Reds started September with three straight wins, the last a 17-hit, 12-run blowout in St. Louis. They took four of their next five but Brooklyn stayed right with them. The excitement spread to the batting race, where Hornsby no longer seemed a shoo-in. As of September 10, his average stood at .358 —16 points higher than Edd's rising mark. Meanwhile, New York's Ross Youngs pulled within a couple points of second.

That N.L. pennant logjam soon became less congested, but not in a good way. Suddenly, the Reds couldn't beat anybody. They dropped five straight, including a doubleheader sweep to bottom-feeding Boston and an error-filled 21–10 embarrassment in Philadelphia. Next came a return trip to Brooklyn, with Cincinnati desperately needing to win the three-game series, preferably in a sweep. Two quick losses squashed that ambition.

The Reds recaptured some pride with an 11–5 success in the series final then lost it completely by dropping eight of their next nine. The kings were dead. Brooklyn took the pennant by seven games over New York, and Cincinnati finished third at 82–71. Most years, that would have seemed an honorable Reds effort but not after winning the World Series. These were supposedly the best players on the planet, yet they shattered in September.

At least Cincy could take pride in its unflappable center fielder, who persevered while everything crumbled around him. No, Edd didn't win the batting title, and he even failed to hold onto second. Youngs shot past him for the silver medal and Hornsby pulled away to an easy gold. But he made a memorable charge, hitting .395 during a 27-game hitting streak that stretched into late September, and finished at .339.

Catching Hornsby was always a long shot anyhow; batting a Cobb-like .370, the Cardinals star won his first of six consecutive crowns. He never bested Roush during the dead-ball days, however, when hitting was more science than slugging. Armed with an old-fashioned, short batting stroke, Edd pounded the springy sphere, but his soaring stats always fell well short of Hornsby's

Nineteen-twenty marked the beginning of a glorious era for baseball. To the delight of most fans and the dismay of traditionalists, offense exploded in the coming years. According to popular theory, the blastoff was lit by a "juiced" baseball that jumped off the bat. Some swear the ball remained unchanged and point to hitter-friendly rule changes. The spitball was outlawed and batters also greatly benefited from a new emphasis on rotating fresh baseballs into games. They saw pitches more clearly when the pill wasn't perpetually stained by dirt and tobacco–rich saliva. Its trajectory became more predictable if it wasn't scuffed up, rubbed raw or smeared with some slippery substance.

But a whole lot of people claimed the ball was different on the inside, too. People who ought to know, such as Edd J. Roush. In a 1960 interview with the *New York Times*, he detailed his frustrating first encounter with the new orb. Taking a typically shallow position in center field, Roush couldn't believe how many drives were sailing over his head.

"When I came to the bench, I turned to our manager and said: 'Hey, what's up? These guys are running me to death. Have they gotten stronger overnight?'" "Didn't you know?" Pat Moran replied. "We're using the lively ball."[4]

Whatever the cause or causes, a future of exhilarating offense awaited. But before the new decade took over, it drove a stake through the old one. About the time Cincinnati fell apart in the pennant chase, disturbing reports emerged about the 1919 World Series. It went beyond rumors now; a Cook County grand jury was hearing convincing testimony in Chicago.

Then, as now, grand jury proceedings were confidential. But the sensational case struck a national nerve so sensitive that the veil of secrecy was lifted and news reporters made contact with nameless court officials, who relayed what they had heard from the witness stand. The next day's papers often carried second-hand quotes — a journalistic sin that should normally evoke an "Objection! Hearsay!" from newsroom editors. These were abnormal times, however. Among the scandal's many actors, some answered questions outside the courtroom by meeting with the press for extended interviews or issued written statements. Mix all that in with the testimony recollections and it became difficult to determine the origin of information.

The grand jury convened because of the Cubs, not the White Sox. Accusations arose after an August 31 game, when the cellar-dwelling Philadelphia Phillies won in Chicago. Sometime before the first pitch, Cubs management received several telegrams and a couple long-distance phone calls from Detroit, all warning of a plot to lose, none with verifiable names or addresses. They might've been bookies. Though the game produced no obvious signs of crookedness, a widely circulated rumor had four Cubs in cahoots with game-fixers. The Windy City became enveloped by a climate of conspiracy ... again.

The *Chicago Tribune* noted, "Undoubtedly the rumor is founded on alleged suspicious things that took place last fall in the world's series between the White Sox and Cincinnati Reds, which caused an investigation that never brought forth proof."[5]

It seemed every powerbroker was spearheading an inquiry at one time or another. Charles Comiskey and Ban Johnson supposedly hired teams of private detectives to hunt evidence, and John Heydler played gumshoe himself. Would conspiracies or conspiracy theories unravel under the pressure of so many prying eyes? Maybe, but baseball moguls had no obligation to share all their findings with the paying public. To keep that public paying, they had to guard any info deemed bad for business.

It would take more than individual investigations to shed light on this dark scandal. In addition to questions of bias, they were undermined by limited scopes of authority. For an extensive public accounting, America wanted and needed a powerful investigative body with the backing of its government, something like a Chicago grand jury.

Subpoenaed to testify on September 23, Giants pitcher Rube Benton dropped a series of bombshells over the next couple days, and not just from the witness stand. He also spoke to reporters. The former and future Red said: (1) Hal Chase and Buck Herzog once offered him money to throw a game to the Chicago Cubs; (2) a well-connected Cincinnati gambler told him that a Pittsburgh syndicate paid $100,000 to fix the World Series; (3) his source pointed fingers at Eddie Cicotte, Lefty Williams, Chick Gandil and Hap Felsch; (4) Chase made $40,000 betting on the Series.

Scurrilous stuff, to be sure, but Benton made no mention of specific crooked plays. Others did. The sordid details poured forth over the next week — some from court, others in sensational newspaper interviews, and some in conflicting accounts. It was a confusing picture of conspiracy, with team ringleaders on one end, New York moneyman Arnold Rothstein at the other, and a whole bunch of shady characters in between. One of those middlemen, Billy Maharg, told Philadelphia reporters that Sox players approached *him* with the fix idea, not the other way around. Cicotte supposedly met him and accomplice Bill "Sleepy" Burns at a New York hotel during the fall of 1919. They made the deal, then used former boxing champ Abe Attell as a go-between with Rothstein. Maharg also detailed the double-crosses — first by Attell, who delivered only a fraction of the promised $100,000 bribe booty, and then by Black Sox players in that Game Three victory.

Some questioned Maharg's credibility. He was, after all, a con man and that last name screamed subterfuge: "Maharg" is "Graham" spelled backward. But even if half his claims were untrue, baseball had a lot of explaining to do.

Finally revealing his own strong suspicions, Comiskey made front-page headlines when he told reporters that he had voiced concerns to Heydler after each of the first two Series games. Speaking on the eve of his grand jury testimony, the N.L. president confirmed Commy's account and expanded on it. "Comiskey said his

First baseman Chick Gandil was identified as the ringleader for crooked White Sox. He's shown here in more innocent times, during his early days with the Washington Senators (Library of Congress).

manager, Kid Gleason, felt convinced some one had 'reached' the Sox players and that they had talked the matter over and felt an investigation should be made. I still believed he was mistaken, but I took the matter up with Ban Johnson later at the game. Johnson replied with a rather curt remark that made me drop the matter."[6]

Also sharing the same news cycle was a Ban Johnson expedition to New York, where the A.L. president met with Arnold Rothstein. The notorious "A.R." reportedly said he knew of the fix but took no part in it.

Then came the day that changed everything. Baseball's black eye turned into a full-body beating on September 28, as Eddie Cicotte and Shoeless Joe Jackson confessed at the witness stand and implicated others. A flurry of indictments quickly followed. Happy Felsch confirmed his own guilt during an interview with the *Chicago American*, admitting to taking a $5,000 payoff. Pictures of the disgraced eight were plastered across front pages throughout the country — Cicotte, Jackson, Felsch, Chick Gandil, Lefty Williams, Buck Weaver, Swede Risberg, Fred McMullin. They faced charges of conspiracy to commit an illegal act, punishable by five years imprisonment and a fine up to $10,000.

It was a sad day for heroes in Chicago, and courtroom moles described their downfall in great detail. Cicotte supposedly broke down in tears while admitting to taking a $10,000 bribe, placed under his hotel room pillow on the night before the World Series opener. He did it for his family, using part of the dirty money to pay off a $4,000 farm mortgage. Cicotte proved a hard bargainer on fix terms, demanding ten grand in advance and getting it. A guilty conscience tortured him ever since.

What about that Game One meltdown when the White Sox ace surrendered six runs in 3⅔ innings? Eddie supposedly claimed he tossed the ball so easy, you could read the trademark. How about Game Four, when he deflected Joe Jackson's throw toward home plate? A deliberate muff, said Cicotte. He also admitted to making an intentional wild throw in the same game.

Shoeless Joe cursed intrusive photographers on his way into the courtroom but came out smiling. Confession was apparently good for the soul. If the weight of the world lifted from Jackson's shoulders, it landed squarely on John McGraw. Waiting his turn to testify, he could barely contain his disgust: "This damned crookedness among men who make more in a week than we made in a year when we fought with our bare hands to keep the game clean."[7]

Speaking publicly that night, Jackson recounted parts of his testimony and admitted to taking a $5,000 bribe. He said he'd been promised $20,000 but never got another dime after the first installment, delivered in a dirty envelope by Lefty Williams. Complaining to Gandil and others, he was shouted down and advised to be content with whatever he got. Some players were promised more and received less, they said. Even more disturbing was Jackson's fear that his testimony could get him killed — not through underworld retribution, but at the hands of a teammate. "Now Risberg threatens to bump me off if I squawk. That's why I had all the bailiffs with me when I left the grand jury room this afternoon.... I'm not going to get far from my protectors until this blows over. Swede is a hard guy."[8]

Though his team sat only one game out of first with three to play, Comiskey immediately suspended all seven dishonored players. The eighth — Chick Gandil — was already serving a suspension for his holdout. He sent letters to the accused, promising reinstatement if they were declared innocent of any wrongdoing and banishment if found guilty. The move ruined Comiskey's chances for another A.L. pennant but enhanced his reputation among the media, which portrayed him as a virtuous King Arthur, wounded by betrayal but determined to cleave evildoers from baseball at any cost. Here was a man of character, a self-made millionaire who put honor before the profit of another World Series appearance. Never mind that his tight-fisted fiscal policy helped create the climate for bribery.

The disgraced eight were only accused, not convicted, so management had every right to keep them in uniform. Then again, an "innocent until proven guilty" approach could have proved a public relations nightmare, especially with those confessions casting a pall over everything.

Not all Chicagoans were disheartened by the swirl of indictments and suspensions. It sparked a celebration among innocent players who had lived under a depressing cloud of suspicion that lumped all White Sox together. No longer would they be forced to share a dugout with men they despised. A carload of players arrived near the courthouse on indictment day and they sent a friend inside for an update. He sprinted back with news that put smiles on everybody's faces. Nemo Liebold hugged Eddie Collins, Collins slapped Amos Strunk on the back, and Strunk swung a playful punch into Mike Murphy's ribs. Next came a rush to telephones and calls to other teammates. A group dinner followed at a downtown restaurant and the party later moved to Collins's Southside apartment. Ray Schalk was out of town but sped back to join the merriment.

Lefty Williams soon came clean and verified what he had already revealed in a sworn statement to Comiskey's attorney. He admitted to accepting $10,000 after the Game Four loss, giving half to Joe Jackson and keeping the rest. Suddenly casting doubt on the entire prosecution was Illinois state attorney Maclay Hoyne. Speaking from New York, where he was gathering case-related information, he said the accused might face only misdemeanor charges of gambling or conspiracy to gamble. They might've done a bad thing, but could the state prove it? And was it even illegal? Illinois law proved hazy on the subject.

As if the Black Sox scandal weren't bad enough publicity, it set baseball men to reminiscing about other ugly incidents from the past. McGraw testified that he had released talented players because they were suspected of throwing games. Former Phillies catcher Charley Dooin claimed those Sox bribes were small change compared to the offers his teammates heard during the 1908 pennant chase. Now touring with a minstrel troupe in Atlantic City, he told the *New York Times* that all payoffs were rejected and one gambler even received a beating for his efforts.

Confirming that story during an interview with the *Philadelphia Inquirer*, former Phillies president Horace Fogel said five players were offered between $1,000 and $5,000 to sit out a series against New York. He also passed along an old rumor about a generous proposition to the late Rube Waddell — $17,000 if he didn't play for his Philadelphia Athletics in the 1905 World Series. The quirky hurler did indeed miss the Series, reportedly because he hurt his arm while tripping over a suitcase.

Benny Kauff testified he had been offered a bribe of $125 "or more" to help throw a game to the Cubs in 1919. He remembered reporting the matter to McGraw, and then delivering several hits at the plate. Teammate Fred Toney made similar claims and Giants owner Charles Stoneham corroborated McGraw's testimony of the previous week.

Baseball's dirty little secret was out. Roaches lurked everywhere, even if they weren't always visible to the untrained eye. Crooks had moved among ball players since the beginning, all the way back to 1877 when four Louisville players were blackballed for throwing games in the National League's second year of existence. The current season fell under suspicion, too, with Ban Johnson relaying a story he heard about Black Sox under orders to lose the 1920 pennant to Cleveland. If they refused, so the story went, gamblers would reveal the dirty business of the previous year. Worse yet, suspicion fell on the upcoming World Series when word circulated of a Brooklyn Dodger dive. A New York district attorney investigated the charge and team president Charlie Ebbets promised full cooperation.

Baseball magnates cringed at each new revelation. With the game's credibility on life support, they had nightmares of empty stadiums and cobweb-encrusted coffers. The current season's profits remained safe, however, as only a few days remained before the start of the World Series. Though decimated by suspensions, Chicago's "Clean Sox" still had a shot at representing the American League, even after Cleveland increased its lead to 1½ games with a September 29 win. Both contenders would wind up with identical 98–56 records if the Sox swept so-so St. Louis and Cleveland split four against a lousy Detroit squad.

Comiskey's crew had a few good bats left. Eddie Collins hit .369 that season, Shano Collins .303 and Ray Schalk .270. Still, it was impossible to ignore gaping holes left by Jackson (.382), Felsch (.338) and Weaver (.333). With limited options at his disposal, Kid Gleason replaced the big guns with small or rusty ones. It was a pockmarked lineup, but even with the loss of Cicotte and Williams, Sox nation could realistically pin its hopes on pitching. Chicago produced four 20-game winners in 1920 and two remained — Red Faber and Dickie Kerr. Neither was up to the task, however, and Cleveland soon clinched.

Nine months passed before the case went to trial. Completed on July 15, 1921, the 12-person jury consisted of two clerks, two machinists, a telephone repairman, stationary engineer, motor company foreman, steel worker, salesman, florist, hydraulic press operator and a stockyards foreman. Most were married, all understood baseball, and none considered themselves serious fans. They formed a judicial dream team, whittled down from about 600 candidates during more than two weeks of voir dire tryouts. In a scene worthy of a ninth-inning rally, loud cheering erupted when the final four were sworn in. Fans couldn't wait to get this show trial underway.

16

Baseball on Trial

I say, gentlemen, that the evidence shows that a swindle and con game has been worked on the American people.... The crime strikes at the heart of every red-blooded citizen and every kid who plays on a sand lot. This country is for sending criminals to the penitentiary, whether they are idols of the baseball diamond or gangsters guilty of robbery with a gun. — Prosecutor Edward Prindeville[1]

With a capacity crowd hanging on every word, assistant state attorney George Gorman outlined the prosecution's case during opening arguments on July 18, 1921. His synopsis: Cicotte and Bill Burns hatched the plan in New York, eight White Sox met in a Chicago hotel room and agreed to throw the Series, Cicotte received $10,000 while Williams and Shoeless Joe garnered five grand apiece, and Arnold Rothstein likely financed the whole thing. Spectators remained properly silent through most of the oration, but Gorman's dramatic delivery sometimes drew an audible reaction — something primitive and innocuous, like a fireworks display might elicit. He couldn't reveal his most damning evidence, however. In an early victory for the defense, Judge Hugo Friend ordered the State to make no mention of grand jury confessions during its opening statement

Charles Comiskey later took the stand and angrily denied a defense attorney's insinuation that he'd once jumped from the National League to the Brotherhood League. Rising from his chair, the aging former player shook a fist and proclaimed that he'd never jumped a contract in his life. The question bore little relevance to the case at hand, but tarnishing Comiskey's halo was sound strategy. Aside from that owner outburst, the day's highlights were limited to a few obvious puns, traded in friendly banter between prosecution and defense:

> "You won't get to first base with those confessions."
> "We'll make a home run with them."
> "You may get a long hit, but you'll be thrown out at the plate."[2]

A day later, the trial hit full stride when Sleepy Bill Burns arrived to testify. Induced by an offer of immunity, he emerged from his Mexican hiding place with lots to say and an eager audience awaiting. Billy Maharg took credit for finding him, telling Philadelphia reporters of a colorful sagebrush search that saw danger from moonshiners' guns and a rattlesnake's fangs. His winding journey ended in remote terrain, south of the Texas border, where he found his old pal fishing at "Devil's River." A former journeyman pitcher who compiled a 30–52 record in five forgettable seasons, Burns played for the White Sox in 1909, and then joined the Reds a year later. With intimate knowledge of both teams in the 1919 Series and baseball in general, he must've seemed an ideal fix broker.

Burns made a grand entrance at court, delaying the proceedings for 15 minutes before walking through the doors with a protective posse of private detectives. He wore a dark green checkered suit, with a lavender shirt and bow tie underneath. The coat didn't last long, discarded minutes into his sweaty testimony. It wasn't terribly hot for a summer afternoon, hitting about 80 degrees outside, but the packed courtroom's combined body heat and the butterflies in his stomach might've contributed to his condition. Looking decidedly nervous during the early stages of this command performance, he wiped his face repeatedly with a handkerchief and rubbed both hands over his balding head. When speaking, he leaned forward with his chin resting on one hand and answered questions in barely audible tones. Burns eventually warmed up to the spotlight, but for now he seemed reticent. A lackluster delivery, however, could not diminish the gravity of his words. With every set of ears straining to hear them, it might've even enhanced the experience.

Abe Attell earned fame as world featherweight champion, then infamy as a fixer of the 1919 Black Sox World Series (Library of Congress).

Burns named Arnold Rothstein as bankroller, with Abe Attell as chief agent. Describing his own role in negotiating with Black Sox ringleaders, he implicated most of the accused players, though Shoeless Joe Jackson's name was conspicuously absent. He told how Cicotte and Gandil approached him in New York with a proposition to sell the Series for $100,000, how the players double-crossed the gamblers when payment was not forthcoming, how they refused $45,000 to drop the fourth and fifth games and vowed to play square the rest of the way. Burns also placed a memorable quote in Cicotte's mouth: "I will throw the first game if I have to throw the ball clear out of the Cincinnati park." That brought a wave of laughter from the room, defendants included. Even Cicotte grinned. In an almost comical twist, Burns remembered encountering Kid Gleason in a hotel hallway while carrying a payoff installment. With that bulky package of cash hidden under his shirt, he said, "Hello Kid," and walked into the players' room.

The day's testimony climaxed with a dramatic courtroom identification. After Burns said someone named "Bennett" played a big role in the conspiracy, the prosecutor asked if that person was in the courtroom.

"He is," Bill answered, prompting a buzz among the spectators as they looked around for the mystery man.

"Do you see him?"

"Yes, he's behind that post. He's the man in the yellow shirt."

Judge Friend ordered the fellow to rise and be identified for the jury, a command that prompted a leaping objection from attorney Max Lusker. Overruled. It turned out that "Bennett" was actually David Zelser, an indicted Des Moines gambler and Lusker client.

Burns endured marathon sessions on the witness stand, his testimony spread over a few days. Multiple defendants meant multiple defense attorneys and several lined up for a crack at him. They attacked the story and sullied the storyteller's character, just as any good lawyers would. Providing a particularly rancorous cross-examination was James "Ropes" O'Brien, a former assistant state's attorney who earned his nickname for sending men to the gallows.

After asking the witness to repeat testimony that he twice met Chick Gandil at Chicago's Warner Hotel, O'Brien shouted, "Don't you know that Gandil never lived at the Warner Hotel in this series? Don't you know that he and other players you say you met at the Warner lived at the Tyson?" In response, Burns said he only knew that the meeting took place at the Warner. A similar exchange took place when testimony touched on an innocent conversation between Burns and a Reds benchwarmer on the morning of Game Three. Though O'Brien said the Cincinnati team was away practicing at that time, Burns stuck to his story.

Toward the end of day two, the witness looked like he might live up to his "Sleepy" nickname, a moniker earned for taking dugout catnaps during his playing days. But even with his body limp and eyes half-closed, Burns answered clearly and defiantly. On his third day at the witness stand, Burns delivered the trial's best comeback line. When a defense attorney asked him, "You don't like me, do you Bill?" he responded, "Sure I do, Ben. You're a smart fellow and I wish we'd had someone like you at the head of this deal. We'd all be rich now."

Overall, prosecutors were thrilled with the Burns testimony, but their joy soon faded when the confessions turned up missing. Also absent from grand jury evidence were immunity waivers, telegrams and private papers. It seemed perfectly obvious and altogether fitting — somebody bought the documents with bribe money, somebody with a lot to lose. Ban Johnson said that somebody was Arnold Rothstein. The baseball magnate claimed he'd uncovered information that, sometime during the previous fall, "A.R." paid $10,000 to a state attorney's office employee for access to those confessions and other vital paperwork.

Vanishing documents did not deal a crippling blow to the State's case, however. Too many people had heard the defendants' grand jury testimony. "We would like to have (the documents)," said prosecution assistant Edward Prindeville, "but the hole they left can easily be plugged up by the testimony of Grand Jurors, court stenographers and others present when the statements were obtained."[3] Re-entered as evidence a couple days later, the confessions painted a picture of decent men who made bad decisions and regretted it.

Though admitting to taking a payoff, Joe Jackson swore that he always played to win. Similarly, Cicotte said he tried his best after the first game. Lefty Williams, however, could claim maximum effort for only one of his three outings. Defense attorneys argued that the confessions were made involuntarily and should be ruled inadmissible. At trial, this critical issue prompted special testimony from otherwise silent defendants. All three confessors said they'd been offered immunity in 1920 and never understood the consequences of signing waivers. Their old grand jury judge begged to differ.

Making a rare appearance in the witness chair, Justice McDonald testified that no promises were made to the defendants. He described his first encounters with each man, hearing their admissions before putting them in front of a jury. McDonald provided colorful detail to a familiar black and white tale. After rejecting an immunity request back then, he granted Cicotte's second wish for discretion; the nervous hurler didn't want teammates to know he was talking and McDonald took him through a back entrance to the courthouse. They met a news reporter along the way, however, and the secret was out.

The judge also confirmed that Joe Jackson did, indeed, get a protective escort with two bailiffs accompanying him while he retrieved his car at Comiskey Park. They apparently remained nearby while he got drunk at a party. That anecdotal addendum came out during Jackson's colorful testimony. He remembered being half-drunk during grand jury proceedings and fully "teed up" the following day. When asked if he had read his immunity waiver before signing it, he replied, "No, they had given me their promise. I'd a' signed my death warrant if they had asked me to."[4] Left unsaid was a far better reason — Jackson didn't know how to read. Though admitting to an emotional experience, Cicotte denied published reports of him breaking down during grand jury testimony. "I didn't weep and wail as some say, but I guess there were plenty of tears in my eyes and the crying I have done inwardly is much greater than the tears which actually came out."[5]

On July 28, it was the defense team's turn to celebrate. Confident that they'd discredited the State's star witness, attorneys suddenly rested their case after exposing a discrepancy in the Bill Burns story. He'd mentioned a morning meeting with the accused, held at a Cincinnati hotel the day before Game One. When Kid Gleason and three other Sox players testified to an early practice that same day, defense attorneys announced that their clients couldn't have been in two places at the same time. They hung a cloud over the prosecution's star witness, then declared victory and quit.

Ridiculing the notion that its case had been damaged, the State contended that a conspiratorial conference could have easily been held before the Sox left for practice. What's more, much of the day's testimony supported prosecution. Ray Schalk reported seeing the defendants together in a hotel room after Game Two, which matched the Burns account.

Also taking the stand were Eddie Collins, Dickie Kerr and Roy Wilkinson — each walking past their former teammates on the way to the witness chair. Some exchanged greetings along the way. They proceeded to deliver bland testimony, used mainly to corroborate the defendants' presence at that aforementioned practice session. Earlier in the day, defense attorneys pointed to White Sox profit leaps as evidence that the accused did not harm Comiskey's business.

Though seven White Sox remained on the hot seat, the once-lofty number of indicted had dwindled over time due to dropped charges, legal escape and indifferent pursuit. A couple brother gamblers — Ben and Louis Levi — were the latest to go free, cut loose for lack of evidence. Fred McMullin was never apprehended but seemed a long shot for conviction. How could he throw a game from the bench? Returning to New York from Canada, Abe Attell beat extradition, as did Hal Chase in California. Meanwhile, authorities showed little interest in hunting down Sport Sullivan and Rachel Brown. Better to pursue the well illuminated than chase such shadowy figures.

Nine defense attorneys were allotted 10 hours for closing arguments. Representing alleged gambler Carl Zork, one lambasted both prosecution and pastime: "Why were these underpaid ballplayers, these penny-ante gamblers from Des Moines and St. Louis, who bet a few nickels perhaps on the World Series, brought here to be the goats in this case? Ask the powers of baseball, ask Ban Johnson, who pulled the strings in this case. Ask him who saved Arnold Rothstein."

Zork needn't have worried. Along with Buck Weaver and Happy Felsch, he had been deemed immune from any guilty verdict. Judge Friend swore he'd order new trials before allowing them go to prison on such flimsy evidence.

Speaking for the prosecution, Prindeville demanded a guilty verdict, with each defendant sentenced to five years imprisonment and a $2,000 fine. Harsh penalties were necessary to protect the country's greatest game. In his final instructions to the jury, Judge Friend explained that it wasn't enough to believe the defendants conspired to throw baseball games. The State had to prove intent to defraud the public and others. After two hours and forty-seven minutes of late-night deliberation, a verdict was reached on August 2. The judge had left, however, so nervous defendants languished another 40 minutes until his return. Their tension evaporated with the announcement of two words: "Not guilty."

Pandemonium enveloped the courtroom, as hundreds of spectators roared with joy. Buck Weaver and Swede Risberg grabbed each other by the arms and yelled, while Lefty Williams wildly shook every hand within grabbing distance. A smiling Cicotte leaped to his feet, pounded Joe Jackson on the back and eventually dashed toward the jury box to give thanks. Other defendants followed close behind, and they soon discovered the admiration was mutual when jurors lifted them on their shoulders in a gesture of triumph.

A flashbulb light show commenced when photographers aimed their cameras at the tumult. As hats and papers flew through the air, bailiffs tried to restore order but eventually gave up and joined the revelers in celebration. Tacitly approving the whole wild scene was a smiling Judge Friend.

Swept along for the ride, Zork and Zelser must have felt like batboys on a team that just clinched a championship. The cheers weren't for them but they had won, too, cleared of charges that portrayed them as conspiring moneymen. On his way out of the courthouse, Chick Gandil fired a parting shot at the man that defense attorneys blamed for inventing a baseless scandal: "I'll give a sailor's farewell to Ban Johnson: Goodbye, good luck and to hell with you."[6]

No longer a major leaguer, Gandil could tweak an A.L. president's nose without fear of reprisal. The other six, however, had a livelihood to return to. Or so it seemed. In truth, they'd only won a highly publicized battle, not the war. Unimpressed by legal vindication, baseball promptly banned them all for life, Gandil and McMullin included.

Ban Johnson: "The trial ... uncovered the greatest crime it was possible to commit in baseball. The fact that the men were freed by a Cook County jury does not alter the conditions one iota or minimize the magnitude of such offenses."

Charles Comiskey: "Cicotte confessed to me that he had been crooked and implicated seven other players. Until they all are able to explain this to my satisfaction, none of them will play with the Sox."

Then came the legendary proclamation from Kenesaw Mountain Landis, baseball's new and all-powerful commissioner: "Regardless of the verdicts of juries, no player that throws a ball game; no player that undertakes or promises to throw a ball game; no player that sits in a conference with a bunch of crooked players and gamblers where the ways and means of throwing game are planned and discussed and does not promptly tell his club about it, will ever play professional baseball."

While Weaver pointed to his 11 hits, .324 batting average and errorless defense as proof of innocence, Landis saw little difference between a ringleader and someone who sat in on fix meetings but apparently did not partake. Both reeked of corruption. Statistics supported Shoeless Joe's contention that he took the money, yet still played to win. His .375 average topped all other batters and he tied for most hits (12) in Series history. But that confession always trumped everything else, even if it did contradict accusations that he took a dive. Jackson sampled the semipro circuit, often under an assumed name, and eventually filed suit for back pay from the White Sox. The two sides settled out of court.

No "Black Sox" ever played another game in the major leagues. Edd Roush sustained stardom for another decade, made the Hall of Fame, and had a monument erected in his honor at Oakland City. The disgraced eight, however, are still more famous. Edd remains a bit player in their cautionary tale.

17

The Swinging Twenties

We never had a good second baseman and shortstop. See, ya gotta have a good combination in there on double plays or you're not gonna win any pennants, that's all there is to it. Your second baseman and shortstop are the ones who get you out of a lot of jams.... We finally got a good second baseman but didn't have any shortstop. Good gosh almighty! The second baseman would get the ball and give it to the shortstop and he'd throw it away at first. What kind of play is that?[1]

Though he never won another batting title, Edd thrived in the 1920s, hitting .332 for the decade and recording single-season highs in hits, runs, doubles, triples and RBIs. Over those same ten years he also became the king of holdouts, and 1921 set his ascension in motion. Missing all of spring training, Edd was still a no-show when Cincinnati opened the regular season on April 13. He had received a huge salary hike to $15,000 following the championship season, but after posting even better stats in '20, felt deserving of another fat increase. Management thought fifteen grand was more than generous.

Days of impasse turned to weeks and Edd missed the entire month before finally agreeing to terms. The Reds sported a 7–9 record when he returned to the starting lineup on May 1. Meanwhile, Heinie Groh sat out so long that he made Roush look like a teacher's punctual pet. Failing to finagle a $12,000 salary, the unhappy infielder signed for 10 grand on June 1 but insisted on an immediate trade. Technically speaking, he couldn't play for anybody until the league removed his name from its ineligible list, a purgatory for those who didn't report to their teams in a timely fashion.

Commissioner Landis gave the go-ahead on June 9, but Groh's reinstatement was conditional — he had to stay in Cincinnati for the rest of the season. No lowly player was going to force a trade on this commissioner's watch. Early reports had Groh gracefully conceding defeat but the mood soon changed. A couple days after hearing that unfavorable ruling, he launched an angry verbal assault against its author. "Judge Landis had no right to order me to play where I don't want to play, nor make me accept a salary that does not suit me. Let him render a square decision in my case. 'Til he does, I am through."[2]

In the space of 24 hours, that lion's roar became a meow. Groh reported for duty on June 12, watching from the bench as his replacement smacked three hits in a 7–1 Reds victory. A day later, he returned as starter for a fading team with a 20–32 record. Unaffected by the absurdly long layoff, Groh smacked seven hits in his first 15 appearances and was batting .460 through 10 games. Cincinnati sure could have used him during the first couple months.

Ray Fisher missed the entire season, opting to take a coaching position at the University of Michigan after the Reds cut his salary. In an amicable parting, President Herrmann reportedly agreed to place him on the "voluntary retired list" but Landis later hit the pitcher with a lifetime ban for jumping his Cincinnati contract. It all worked out for the best; he became a Wolverine legend over the next 37 years and Ann Arbor folk still see his name every time they walk into Ray Fisher Stadium.

Things had looked so promising for 1921. The everyday Reds lineup seemed potent and a couple of winter trades revamped the pitching staff. Cincinnati dealt Jimmy Ring and Greasy Neale to the Phillies for veteran Eppa Rixey, a tall southpaw who would become the best hurler in franchise history. Dutch Ruether went to Brooklyn for another accomplished veteran, Rube Marquard. The Reds fielded an impressive-sounding rotation of Marquard, Rixey, Luque and Donohue.

But that Ohio River battleship never left port. One horrible month sank all hopes, as Manager Moran helplessly watched his boys post a pitiful 7–19 mark in May. They showed a June pulse, winning eight of nine at one point, but followed with 10 losses in their next 11 games. Rounding out a disastrous year, Edd was twice sidelined by leg injuries.

There would be few bright spots during the season. Near the top of a depressingly short list was a July 25 exhibition game against Babe Ruth and the New York Yankees. More than 16,000 fans turned out for an up-close look at the phenomenal slugger who'd reached mythic stature with a mind-boggling 54 homers the previous year. He would finish at 59 in 1921. Despite the daunting dimensions at Redland Field, Ruth did not disappoint, belting two tape-measure shots.

Though Cincinnati won, 9–8, this day belonged to the Babe. With the bases loaded in the fifth inning, he blistered one high and deep over Edd Roush and the center field fence, a magnificent and unprecedented feat. That distant barrier stood more than 15 feet high and precisely 402 feet from home plate. No major leaguer had ever hit it on the fly, much less sent one above and beyond. Ruth drilled another into the right field bleachers during the seventh inning and nobody had ever done that, either, except for the occasional drive that *bounced* over the fence.

"Babe simply and modestly came along and achieved what had been believed impossible," the *Cincinnati Enquirer* proclaimed. "Ruth demonstrated to the satisfaction of every rooter present that he is absolutely in a class by himself as a propeller of the spheroid. Here comes the big fellow onto a field which he had never seen before and in a single game he twice accomplished a feat for which the heaviest hitters in the National League have been vainly striving for 10 long years."[3]

Edd launched the first long ball of the day, rapping one to deep right in the first inning. It looked like a one-hop homer before a fan reached out and

Babe Ruth played against Roush during spring training games. He also swung through Cincinnati for the occasional mid-season exhibition (Library of Congress).

grabbed the ball as it bounced toward the bleachers. He settled for a ground-rule double. In a perfect ending to a perfect afternoon, Pete Donohue struck out Ruth in the ninth inning. Cincinnati fans got what they came for—an exciting win for the home team and, more importantly, eyewitness memories of the phenomenal Babe Ruth at his best. An *Enquirer* caricature showed him hitting the homer over "Eddie" Roush, with the caption, "Here's one you'll be telling your grandchildren about."

As it turned out, not just *Edd's* grandchildren, but others too. From that Oakland City backyard, the aged Hoosier spoke from first-hand experience when he described the Babe. His assessment was peppered with criticism: "(Ruth) was a good hitter, now don't misunderstand me. But he wasn't much of an outfielder. All the ground he covered is what he stood on."

Roush compiled a career-best .352 in 1921, good for second behind Hornsby's .397. Emerging from a logjam of runner-up candidates, he hit .539 over the last 10 days of the season.

1922

Edd took the holdout crown back from Groh in 1922, as days turned into weeks and weeks became months. Newspaper reports had him demanding a three-year contract at $18,000 per season. At first, his absence seemed a death knell to the Reds, who lost 10 of their first 11 games. But while Edd cooled his heels, the Reds bounced back to respectability and pushed past the .500 mark, an inspired effort for a team without its sparkplug.

Groh was gone, too. He finally got his desired trade during the winter and Manager Moran received George Burns in return. Cincinnati made out well on the exchange, as Burns came off a strong season of 111 runs scored, .299 average and a league-high 80 walks. Over the course of 10 full seasons in New York, he led the N.L. in scoring five times and twice topped the circuit in stolen bases. Filling the center field void left by Edd's long absence, Burns produced similar numbers for the Reds.

Rounding out a particularly strong outfield, Pat Duncan hit .328 on the season and unheralded George Harper burst into prominence with a .340 average. Their emergence may explain why management didn't blink during Edd's contract negotiations. But could a loaded outfield offset all the infield question marks? Already crippled by Groh's departure, the Reds also traded away veteran shortstop Larry Kopf and a key reserve. Now they'd have to rely on aging Jake Daubert and a bunch of greenhorns.

With a holdout that lasted months, Edd had plenty of time to hunt and fish in 1922 (Roush Family Collection).

Edd finally capitulated in late July, applying to Commissioner Landis for reinstatement, traveling to Cincinnati for a hat-in-hand conference with President Herrmann and signing a prorated pact in front of the team's board of directors. He agreed to a 10-week contract that would expire at season's end, then went straight to the clubhouse, donned a Reds uniform and joined his teammates for an in-progress game against the Giants. As the Reds prepared to bat in the bottom of the fifth, Moran sent him to coach first base.

"Then came a storm of applause which surpassed anything ever heard before at the yard," wrote the *Enquirer*. "The bugs cheered and rocked in their seats in glee, giving Eddie a tremendous ovation, which showed how popular his playing in past years has made him with the rooters."[5]

A day later, the Yankees returned to Redland for another exhibition and Babe hit one more into the right field bleachers, only farther this time. Yet, once again, the home team emerged victorious, taking a 5–3 decision in seven innings. Approximately 7,000 fans turned out for this exhibition, less than half the total of the previous year's matchup. Some said Ruth's star power wasn't what it used to be. Suspended by Commissioner Landis for unapproved barnstorming, he missed the first five weeks of the 1922 season and would finish with 35 homers, a paltry total compared to his two previous campaigns. Nonetheless, the great Bambino's traveling circus always created excitement in Cincinnati.

Providing additional drama to the latest meeting was an empty visitors dugout. The Yankees train arrived four hours late, so a fleet of taxis rushed them directly to the ballpark. Start time was delayed 90 minutes. When the New Yorkers finally arrived, photographers scurried to get shots of Ruth, and one posed picture showed the Babe shaking hands with Eddie Roush. That was the highlight for Cincinnati's superstar; he watched this one from the bench.

Pressed for time, the Reds called it quits after 6½ innings and rushed off to catch a 6 o'clock train to Philadelphia — site of their next game. Edd made his season debut in game one of a July 26 doubleheader against the Phillies. It was a pinch-hitting appearance, the first of many before he finally regained his starting position on August 10.

Nobody ran away with the pennant while Cincinnati struggled. As of August 13, New York led St. Louis by a half-game and owned a 4½-game cushion over red-hot Pittsburgh, winner of 13 straight. Chicago sat 5½ back, while the Reds' 58–53 mark put them fifth with a deficit of 7½ games. Jumping back into the hunt, Roush and company took 10 of 13. They still stood in fifth place and trailed New York by a bunch but the rest of the pack had come back to them. Only 1½ games separated second place from fifth.

On September 4, the Reds swept a home doubleheader from Chicago and moved into fourth. With 10 days left in the season, they embarked on another hot streak; Cliff Markle tossed a shutout at Boston, then Cincinnati bats exploded for 30 runs in a three-game sweep at Philadelphia. Hitting proved a constant for this team, and it finished the season with a club-record .296 batting average. At the top of the lineup, that Burns-Daubert-Duncan-Roush foursome compared favorably to the N.L.'s most formidable combos. The bottom part had pop, too, featuring such .300 hitters as Bubbles Hargrave, Babe Pinelli and Lew Fonseca.

Finishing with 93 wins, New York took first by a comfortable margin but the battle for runner-up went down to the final day. Hosting Pittsburgh for an October 1 doubleheader, the Reds scored two in the bottom of the ninth to win a 5–4 decision in game one. They took the second contest too, as Eppa Rixey picked up his 25th victory of the season. The sweep moved Cincinnati into second with a final record of 86–68 — an impressive mark, considering the team's terrible start. One game back in a tie for third were Pittsburgh and St. Louis.

Before calling it a year the Reds launched a Midwestern exhibition tour, bringing their "A" team to play the locals at small city ballparks. They scheduled an October 4 stop at a town Edd once played for — Washington, Indiana. From there, he could make a quick visit home to Oakland City.

Fresh off a 48-hour stop in Lawrenceville, Illinois, the Reds arrived by B&O Railroad on game day. They met a Grays squad that included a fellow named Roush — *Fred* Roush. Edd's brother swung a powerful bat for Washington's town team. The contest was not a serious affair and Fred became the butt of one joke after grounding to third. Instead of throwing directly to first base, Babe Pinelli tossed the ball to his shortstop, who threw to the second baseman, who finally fired to first. Even after all that, Fred couldn't beat the throw(s). Though angered by Cincinnati showmanship, he managed to keep that Roush temper from boiling over.

The Reds endeavored to entertain, not humiliate, and they bore down just enough to deliver a 10–5 win. Before departing on an evening train to Ohio, Edd told friends they'd just watched the next National League champions. "We've got a bunch of real ball players now and if Herrmann will just keep them all together for next year the Reds will finish first in the National League next year."[6]

1923

> *You're not gonna tell a owner what to do. They don't ask nobody for advice. Jesus Christ! They tell ya! ... You couldn't tell them anything. You tell them something and they look at you like you was nuts.*[7]

The eyes of the world turned toward Egypt when archeologists opened King Tutankhamen's opulent burial chamber in February. Dead for more than

3,000 years, the former child monarch raised no objection to the intrusion at his exclusive "Valley of the Kings" address. Granted, it was huge news but two months later it became *old* news, upstaged by another monumental opening. They called this one Yankee Stadium. Referring to the king of baseball, some nicknamed it "The house that Ruth built" and fans would see wonderful things at this Bronx palace.

Between those two milestone events came a lesser drama — the annual Roush holdout. He demanded $25,000 and the club would go no higher than 15 grand. His asking price made him a pariah on the trade market, too. The salary showdown took a new twist when the Reds fined Roush $50 for every day missed at training camp. Edd steadfastly refused to sign any contract that included a provision for penalty payment. As opening day approached, the running total had reached about $1,500.

On April 10, he reportedly met with the club's board of directors and made a counteroffer for a three-year deal at $16,000 per season. Management refused to move, sticking to its original offer of $15,000 for one year minus the fines. Edd quietly picked up his hat and left the room. He later spoke publicly about a plan to sign with some industrial team at a big steel plant.

Local press announced an end to the impasse on April 15, with management winning the stare-down. Edd signed a one-year contract at the same terms club officials offered him the previous fall. He presented Garry Herrmann with a gracious letter of surrender, saying he liked Cincinnati, was anxious to rejoin the team and did not want to play outside organized baseball. The proud athlete did throw in one final jab. "Probably I was mistaken in my original demand for $25,000 a year, although I am free to say that I really did not expect to get that amount. On the other hand, I believe the club was mistaken in trying to inflict a fine of $50 a day against me because I do not believe that such a fine could be inflicted until I had signed the contract. In other words, I believe that both sides were wrong to some extent."[8]

Now Cincinnati could direct its entire focus on the April 17 season opener at Redland Field. The opponent — Rogers Hornsby and his St. Louis Cardinals. Fans clamored for seats, creating the greatest ticket demand in memory, and the grandstand sold out before Thanksgiving. Interest proved so great that the club boosted crowd capacity by installing temporary seating in left field and near the grandstand. About 4,000 standing-room tickets went on sale and reserved-seating customers were encouraged to arrive early to avoid the "crush and confusion."

A chilly day seemed warm when the Reds won an exciting debut in extra innings. Ivey Wingo scored on a George Burns single in the bottom of the 11th, giving the Reds a 3–2 triumph. Edd watched it all from the pine, which seemed fair considering that he'd only recently joined the team. He made brief appearances the following two days, then cracked the starting lineup on April 20.

Another tight pennant chase was about to commence. Locked, loaded and determined to defend their World Series title, the New York Giants showcased an imposing cadre of hitters — George Kelly, Frankie Frisch, Dave Bancroft, Heinie Groh, Ross Youngs and Irish Meusel. Pittsburgh was loaded, too, led by Pie Traynor, Max Carey, Clyde Barnhart and Charlie Grimm. But neither team's pitching staff compared to Cincinnati's.

The Reds got off to a slow start, splitting their first 26 games and then dropping seven of eight. Just like the previous season, they'd have to climb out of a hole to join the pennant race. Unlike 1922, Edd Roush was there with a rope.

Cincinnati reeled off six straight victories, dropped a couple one-run decisions, and embarked on another long winning streak. Edd went supernova, stinging nine hits in 13 at-bats as the Reds took four straight, then batted .412 while the streak stretched to nine. Brooklyn's Dazzy Vance brought the run to an emphatic end on June 17, tossing a one-hit shutout in a 9–0 slaughter at Redland Field. The future Hall of Famer came within an eyelash of a no-hitter, losing it when Sammy Bohne singled with two outs in the bottom of the ninth. Unfazed, Cincinnati rebounded to beat the Dodgers three straight times. Highlighting the mini-run was Dolph Luque's 11-inning shutout, stretching his scoreless inning streak to 25.

Twelve wins in 13 games — a magic elixir for the Reds' pennant-chasing blues. Most of their success came in friendly home confines, though. How would they handle the upcoming 29-game road trip? They took 16 of the next 23 contests and moved into second place, 4½ games behind the Giants. The victories continued rolling in but McGraw's league leaders were hot too and refused to surrender the high ground, though their pursuers did pull within a couple games at one point.

Around the same time, America turned its attention to San Francisco where president Warren Harding lay on his deathbed. Stumping for United States participation in the World Court, he had to cancel his entire California itinerary after falling ill. Doctors suspected ptomaine poisoning at first, then diagnosed him with pneumonia and heart complications. A couple days of slow improvement created cautious optimism and Harding reportedly talked of returning to Washington. He died on the night of August 2 while the first lady read to him from the evening newspaper.

The sports page might've carried results of a Reds 2–0 triumph, their last success for quite awhile. Going ice cold, they lost five crushing games in an August homestand versus New York, with the normally unhittable Luque getting shelled twice. Only three games back at the start of the series, Pat Moran's crew dropped eight games out of first.

Cincinnati showed little fight, except for a brawl that broke out during the eighth inning of the August 7 finale. It started after Luque threw one high and tight, near the head of Ross Youngs. New York's bench erupted in howls and a fellow named Casey Stengel was accused of saying something particularly harsh toward the Cuban pitcher. Luque walked unhurriedly to the Giants bench and threw a punch at the still-seated Stengel, who ducked and took a glancing blow off the shoulder. Before the two could properly engage, Youngs arrived and put Luque in a chokehold, dragging him away from the fray.

A serious face for a serious player (National Baseball Hall of Fame Library, Cooperstown, New York).

To his credit, the powerful Texan made no attempt to strike his captive. Still, the area saw a volatile mix of onrushing players, police and fans. Things eventually calmed and a couple cops led Luque back to the Cincinnati side, though he didn't stay there long. That volcanic temper erupted again and he headed back toward the Giants bench, this time with a bat in hand. Police intercepted him.

Where was Roush during all this? Throwing gas on the fire, though press reports differ on the volume of accelerant.

New York Times: "Eddie Roush, who had come in from centre field, took a punch at Stengel, but was repulsed by other Giant players before Stengel could get in a blow at him."

Cincinnati Enquirer: "Roush had come in from the outfield and was advancing on the Giant bench with the evident intention of giving Luque all the aid and comfort in his power, but he was intercepted by (Babe) Pinelli and other Red players before he could commit an overt act."

Luque and Stengel were ejected but Edd got to stick around. A week later the Reds went to the Polo Grounds and took four of five, then won nine straight to close within 3½ games of first on August 27. Just when it looked like Cincinnati might have another World Series in it, fate took an ugly turn during the stretch run, or "dame fate," as sportswriters liked to call her. Edd missed a couple weeks with a broken rib, shortstop Ike Caveney called it quits because of a similar injury, Jake Daubert sat out awhile after getting plunked by a pitch, and backup first baseman Lew Fonseca saw his season end in a violent basepath collision.

Edd's injury proved mystifying because nobody seemed positive when it happened. Most likely, it was the wild pitch that Burleigh Grimes bounced off him during an August 24 game in Brooklyn. He later aggravated the injury while heaving a heavy suitcase onto a baggage truck. On August 31, X-rays showed a fracture of the eighth rib on his right side.

The Reds went into a tailspin, losing nine of 14 in Roush's absence, but New York failed to capitalize. It was similar to that September 14 heavyweight clash at the Polo Grounds, where big Luis Firpo knocked Jack Dempsey through the ropes in the first round. Climbing back into the ring, Dempsey made it to the bell and won by knockout in round two. The Reds climbed back into the race and won nine of 10, capping things with a September 24 win over the Giants at Redland Field.

Now sporting a 90–59 record, they trailed by three games with mighty Eppa Rixey slated to pitch the following day. A sore arm sidelined the veteran, however, leaving Luque to fill in on short rest. Cincinnati fell, 3–2, and that hard-fought defeat marked the beginning of the end. Dropping four of their final five, the Reds settled for bridesmaid while the 95–58 Giants took the flag by 4½ games.

Once disappointment wore off, Reds rooters could take pride in one of the finest seasons in franchise history. Their heroes produced 91 wins — a wonderful total during the era of 154-game schedules. Luque became the National League's best pitcher, leading the circuit in wins (27) and ERA (1.97), and a strong argument could be made for Rixey as second-best. Throw in 21-game winner Pete Donahue, along with dependable Rube Benton, and Cincinnati could have laid claim to the finest rotation in baseball. It was reminiscent of the championship year.

Meanwhile, Edd maintained his position as one of the league's elite hitters. He led a Cincinnati offense that featured three players hitting well over .300 and one eagle-eyed batsman (George Burns) who took more walks than a Bedouin nomad. Going 3-for-4 on the final day of the season, Roush pulled into a tie for third with Brooklyn's Jack Fournier, both hitting .351. Hornsby's .384 took top honors while St. Louis first baseman Sunny Jim Bottomley ranked second at .371.

Another all–New York World Series ensued, though not all at the Polo Grounds. Hosting half the Fall Classic contests was nearby Yankee Stadium. Edd picked McGraw to win and said so in print. Penning a newspaper column on the event, he wrote, "The 1923 world series will be won, I believe, by the best team in the best league, the Giants. Events of the last few years have convinced me the National League is a stronger organization in team strength at least, than the American League."[9]

The Yankees prevailed in six games.

1924

Many a time I never slept all night. Well, it was so god damned hot you couldn't sleep. Hell no! But what are you gonna do? You didn't have air conditioning or anything like that back in those days. You sat there and sweat, that's all![10]

In a wintertime transaction, the Reds bolstered an already-strong pitching staff by purchasing Carl Mays from the world champions. The submarine-style hurler was notorious for a 1920 tragedy that ended the life of Cleveland shortstop Ray Chapman. Drilled in the head by a Mays fastball, Chapman collapsed and died the next morning. That tragedy shadowed Mays for the rest of his career and every inside pitch raised eyebrows. He won 20 games for another fantastic Reds rotation.

Remarkable news surfaced on the Roush front — there would be no hold-out in 1924. What's more, steps were taken to prevent future salary showdowns when Edd signed a rare three-year deal at $19,000 per season. Once again, Cincinnati fans bubbled with optimism.

Dame fate gave them a sobering slapdown, however, as Pat Moran fell seriously ill at the start of spring training in Orlando, Florida. He felt sick on the long train ride down but still hoped to lead practice for early arrivals. After a restless night on March 2, Moran became too weak to leave bed the following morning. Summoned for treatment, a doctor predicted recovery within 48 hours, but the Reds skipper remained bedridden a day later. Further examination showed he had "some

One of baseball's most respected managers, Pat Moran died during spring training in 1924 (Library of Congress).

weakness in the kidneys" and a "severe attack of acute indigestion." The physician still anticipated a return to health, however, and vetoed a suggestion that his patient be moved to a hospital.

Patrick Joseph Moran died on March 7 at the age of 48. Accompanied by Ivey Wingo and George Harper, the body was taken by train to his hometown of Fitchburg, Massachusetts, for funeral services. Tributes poured in from all over the country.

Former umpire Charles Rigler: "No man ever fought harder on the ball field for victory and no man more quickly forgot the differences born in battles than Pat Moran."

Yankees manager Miller Huggins: "Pat Moran was a friend, neighbor, confidant — a genial soul who was loved by everybody who came in contact with him.... As a strategist he was a marvel and I don't think he ever got credit for his true abilities."

After tending Moran's bedside until the very end, coach Jack Hendricks took over as Reds manager. He owned 18 years of minor league managing experience and one season in the majors, a 1918 stint with the St. Louis Cardinals. It was Hendricks, in fact, who filed formal protest over a disputed loss to Cincinnati and unwittingly cost Roush a batting title.

Perhaps motivated by the tragic turn of events, Reds players arrived at camp in droves. When six more rolled in shortly after 5:00 P.M. on March 9, the team lacked only one player for a complete roster. That missing man was Jake Daubert, who'd sent a telegram saying he would get there the next day. Roush actually arrived early for spring training.

The season started with a bang as a record crowd of 35,747 watched the Reds come from behind for a 6–5 victory over Pittsburgh. Edd went hitless but drove in the game-winner on a ninth-inning sacrifice fly. The Pirates took a 1–0 decision the following day, producing the game's lone run in the top of the ninth, then Cincinnati prevailed in the rubber match by scoring twice in the ninth en route to a 3–2 triumph. Three games, three thrillers and two happy endings; maybe this was the year.

Things were about to take a frustrating turn for Edd. On April 20, he strained his side while swinging at a pitch and missed the next eight games. The Roush-less Reds won four straight, however, and moved into first place with a record of 7–2. Upon his return, they took seven of nine games and replaced New York atop the N.L. standings. Hitting .273 during that stretch, Roush didn't exactly carry teammates on his back but they prospered with their star back in the lineup.

Success proved fleeting, as Cincinnati fell to the middle of the N.L pack in May. Things went from bad to worse during a trip to St. Louis, with some familiar names bitten by the injury bug. Fonseca broke his arm while sliding into second base and Daubert took a fastball off his head — the eighth such cranial collision of his career. He eventually walked off the field with help from a couple teammates and left for a hospital soon afterward. In that same game Edd strained a leg muscle while making a leaping catch of a fly to deep right-center. He limped to the Reds bench, destined to miss nine games.

Crippling losing streaks continued over the next couple months, with Cincinnati dropping 10 of 12 in June and 7 of 10 during July. Of course, the Reds also enjoyed stretches of success but not enough to make a serious pennant run. They finished fourth with a record of 83–70, 10 games behind those incessantly excellent Giants. That wasn't bad considering the injury cavalcade, yet it still proved a bitter pill to swallow. The Reds fielded a championship-caliber pitching staff, with the lowest team ERA in baseball, but only one club scored fewer runs.

Edd did his part, batting .348 with a league-best 21 triples and team-highs in runs (67) and RBIs (72), impressive numbers for someone who missed about 30 games with injuries. Rogers Hornsby ascended Mount Olympus and strode straight into Valhalla in 1924, his absurd .424 batting average serving as entry ticket and backstage pass. Even Cobb never hit that high. Though 76 points behind, Edd stayed among the league elite and finished fifth.

Justice prevailed at the World Series when the Washington Senators won a title for Walter Johnson, their aging superstar and all-around nice guy. On the morning of Game Six, tragedy struck the Reds again. Jake Daubert was dead. He'd never fully recovered from an appendicitis operation, conducted a week earlier at Cincinnati's Good Samaritan Hospital, and an October 8 blood transfusion did nothing to improve his deteriorating condition. He died around 5:00 A.M. the following day with his adult son, a close personal friend, and teammate Lewis Fonseca at bedside. Exhausted from a three-day vigil, Daubert's wife was taken away for treatment after collapsing in his hospital room. Minutes later, her husband passed away. He was only 40 years old.

"Daubert was never able to rest properly after being hit on the head in that St. Louis game," Dr. Harry Hines said. "Even after the operation, when he was very weak, he could not sleep, though he tried desperately. The strain of being constantly awake and the sufferings caused by his disordered stomach undermined his constitution and led to his death."[11]

After taking that head shot, Daubert sat out for about a month before making a fairytale return, lashing a bottom-of-the-ninth, game-winning double against the same guy who'd drilled him — Cardinals ace Allan Sothoron. But he still wasn't right, and after bouncing in and out of the lineup, went home to Pennsylvania for a few weeks of rest. Daubert looked like his old self from August through mid September, hitting .333 in 150 at-bats, then left the team with a week left in the season. He did not have long to live.

In the space of one season, the Reds had lost their manager and team captain.

1925

> *Of course I was always the guy, if anybody got in trouble, I was always the one who had to take 'em to the hotel or get 'em a train or some dang thing. I was always in the wrong place all the time. I never could figure that out.*[12]

Spending a quiet winter back in Oakland City, Edd planned another early showing at spring training but had second thoughts after his wife's brother suffered a grisly injury in a coal mine. It happened on January 29, while Arch Swallow was handling coal cars at the bottom of a Gudgel Mine shaft. Two loaded cars hit him from behind, trapping his body against the ones he'd been pushing ahead. Rushed to the hospital in Princeton, Swallow survived the encounter but his right leg was crushed beyond repair.

In the minutes before all hell broke loose, perhaps he thought about his missing dog. A couple days earlier the *Oakland City Journal* ran his lost-and-found ad, offering a reward for the return of a white and lemon-colored hound. Now he was about to lose a leg. Such tragedies were all too common; a journey through time and newspaper archives shows a steady stream of victims, including some who died in the dark depths. All were deemed acceptable casualties, the unfortunate but unavoidable human toll for fueling society. Little has changed.

Swallow's leg never healed, and he agreed to have it amputated on February 23. Edd stuck around to provide moral support during the family crisis. After arriving in Orlando on March 8, he received orders to report to his manager's hotel room. Was he in trouble with Jack Hendricks?

"Eddie, I would like to have you act as field captain of the team this year," said Hendricks. "Will you accept the appointment?"

"Yes," Roush responded.[13]

The man of a million contentious contract negotiations was a heartbeat away from management. On the bench, he'd be considered an adviser and assistant manager. On the field, he'd deal with umpires in cases of dispute. "Eddie is one of the hardest workers and most loyal players I have ever seen on a ball club, and I look for a lot of help from him this season," Hendricks told the press. A closer look reveals further logic behind the selection. He was a nine-year veteran and the only position-player remaining from the 1919 championship team.

A couple of first-rate coaches were added to the payroll, too. Everything fell into place for an encouraging spring training but it didn't carry over to the real season. Despite a rip-roaring 8–3 start, the 1925 campaign proved a bust. Cincinnati led the league in team ERA for the third straight season but still couldn't score enough runs. Though spending a few days in first place, the Reds fell out of contention early and finished third, 15 games behind the Pirates. Hitting .339, Edd dropped from top-five grace but stayed among the league's 10 best batters.

Reds pitchers were simply amazing. Though saddled with a mediocre 16–18 record, Luque posted the league's lowest earned run average at 2.63, while Pete Donohue and Eppa Rixey won 21 games apiece and finished among the top four in ERA. Suffering from a sore arm, Carl Mays appeared in only 12 contests and went 3–5. Would a healthy Mays have made a difference? Not without an offense.

1926

> *I played against (Lou Gehrig) in spring. The first game I played against him, I never even stepped on first base. There wasn't any place. He had his leg and everything else all over it.... If it had been in the (regular) season, I'd have cut his leg off. WRAY radio interview in Princeton, Indiana*

Still in need of a strong presence at first base, the Reds purchased Wally Pipp from the New York Yankees. He lost his starting job the previous summer after sitting out a game because of a headache, or so the legend goes. This much is indisputable: Pipp's young replacement proved so capable that he couldn't get his job back. That substitute's name was Lou Gehrig and he went on to play 2,130 consecutive games while becoming one of history's greatest sluggers. Pipp achieved his own brand of immortality as the guy who gave way to Gehrig. His name became synonymous with any scenario where a sub surpassed the starter, even for a day. Eight and a half decades later, getting "Pipped" is still part of sports lexicon.

None of it is fair. Pipp had a good run in New York and contributed to the first World Series title in Yankees history. Dismiss the notion that he showed weakness by taking a day off; this is the guy who decked Babe Ruth during a dugout disagreement. He had a reputation as one of the toughest men in baseball. Gehrig's ascension was inevitable, and with the Yankees suffering through an unusually bad season, it seemed an opportune time to take a look at young prospects. Other second-stringers cracked the lineup that day, too.

The discarded Pipp arrived at Orlando training camp on the night of March 8, with Edd preceding him by several hours. It would be a memorable season for the Reds. Establishing themselves as early frontrunners, they won 14 of 16 in May but an early–June slump brought them back to earth. Rebounding to take 12 of 14 at month's end, Cincinnati punctuated the streak with a five-game sweep of the world champion Pittsburgh Pirates. One of those triumphs came by the score of 16–0.

When the sun rose on July 1, the Reds owned a 43–27 record and 3½-game cushion over second-place St. Louis. This was starting to look serious. A cooling-off period followed but they still clung to a small lead on July 18.

So long a team weakness, hitting became a strength. Edd's average hovered near .330, which ranked lowest among Cincinnati outfielders. Former pitcher Rube Bressler jumped into prominence with the bat, hitting in the low .370s as a part-time outfielder and full-time utility player. Meanwhile, rookie left fielder "Cuckoo" Christensen joined the starting lineup in midstream and blistered pitches at a .350 clip. The quirky kid looked like another Edd Roush. Right fielder Curt Walker led the team in hits while posting a .332 mark and catcher Bubbles Hargrave toyed with .400, though he had far fewer at-bats than the true league leaders.

Suddenly, a brutal homestand put the Reds in a tailspin — eight losses in 11 games against St. Louis, New York, Philadelphia and Brooklyn. Nevertheless, they still led Pittsburgh by two games and the Cardinals by 2½. In the midst of this came a special ceremony honoring Edd's decade of excellence in Cincinnati. Officials set aside July 21 as "Roush Day" at Redland Field and, in addition to the accolades, he received one doozy of a gift — a handsome Sedan automobile. With a Wednesday crowd of 8,000 watching, Father Francis Finn sang Edd's praises during the big presentation speech, and then a local judge spoke briefly before handing over some lesser prizes.

The Roush family got in the act, too; Essie accepted a chest of silverware while young Mary settled for a baseball glove, presented to her by a Cincinnati city councilman. It wasn't exactly the most practical gift for a young lady closing in on her ninth birthday, but daddy may have found some use for it. Also attending the gala was the widow Roush, Edd's mother. Laura joined her family in that shiny new car for a ceremonial cruise around the ball field. Adding to the ambience of sight, sound and scent were several bouquets of summer flowers and mellow music from two house bands. According to pastime lore, a venerated ballplayer never performed well on his day of honor. Dismissing the superstitious cliché with two swings of his club, Edd rapped a pair of run-scoring singles in a 6–4 win over the Boston Braves.

Pittsburgh moved into first and stayed there through most of August. These were the Pirates of Pie Traynor, Max Carey and Paul Waner, all future Hall of Famers. Cincinnati responded with its best stretch of the season, winning 13 of 14 from August 11 to 28, but it was only good enough to pull even.

Hovering one game back were the St. Louis Cardinals of Hornsby, Bottomley, Jesse Haines and Taylor Douhit, the first three destined for Cooperstown induction. Beating Hornsby's crew twice in early September, the Reds took over first before surrendering it back to St. Louis the following day. They went on to lose five of the next six and dropped 2½ back.

Suddenly a resurgence occurred when Cincy won two at Pittsburgh and took the first three at Ebbets Field. Now the top two contenders sported identical marks of 82–60, with Pittsburgh trailing by 2½. When Carl Mays tossed a five-hitter on September 14, the Reds moved into first. It was only a half-game advantage — St. Louis had the day off — but any mid–September lead holds significance.

After finishing a five-game sweep in Brooklyn, the Reds moved to the Polo Grounds and took a 3–0 decision behind the four-hit pitching of Pete Donohue. It made eight straight victories, yet they still couldn't create any breathing room. The Cardinals won a doubleheader at Philadelphia that same day and knotted the race again. With nine games remaining, both teams sported marks of 85–60. Sinking 4½ behind, Pittsburgh fell out of contention.

Though the stage seemed set for an epic finish, neither contender cooperated. Cincinnati dropped six straight against weak competition and St. Louis played .500 ball over its final eight games, including a season-ending 2–1 loss to the Reds. The pennant went to the lesser of two chokers. In Hornsby's first full season as manager, St. Louis backed into first with a final mark of 89–65, two games better than Roush and crew.

Heading into 1926, the Cardinals were a franchise with a long history of failure and it seemed unlikely that anything would change. Yet hope abounded during training camp and carried through to October, when they beat the mighty Yankees for World Series supremacy. "We felt confident from the beginning," Hornsby said. "It was confidence that won for us; that's half of any battle.... We may not be a great team but no one can say we are not a game team."[14]

Edd finished with a .323 batting average, his second lowest in 10 years but still top ten worthy. His lowest occurred in 1919 when he led the league at .321, but in 1926 Edd didn't even lead his own team. After four consecutive seasons at .300 or better, Hargrave won the National League batting crown with a lofty .353. And though the "Bubbles" nickname sounds unbefitting a big leaguer, it's no worse than the one of his kid brother "Pinky," a part-time catcher for the St. Louis Browns.

Roush wasn't the Reds second-best batter, either. That honor went to another nickname all-star — Cuckoo Christensen. Playing in 114 games, the flighty rookie outfielder gave Hargrave a run for the title before finishing three points back in second place. His .350 mark far surpassed the efforts from stalwarts such as Hornsby and Roush. Reds management practically drooled over Christensen, anointing him the heir apparent in center field. If only they could have peered into a crystal baseball and witnessed his future. The Cuckoo clock had one year left and it was a bad one. He suffered a sophomore slump in '27, got benched, ended with a .254 average in 57 games and never played major league ball again.

Keeping with an annual off-season tradition, the Roush name was tossed around in trade rumors. Press accounts frequently portrayed him as a man with one foot out the door, usually on its way to John McGraw's dugout. In 1920 it was Roush and Larry Kopf to the Giants for Ross Youngs. Edd went all over the place during December of 1921; first the Cubs bought him, then club president Herrmann announced he'd probably deal his star to the Cardinals, and then a newspaper story predicted Edd's imminent purchase by the Giants. Two winters later New York was still angling for Edd, willing to part with first baseman George Kelly and benchwarmer Billy Southworth in return. Herrmann dismissed that notion but said he'd agree if Frankie Frisch were substituted for Kelly.

Weary from endless conjecture that never came to fruition, the *Zanesville* (Ohio) *Times Signal* wrote,

> The Great American Jackass still develops most prominently in New York, and is typified by the writers who annually announce that Edd Roush will be traded to the Giants. Once more the Manhattan scribes solemnly assert that Roush will be given for (Bill) Terry — that the best and most firmly established star of outfielders will be exchanged for a first baseman who is as yet a dubious quantity. The same blithe cousins to a horse also announce that Bubbles Hargrave will be included in the deal. What a run on thistles and baled hay there ought to be in New York this winter!

Yet the rumors persisted. Shortly after completion of the 1925 season, a *New York World* article reported an upcoming deal of Roush and Hargrave to the Giants for Kelly, outfielder Emil Meusel and catcher Frank Snyder. The *Syracuse Herald* claimed New York coveted Roush or Luque, but wasn't willing to give up Kelly in return.

Sportswriters didn't fabricate all those hot stove stories. McGraw made it abundantly clear that he desired Roush's return to the Giants fold, so clear at one point that Commissioner Landis rebuked him for tampering.

18

McGraw and Roush:
A Marriage of Inconvenience

I wouldn't sign a contract with McGraw. Well, I knew what he was like, see. Call you all sorts of names if you made a bad play. I was with him that half a season in '16 and I knew doggone well that if he started in on me, someone would get hurt.[1]

In February of 1927, speculation finally merged with reality. Six and a half months after that "Roush Day" tribute at Redland Field, Edd was dealt to the Giants for George Kelly and cash. With one cold transaction, Cincinnati lost its greatest player, most experienced veteran and last true link to the 1919 champions. The trade made sense on some levels and mystified on others. John McGraw did need an outfielder and Cincinnati seemingly had a surplus, but the Reds already owned a decent first baseman. Though his .291 batting average was nothing special, Wally Pipp's 99 RBIs ranked fourth best in the league.

Kelly owned a great resume, highlighted by co-starring roles on Giants pennant winners. A perennial .300 hitter, he became an RBI machine, leading the league twice and averaging 110 from 1920 until 1925. He also averaged nearly 20 homers over a five-year span, significant power numbers for that era. In 1926, Kelly kept the average at .303 but dropped to 13 homers and 80 RBIs, still solid stats but perhaps evidence of a downturn. So the Giants shipped him out and promoted an unheralded kid to starting first baseman. The youngster's name was Bill Terry, and that all worked out pretty well for New York.

As much as anything, the trade might have been a cost-cutting measure for the Reds. Edd's three-year contract was up and he pushed for another lucrative, long-term deal. Those salary wars seemed necessary evils in the past, but now Roush was almost 34 years old. So it was off to the Big Apple for Edd, with McGraw finally catching the one that got away. Or to be more precise, the one he threw back.

Life could have been so different for that Hoosier hero if he had remained with the Giants. A superb batter and elite fielder, thrilling fans in the nation's biggest city while inspiring flowery prose on pages of legendary newspapers.... Maybe "Roush" would've been mentioned in the same breath with Gehrig, DiMaggio and Mays. Or maybe he never would've fully blossomed under McGraw. Speculation aside, one thing was abundantly clear: New York City's sports scene had certainly changed in the decade since Edd last wore a Giants uniform. For starters, the Polo Grounds now hosted *two* teams called Giants — one a professional football squad. Then there were the Rangers, flourishing in the National Hockey League and poised to launch a season that would end with their first Stanley Cup.

Edd wasn't the same fresh-faced and fresh-legged kid McGraw met in 1916. Then again, that kid was all potential and no experience. Roush returned as an accomplished veteran and proven winner — qualities worth paying for. The Reds certainly could've used them. Over the next dozen years, they fell from grace and landed in that non-contenders graveyard known as the "second division." Coincidentally or not, the team's demise coincided with a certain trade that rocked the baseball world.

Keeping with the persistent theme of Edd getting overshadowed, the Giants pulled off another deal that sparked greater fanfare. This one brought the magnificent Rogers Hornsby to New York and sent Frankie Frisch to St. Louis. Why would the Cardinals even think of unloading the guy who'd just given them a world title? The answer was his repellant personality and demand for more money. He looked at people with "go to hell eyes," according to one observer.

Hornsby's deal faced a monumental stumbling block. He owned stock in the Cardinals, and that seemed a major conflict of interest. The league office issued an edict that forbade players from holding stock with one team while playing on another. McGraw then threatened legal action against N.L. President Heydler. They say Hornsby eventually accepted a $100,000 offer for his stock.

Sparkling resume aside, some justifiable doubts emerged about Roush and his return. What about injuries, age, and overall durability? How much did this two-time batting champ have left in the tank? All fair questions regarding someone who had just posted his worst batting average of the live ball era. Still, that .323 looked awfully good for an off-year and, more significantly, he reached a career high in runs scored (95) while recording his fourth-highest total for RBIs (79). Edd wasn't over the hill yet, which proved fortunate for the Giants. He would fill a center-field void that existed ever since New York traded George Burns to the Reds in 1922. Or would he?

Lost in the wheeling and dealing was a gargantuan stumbling block: Edd did *not* want to play for McGraw. He remembered how insulting the man could be and doubted they could coexist. Not that Edd was even remotely intimidated; he just shuddered at the possible consequences if McGraw provoked him. With that mindset as a starting point, a stubborn holdout was born. Approaching the twilight of his career, he demanded high-noon terms — lots of money and a multi-year pact. Though management scoffed, one big name was in his corner. "I think it stinks," Hornsby said of the Giants outfield. "They got to get Roush out there to keep those clowns from knocking their heads together, and if they don't they're crazy, no matter what they have to pay."[2]

Babe Ruth made earlier headlines with his unthinkable insistence of $100,000 a year and soon accepted a three-year, $210,000 package. Would Roush compromise, too? While the Giants trudged through spring training in Sarasota, Florida, he laughed off an offer for $19,000 a year and said he'd rather spend the summer fishing. Edd had reportedly requested the same terms from Cincinnati management, which rejected his proposition for $57,000 over three years. He wouldn't reveal his asking price to the press but reliable sources said the Hoosier demanded a three-year deal worth a whopping $30,000 per season.

One of those sources was Giants owner Charles Stoneham, who grew increasingly agitated by Edd's inflexible approach. After all, he had generously agreed to pay the salary that Roush couldn't get in Cincinnati and even upped the ante by $1,000. Edd said twenty grand wasn't enough and Stoneham refused to pay one penny more. What's more, the chief threatened to make an example of his wayward warrior if he didn't report by April 12.

Edd put himself in danger of incurring heavy fines, suspension and a spot on baseball's ineligible list. A similar situation played out in the Bronx, with Yankees ace Herb

His long holdout finally at an end, Roush signed a lucrative contract with the New York Giants in 1927. Manager John McGraw sits behind the desk in this photo while lefty Edd poses with a pen in his off hand (Roush Family Collection).

Pennock holding out at his silver fox farm in Pennsylvania. They both went out on limbs, but that's where the cabbage was.

Roush returned with a veritable cornucopia on March 31, agreeing to a lucrative accord after two short conferences with McGraw in a Chattanooga, Tennessee, hotel room. The Giants had just left Florida the previous evening, embarking on a whistle stop tour toward home with exhibition games slated for Tennessee, Alabama and Georgia. Describing the scene in detail, newspapers reported that Edd leaned back comfortably in a chair and quietly negotiated while smoking a big black cigar.

McGraw seemed quite the appeaser during an interview with the *New York Times*. Among other concessions, he went along with one of Edd's reasons for avoiding southern sojourns to training camp. Those sandy ballpark fields were murder on someone with a long running stride. More significantly, he appeared perfectly comfortable with the lofty salary demands. "Roush was very sincere and told me frankly that he would rather play in Cincinnati than anywhere else and he has a home there and his daughter goes to school there and he said he would want more money to play elsewhere. That's all right. He wanted more and he is getting it. I don't blame him."[3]

As an octogenarian, Edd still beamed with pride when reflecting on that ancient transaction. Sans the cigar, he leaned back and softly crowed, "Well, in New York over there in '27, '28 and '29 I had a three-year contract for

Roush slides home in a cloud of dust during a Giants spring training game (Roush Family Collection).

$70,000. That's $23,333 and I think they lost a third cent, but anyhow ... I got the most money than anybody in the National League at that time."[4]

A day after signing, he set tongues to wagging. Everybody knew Roush didn't need much time to get into baseball shape but his spring debut seemed surreal: two hard-hit balls, two defensive gems and all of it packed into a relatively brief appearance. Though hitting the ground running, Edd was also careful to pace himself. He played short, three-inning stints before pronouncing himself fit for extended action.

By the time the Giants returned home, old Roush looked as good as ever. In an April 9 exhibition game versus the Washington Senators, he lashed three hits during his latest Polo Grounds debut. The season opener arrived three days later at Philadelphia, where McGraw filled out a lineup card that featured three fearsome bats in the middle of the order: Roush third, Hornsby fourth and Bill Terry fifth. At the time, Terry didn't scare anybody. The New York press complained he was no George Kelly, and that assertion proved correct. Terry became far better. They headed in different directions, Kelly winding down an outstanding career and Terry beginning a legendary one that culminated with a .401 batting average in 1930.

Opening the '27 season with seven road games, the Giants won four of them — no thanks to their new center fielder. Roush had a miserable time of it, producing only four hits in 32 plate appearances, and things didn't get any better when the team returned home. Receiving a nice welcoming ovation from fans before his first Polo Grounds at-bat, he proceeded to fail in all five plate appearances. But the Giants still won that April 20 opener, topping the Phillies in front of 50,000 faithful, an attendance figure that could only be dreamed of back in Cincinnati. Roars filled the air as Mayor Jimmy Walker approached the mound for the ceremonial first pitch and the cheering never fully subsided until the last out went into the books. Was there a better baseball city on the face of the earth?

Three key additions to the 1927 New York Giants. From left, Burleigh Grimes, the great Rogers Hornsby and Edd Roush (Roush Family Collection).

Edd flopped the following day as well, dropping his average to an even .100. A three-game benching followed before he began to find his stroke, homering in a 4–3 win on April 28, going 3-for-4 on April 30, and posting another three-hit game in early May. Thus began Roush's slow rise to respectability. It took a long time to repair batting-average damage and there would be setbacks along the way. His freefall, however, was over and bad stretches would be countered by good ones.

New York jumped out to a strong start, sitting atop the standings through April and much of May. Among the successes was a sweep of visiting Cincinnati. After one of those triumphs, Edd sat down and talked to some of his former Reds teammates. The scene angered McGraw, who always discouraged players from getting chummy with the enemy. A half-century later, elderly Edd reflected on the inevitable confrontation: "He called me in there and he said, 'Roush, I saw you socializing with the opposition.' 'Well,' I said, 'what in the hell are you gonna do about it? We talked (because) we played together for years but when this ball game starts, all friendship ceased.'"

Everything seemed friendly when the sun rose above the Polo Grounds on May 18. Winning six of their last seven contests, the Giants held a four-game lead over second-place Chicago and owned four of the league's top five hitters. After playing a June 1 exhibition against McGraw's alma mater, St. Bonaventure College, the Giants traveled to Cincinnati and split a four-game set. In an admirable homecoming performance, Edd celebrated by spearheading a two-run rally that gave New York a 12-inning triumph in game one. Things went downhill after that and he left town with only two hits in 18 appearances. Recuperating from appendicitis surgery, George Kelly did not play for the home team.

The Giants, Cardinals and everyone else found themselves entirely overshadowed by a prominent visitor during their July 18 game at St. Louis. Watching from a special box seat alongside the home team's dugout was Charles Lindbergh, fresh off his historic transatlantic solo flight to Paris. Just a few days earlier he rode an open-air car down Manhattan's Fifth Avenue while millions cheered their throats raw. "Lindy" soaked up similar adoration at other major cities, including St. Louis on this game day.

Arriving 20 minutes late at Sportsman's Park, Lindbergh was greeted with a deafening roar from 40,000 fans. Officials presented him with a Golden Pass, good for free entry to any National League stadium. In the circuit's half-century history, only two other men were similarly knighted — President Calvin Coolidge and New York Governor Al Smith.

Lindbergh led a pre-game mini-parade that strolled to the outfield flagpole, then returned to home plate. Settling into his seat of honor, he watched the first three innings, and then departed to another loud salute.

Fans finally focused on the diamond and watched St. Louis take a 6–4 triumph. It was New York's seventh loss in eight games.

After a strong start the Giants struggled for two months and dropped to fourth, consistently hovering around .500. Their pitchers surrendered too many runs and an explosive offense could only take them so far. Meanwhile, those pesky Pirates formed a nice blend of both, which carried them to the top of the N.L. The pennant chase soon fashioned into a three-horse race, with Chicago and St. Louis hot on Pittsburgh's heels. New York trailed by several lengths and that frustrated fans who expected better results from the blockbuster trades.

On July 3, the *Times* diagnosed what was wrong with the Giants: Bill Terry cared only about hitting .300, Hornsby was disgusted with his teammates, Fred Lindstrom had a bad back, George Harper was too slow, none of the catchers could play, the shortstop suffered brittle knees, the bench lacked depth, and their pitching staff reeked from top to bottom. What about Edd? "Roush got off to a bad start and evidently doesn't care." One day later, he drilled game-winning hits in both ends of a doubleheader sweep against Boston.

Though the team continued to struggle, a criticism ceasefire was called for July 19, the day devoted to celebrating McGraw's 25-year anniversary as Giants manager. Presented a silver cup by a delegation of dignitaries, he heard wild applause from 25,000 fans at the Polo Grounds. Accompanying Mayor Walker in pre-game ceremonies were explorers Richard Byrd and Clarence Chamberlin, Commissioner Landis, George M. Cohan and former heavyweight champion Jim Corbett. Earlier in the day, Eddie Cantor headlined some clownish exhibition baseball between two teams of Broadway actors. Only in New York.

Unsentimental to the end, the Chicago Cubs gave McGraw an 8–5 beating. His Giants soon vaulted back into contention, however, starting with a late July stretch of six wins in seven games. Then they went thermonuclear, taking 19 of 22 and pulling within a half-game of Pittsburgh on September 8. The Pirates proceeded to build a little breathing room, but New York took three of four in Pittsburgh and closed the gap to 1½.

McGraw's men would come no closer. Pittsburgh swept a twin bill at Chicago and took a rain-shortened victory the following day, while New York lost one and tied another. Suddenly the divide stood at 3½ with five games to go. Though the Giants won four down the stretch, it wasn't enough. The Pirates claimed the pennant with a final record of 94–60 and St. Louis slipped into second at 92–61, a half-game better than New York's 92–62.

That down-to-the-wire success earned the N.L. champs a berth as World Series sacrificial lambs. They were swept by a team that still merits serious consideration as the best of all time — the '27 Yankees, with their "Murderers' Row" of Ruth, Gehrig, Combs, Meusel, and Lazzeri. Less famous, but also devastating, was a pitching staff that posted the best team ERA in baseball.

With all due respect to other borough teams, the Yankees now owned New York City. They were just too good and too entertaining. But baseball stallions roamed the Polo Grounds, too. Though a Giant-come-lately, Hornsby posted fantastic statistics while finishing second to Pittsburgh's Paul Waner in the hitting race: 367 batting average, a league-leading 133 runs and 125 RBIs. Terry broke out with corresponding numbers of .326, 101 and 121. Edd recorded a .306 mark and one tremendous comeback from the dark days of spring.

1928

> *I'd tell (sportswriters) a story, you now, about baseball. When it come out in the paper, it didn't sound like anything I said. Why thunder! Switched it around to suit themselves. I finally got so I'd say, "Write your own damn story, I'm not gonna fool with it. You don't write what I tell you. You (might) as well do it your own way to start with."*[5]

Despite his remarkable debut season at the Polo Grounds, Hornsby was traded to the Boston Braves for a couple .288 hitters. It put to rest rumors that he would succeed the ailing McGraw as manager. "Mac" still led the team when spring training opened in Georgia, but this season would prove oddly hazardous to his health. A foul ball drilled his foot during camp, and though no bone was broken, he had to avoid walking for awhile. On May 14, a car clipped McGraw as he tried to cross the street near Wrigley Field. Once again no broken bones, but the painful collision required much rest and recuperation.

Edd reported to camp March 13 and quickly whipped himself into shape. Replacing Hornsby at second base was Andy Cohen, a youngster who achieved a modicum of fame as a Jew in a Gentile game. In sports, as in entertainment, Jews commonly changed their last names to fit in but Cohen kept his and prospered from it. With publicity dollar signs in his eyes, McGraw plucked Andy from the Texas League and gave him 35 at-bats as a utility infielder in 1926. Sent to Buffalo for further minor-league seasoning, he was hailed by the Jewish community and honored with an "Andy Cohen Day." Home and away, he became guest of honor at a series of short ceremonies in International League cities. Admirers showered him with gifts.

When Hornsby's deal went though, the time seemed ripe for appealing to that huge consumer market of New York City Jews. Starting at second base, Cohen got off to a great start in the season opener, drilling a two-run double with New York trailing by one in the bottom of the sixth. Adding impact to the debut was his team's opponent that day — the Boston Braves and their new player-manager, Rogers Hornsby. In a take-off of the famous "Casey at the Bat" poem, United Press circulated "Cohen at the Bat." Though paying tribute to the man, it also contained some unflattering generalizations: "...then from the stands and bleachers, the cry of 'Oy-Oy' rose, for up came Andy Cohen half a foot behind his nose." Cohen hit .274 that year, 113 points behind Hornsby's league-leading mark.

The 1928 season saw another tight N.L. pennant race, with the Cardinals edging New York by two games and Chicago by four. Over in Yankee land, the city bullies put another notch on the dynasty belt by beating St. Louis in a second consecutive World Series sweep. Gothamites took pride in their National League sons, too. Winning 93 games, the Giants put together a campaign that compared favorably with the franchise's glory years of the early '20s.

One particular player, however, would not remember the season fondly at all. Sidelined by torn stomach muscles, Edd Roush appeared in only 54 games and hit a paltry .252. Off-field issues surfaced, too, most notably a publicized quarrel with acting manager Roger Bresnahan. Pressed into duty after McGraw's vehicular mishap, the former Giants catcher flexed his newfound muscle by suspending Edd in late June. Vague official statements shed little light on the source of conflict, but it was understood that the bland "breaking team rules" refrain could be narrowed down to missing an 11:30 P.M. curfew. Edd supposedly gave a tongue-lashing to the interim boss, which might have cemented disciplinary action.

Popular opinion said it was indignant Roush's idea to part ways, with the punishment just an afterthought. Another report had him showing up at the Penn Station train terminal, and then informed he couldn't accompany the team to Philadelphia. Either way, a five-game suspension went on Edd's permanent record.

According to newspaper accounts, he threatened permanent retirement and planned to go over Bresnahan's head to McGraw. The storm blew over, however, and Roush quietly returned to the dugout after serving his sentence.

Edd's eruption came on the heels of irritating rumors that he'd been "dogging it." According to anonymous gossip that reached the ears of newspapermen, he was prone to faking or exaggerating injury, especially when Giants batters had to face a tough southpaw. It was the worst kind of character assassination for a baseball warrior.

1929

*Roush at the moment is far and away the most expensive and frag-
ile piece of bric-a-brac McGraw has had on his hands in several years.
Also, it is generally felt, a large measure of the Giants' success this year
will depend on whether this star will regain his strength and former effec-
tiveness.—John Drebinger,* New York Times[6]

Edd had surgery on that nonexistent stomach injury during the offseason and spent the winter recuperating. Reporting to spring training on March
11, he looked fit but nobody expected him to exert himself. The Giants wanted
their center fielder healthy for opening day.

Training camp moved to San Antonio in 1929 and the Giants scheduled
an exhibition game at the Texas border town of Laredo. A little farther south
lay some volatile Mexican territory, where rebel revolutionaries were said to
roam. Journalists arrived in town, pens poised to leap into action if civil war
erupted. But for the moment, at least, all focus centered on a baseball game
between the San Antonio Bears and New York Giants. "The Mexicans from
neighboring Nuevo Laredo, which is just on the other side of the bridge, also
decided to pass up their revolution for the day and helped swell the crowd to
a total of about a thousand," wrote one correspondent. "For, after all, a revolution is something the Mexicans can put on most any time, whereas this
was the first time in their lives they had ever seen John McGraw and his
Giants."[7]

If only the upcoming season had proved as compelling. A well-traveled
Hornsby landed in Chicago, where he won another batting title and led the
Cubs to a runaway pennant. Hitting .380 with 156 runs, 39 homers and 148
RBIs, the "Rajah" looked like he could go on forever. The champs also saw
great performances from all three outfielders — Hack Wilson, Kiki Cuyler and
Riggs Stephenson. When the dust settled, Chicago emerged with 98 wins and
double-digit separation from the nearest contender. McGraw's boys crafted
a decent season, winning 17 more than they lost, but that put them a distant
third.

Still, the New Yorkers witnessed a couple milestones of sorts. At the tender age of 20, outfielder Mel Ott lit up the league, hitting .328 with 138 runs,
42 home runs and 151 RBIs. Bill Terry broke through, too, his .372 average
rating 46 points higher than his previous best. Over the next several years,
those golden boys formed one of the best hitting tandems in baseball.

Another significant side story revolved around the reemergence of one
Edd J. Roush. After watching him sit for most of the previous season, skep-
tics doubted the 36-year-old could return to form. Though he did miss a
chunk of summer because of a leg injury, Edd appeared in 115 games and

totaled 450 at-bats. His .324 batting average outshined every Giant starter except two — Ott and Terry.

Roush certainly had his moments: a five-hit game in May, a 17-for-34 stretch during June, and a game-winning homer in August. Then came a fitting final salvo on the last Sunday of the season. Ott and Philadelphia's Chuck Klein were tied for the home run lead when the Phillies came to town that day, but Edd Roush became the only man to circle the bases. He also belted a double and a triple while leading his young charges to a 4–2 victory. So often a target for criticism, Edd was praised to the heavens on this day.

In its October issue, *Baseball Magazine* called him the last of the great place hitters — a scientific batsmith in a new age of blind slugging. It wasn't just Ott and Klein swinging from the heels; power numbers increased across the board. Hornsby and Wilson belted 39 homers apiece for the Cubs, while Bottomley and Chick Hafey each launched 29 as Cardinals. Complementing Klein in Philadelphia, Lefty O'Doul delivered 32 round-trippers.

When Roush was winning batting titles, a fellow could lead the whole National League with a dozen homers. That, however, was a different era, and modern players showed little interest in the old ways. "Many batters have criticized place hitting," Edd told his interviewer. "There's some excuse for it now, with the lively ball and all the slugging. But even now place hitting would pay if a fellow could do it. Those who criticize the system merely admit that they can't do it."[8]

19

Holding Out and Holding On

Along about this time of year
Without the slightest doubt,
The baseball world is due to hear
Ed Roush is holding out.
— *George E. Phair,* New York American[1]

If they pay me the money I will play, if they don't I won't. It doesn't
make any difference either way.—Oakland City Journal[2]

1930

With that lucrative three-year contract now expired, Edd started the new decade by threatening to retire rather than surrender his position as one of the game's best-paid players. Oft-injured and closing in on his 37th birthday, he didn't warrant big money anymore, but this was about principle, not cost logic, and Edd Roush never moved backward.

Disregarding management's offer the previous fall, he remained unmoved as spring approached. Asked to take a substantial cut, Edd refused. One news story quoted a paltry $7,500 offer, prompting a strong denial from club officials. Most put the figure at 15 grand. John McGraw wired word to the Roush home in Oakland City, promising drastic action if he didn't report to camp. When no reply arrived, someone suggested that maybe he didn't receive the message. "How could anybody help getting a telegram in Oakland City, Indiana?" McGraw responded.[3]

The town's local newspaper reported that the two sides were $5,000 apart, with Edd asking for $20,000 and his team offering $15,000. Finally, in late March, negotiators withdrew their previous offer and replaced it with something less favorable. Their message: the longer you hold out, the less money you get.

On April 7 the Giants staged an exhibition game in Evansville, bringing holdout and boss within a short drive of each other. Edd came down that morning and shook hands with some of his teammates in a hotel lobby. McGraw walked by and the two combatants exchanged the briefest of pleasantries: "Hello Mac." "Hello Eddie." Roush watched the Giants lose an 11–10 decision to the Chicago White Sox and then went home, no closer to an agreement. He remained AWOL when the Giants opened their season in front of 50,000 fans on April 15.

Weeks turned to months and months turned into an entire season. The retirement threat was no bluff and McGraw felt just as strongly about guarding the team coffers. Looking back, it seemed an awfully bad time to embrace unemployment. The stock market crashed shortly after the 1929 season ended and America would soon sink into economic quicksand of the Great Depression. Nobody could've imagined the depth and duration of the hard times ahead.

Edd's family did not suffer, however. These were the days and years when they ate the fruit from all those salary wars. Their patron had ample money, owned stable investments, and everything the Roushes needed was at their fingertips in southern Indiana. So much for the old chestnut that a boy can't be kept on the farm when he's seen the city. As far as Edd was concerned, urban folk could keep their bright lights, big crowds and tree-less neighborhoods. But what would a baseball legend do with so much time on his hands? "Oh, just fool around," he answered. "There is always plenty to do."

The Roushes made a seamless transition to life outside baseball, as the local society page could attest. Sometimes it was just brief mention of a slumber party, trip to Evansville or hosting out-of-town visitors. On May 27, they earned significant ink for throwing a bridge party — not something that would've drawn attention back in New York, but such was the refreshing lilt of small-town life.

The holdout allowed Edd to spend more time with his twin and both participated in early-summer benefit baseball games between Oakland City and Princeton. Accompanied by miserable humidity, July arrived like a blast furnace. It was southern Indiana's worst heat wave in nearly 30 years and Oakland City witnessed a high of 108 blistering degrees. In his first summer vacation in nearly two decades, Edd spent it in an oven.

Relief arrived by mid-month but the cycle would repeat itself, spawning powerful thunderstorms. Heat, rain, wind, lightning, felled tree limbs — all as much a part of southern Indiana summers as sweet corn and baseball. In late August the Gibson County Fair kicked off at Princeton, drawing many Oakland City residents to evenings of fireworks, band music, concessions goodies and races between horses or automobiles. Folks still had a few bucks in their pocket at this early stage of the Depression.

September's focus switched to football, as Oakland City College prepared for the upcoming season with two-a-day practices, and World Series action took center stage in early October, with hundreds of locals tuning in for the battle between the Philadelphia Athletics and St. Louis Cardinals. Some followed the action while shopping, as merchants cranked up the volume on in-store radios. Not long after Philly took the title in six games, Edd played an exhibition in nearby Winslow where a weekend festival was in full swing.

One late night in November, Oakland City Boy Scouts embarked on their annual opossum hunt. Accompanying the youngsters and scoutmasters was an avid local hunter named Edd J. Roush. A month later, the dress turned formal when his widowed father-in-law remarried.

It turns out there really *was* lots to do in farm country.

Back during mid-summer, the *Oakland City Journal* ran a recurring item that drew national attention: "For Sale — A Studebaker 6-cylinder sedan, in good condition. Edd J. Roush." It sounded an awful lot like his "Roush Day" gift from 1926 and some saw the ad as evidence that, without a baseball salary, he had fallen on hard times. Edd just laughed it off during an interview with a news service sports editor. "You know, I learned long ago not to believe half of what some sports writers write about ball players because half of them don't know what they are writing about. The truth is I have three automobiles and decided to get rid of one because operating two of them keeps me busy."[4]

No mention was made of his February advertisement that put the Roush Pool Room up for sale. Leasing the bottom floor of the Washington Hotel since 1926, Edd apparently couldn't find any buyers for the space, four tables and fixtures in fine condition. Sometime around September he added bowling lanes to the property and soon afterward the hotel proprietor filed suit against Edd, asking for $15,000 damages and a permanent injunction. Yet when Thanksgiving approached, Roush Pool Room was offering a dressed turkey to the player who rolled the best bowling score.

1931

> *No, I never got in any fights ... to tell you the truth, they didn't start a fight with me for the simple reason that next time I came down there I was liable to cut their ears off. I could handle them spikes and mine were sharp and long and when I hit a fella, I hit him hard enough that they usually took him out of the game to patch him up.*[5]

While Bill Terry held out, John McGraw received some positive news on another front in early March. Edd Roush was a Giant again, sort of. Reinstated to active status by Commissioner Landis, he automatically reverted to Polo Grounds property. But Edd still refused to work for the Giants — not at reduced salary — and he settled in for a contented retirement.

Then came a pleading voice from the past. It belonged to Reds owner Sidney Weil, who'd lost a bundle in the stock market crash, and encouraged a return to the place that made Roush famous. The Giants could have nixed the proposition but had nothing to gain by keeping a ghost on their reserved list. They were willing to cut ties for the waiver fee.

That potential crisis averted, Weil soon faced a larger stumbling block: Edd didn't want to play for him, either. Nothing personal, but the team stank and an aging icon wouldn't improve things any. Having recorded only one winning season in the past four years, Cincinnati went 59–95 in 1930 and the current team looked just as bad, if not worse. How much could Edd help the league's worst offense? A porous pitching staff was certainly beyond his repair.

Weil desperately desired a turnstile-turning persona and told the Red hero to name his price. Edd proposed a figure of $15,000, thinking it would dissuade his ardent pursuer. It didn't. Weil agreed on the spot and Roush committed to a one-year contract on March 26.

"So I said, 'Well, I'll come over and help ya a little while and if I get tired, I'll quit.' I went over there and he wouldn't let me quit.... I said, 'You haven't got a ball club. If I hit .500 and hit that ball like I used to, you still wouldn't beat anybody.' He said, 'I know, (but) you're a drawing card.' And I said, 'All right, I'll stay with ya.'"[6]

The Roush signing immediately unleashed a flood of rumors that he would not only take over center field but eventually the entire team. Manager Dan Howley pushed for the acquisition, however, and it's hard to believe he would sow the seeds of his own unemployment. Edd had more pressing matters to worry about, like the daunting challenge of getting that 38-year-old body back into baseball shape. Six days passed before he joined the Reds, who'd already embarked on an exhibition tour. After a brief connection with new teammates, Roush stayed behind in Georgia while the Reds continued their barnstorming trek. There, he trained with an Eastern League minors team.

In years past, Edd's bosses found themselves consistently amazed by his

Edd was at the end of his rope in 1931 but squeezed one more season from his 38-year-old body (Roush Family Collection).

knack for instant acclimation at spring training. Now, management encouraged him to take it slow and avoid undue strain. It was, after all, the old guy's first serious workouts since 1929 and he didn't wear rubber leg supports because they looked pretty.

A year earlier, Weil paid cash for another famous graybeard named Harry Heilmann. In his prime at Detroit, Heilmann was the American League version of Rogers Hornsby — posting averages as high as .403, .398, .394 and .393. Though the 35-year-old hadn't breathed that rarified air lately, he still wielded an explosive bat in 1930, hitting .333 with 79 runs and 91 RBIs. Unfortunately, Heilmann also had a bad case of arthritis and never played a single game in '31.

With only two weeks worth of pre-season conditioning, would Roush's body break down, too? As the April 14 opener drew near, he assured everyone that he felt fine and his legs could withstand the daily grind. Simple ceremonies preceded the debut, and Cincinnati players were presented with a mass of flowers, shaped like a huge baseball. That must have been how big the real ball looked to St. Louis batters, who ripped 10 hits in a 7–3 victory.

Edd received a big ovation upon making his first plate appearance in the opening inning. Four-and-a-half years had passed since he last wore the Red uniform, not nearly long enough to dim memories of brave deeds. But this Eddie Roush bore little resemblance to the mid–1920s version. He went 0-for-4, thrice retired on easy fly balls and reaching base on a fielder's choice grounder.

Looking back at Cincinnati's 1931 season, one good thing emerges from the ashes — at least death came quickly. After dropping their first five games, the Reds beat Pittsburgh, lost seven straight, beat Pittsburgh again, and lost another five in a row. That made for a 2–17 start. A brief period of competence followed, and then 12 defeats in 14 games. By the end of May, Cincy's fate was already sealed. Nobody bounces back from an 8–30 start.

Between loss number 24 and 25, Edd stirred up a hornet's nest during a May 26 home doubleheader with the Chicago Cubs. In game two, he spiked first baseman Charlie Grimm while trying to beat out a slow grounder, and the benches emptied. The stampede started when both men began exchanging angry words. In the *New York Times* version, Grimm thought the wounding intentional and dropped into a fighting stance. Meanwhile, Hack Wilson led the charge out of the Cubs dugout.

Built like a fire hydrant, the short and burly 190-pounder stood one year removed from a league-leading 56 home runs and all-time record 190 RBIs. His numbers dropped way down in '31, however, and he sat out both games on this day. That's what Edd was supposed to do, too. He'd been given the day off to rest tired legs but was pressed into action when a sore arm sidelined the game one center fielder.

According to the *Chicago Tribune*, Wilson leaped into action after hearing Roush threaten to punch his already-injured comrade. He supposedly approached Edd and declared, "It is not my purpose to pick on broken down old men. But I urge you to pick five of your teammates for your side and I will thrash the whole delegation." It's quite the wordy battle cry for someone at ground zero of an impending riot, so take that quote with a grain of balk. The *Tribune* also has "the dark skinned Cincinnati outfielder" looking intimidated by Wilson and warned to avoid train depots where he might encounter the muscular brawler. Back in Cincinnati, the site of the brouhaha, newspapers reported nothing of the sort.

Credit went to the three-man umpiring crew for rushing into the middle of the melee and preventing fisticuffs. When things quieted down, the contest proceeded without any ejections. Grimm, however, was just as good as ejected. He limped to the dugout and did not return.

The spiking was no accident. Edd freely admitted it 47 years later, flashing a devious grin while speaking of old-school retribution for knockdown pitches. In his version, the Cubs were locked in a pennant race at the time and ended up losing it, all because some pitcher wanted bragging rights for making Roush eat dirt.

> So I walked halfway out there (to the pitcher's mound) and I said, "Let me tell you something, you big so and so, you couldn't hit me in the head with a handful of (buck) shot. But I'll tell you one thing, you won't have enough players to finish this ball game if I get to 'em." Hornsby was playing second base and he was playing deep. I slapped the ball on the ground so the pitcher couldn't get it and I got to first base just ahead of the ball. Grimm's out there reaching for the ball and I stepped right there (on his leg) and the other foot was up in (his chest). Grimm hopped around there and, of course, they come off the bench and I kept backing up. Don't let nobody get behind ya when you get in a thing like that.
>
> ...We beat them five straight ball games, beat 'em right out of the pennant just because that guy wanted to go back home and say, "That Roush. I knocked him down twice." Why I never hit so much in a five-game series in my life. They only got me out two or three times.

A glance at the historical record shows an entirely different outcome. Beginning with a double defeat on that day in late May, Cincinnati actually lost three of four to the visiting Cubs. But elderly Edd's memory wasn't far off; he'd just combined two separate stories into one. Long after their brouhaha, the Cubs traveled to Cincinnati and dropped five straight, from August 30 to September 5. Roush blistered the ball at a .423 clip during that stretch.

Trailing league-leading St. Louis by double digits, the Cubs weren't exactly embroiled in a tight pennant race before their embarrassing meltdown, but cellar-dwelling Cincinnati crushed all vestiges of hope and sent them spiraling eight games behind New York in the race for second. It was a fantastic week and rare source of pride for an exceptionally bad team.

Immediately following the series finale, Redland played host to an old-timers game. Cy Young threw an inning, as did Three Finger Brown and two members of Cincinnati's 1919 champs — Slim Sallee and Hod Eller. Bedford Bill Rariden saw action behind the plate. Fans had to wonder whether these rusty retirees were still better than the current crop of Reds.

Cincinnati made a run at 100 losses but came up four short, finishing 58–96 and 43 games behind pennant-winning St. Louis. Edd played in 101 games, hitting .271 with 46 runs and 41 RBIs. Among N.L. starters, those numbers put him closer to the bottom than the top. Modern baseball belonged to men like Bill Terry, Mel Ott, the Waner brothers and Carl Hubbell. In the same year Willie Mays and Mickey Mantle were born, the Edd Roush era came to a sputtering end.

He played sparingly in the final three weeks, missing long stretches while management put younger men on the field. After a seven-game absence, Roush started the season finale against pennant-winning St. Louis. Exiled to left field, he caught five fly balls and went 2-for-3 at the plate with a triple and RBI — an improbable yet entirely fitting end to a season and career. The Cincinnati symbol took off his uniform for the final time that day and joined about 8 million other Americans in unemployment.

20

An Active Depression

Nowadays, it's a rare thing to find a player who can hit behind the runner or drop down a bunt wherever he wants. In the old days players were taught to hit to all fields but now they are nearly all one-field bat- ters.... Everybody goes up there taking a full swing and you rarely find anybody choking the bat and punching one over the infield to a certain spot. This free hitting may produce more home runs but it produces fewer smart plays.—Edd Roush interview with International News Service, *1938[1]*

Reds management made it official in January of 1932, announcing the unconditional release of Edd Roush. Even in a best-case scenario the 38-year-old couldn't have drawn much salary or playing time, so better to end it now and embrace retirement.

Back home, someone was trying to grab $15,000 worth of his nest egg. Regardless of misspellings, the Lawrence Hurt vs. "Edward Rousch" lawsuit continued a slow trek through the local circuit court. Hurt said his hotel's annual income had dropped by more than half since Roush moved that pool hall/bowling alley into the two-story, brick building. Noise and loitering riffraff were supposedly hurting business for his 28 rooms upstairs and caused property value to drop. Edd's defense team filed a series of counter motions.

In May of 1931 the plaintiff asked for a change of venue, claiming there was no chance of a fair and impartial trial in Gibson County. "Defendant has undue influence over the citizens of said county," read one part of the motion. "An odium attaches to this plaintiff in said county on account of local prej- udice," read another. The case moved to neighboring Pike County and another couple years passed without resolution before the parties reached an out-of- court settlement in February 1933.

Edd didn't ditch baseball altogether during 1932, his first year of perma- nent retirement. On August 22, he returned to Redland Field and joined more than 100 former major leaguers for another old-timers day. A vast majority

"

of them wanted to play in the exhibition game between graybeards: Honus Wagner appeared at shortstop, Tris Speaker took a spot in the outfield, Cy Young pitched a bit and Chief Bender saw some mound action, too. Named captain of one team, Edd watched his charges drop a 6–4 decision. A month later, gossip circulated about Roush as a serious candidate for Reds manager. Current skipper Dan Howley was wrapping up his third straight season of 90-plus losses, a miserable streak that screamed for change.

At home, the Roush brothers headlined an Oakland City team that traveled south to Evansville's Bosse Field for an October game with the Ellis All-Stars. Even in these times of economic duress, organizers could drum up sufficient support for the occasional exhibition contest but the Depression was killing major league baseball. Though still thriving through 1930, the game soon suffered precipitous drops in ticket sales. With national unemployment reaching an eye-popping 25 percent in 1933, fewer folks could afford an afternoon at the ballpark. And that figure didn't include the growing subset of working poor, those who were forced to take wage cuts or reduced to part-time employment.

One year earlier, attendance fell below seven million — the worst since 1919. With a decade's worth of "lively ball" gains wiped out in the span of a couple seasons, owners tried to compensate by trimming rosters and slashing salaries. Even Babe Ruth and Commissioner Landis took sizeable pay cuts.

Edd got out just in time. If the great Bambino lost all leverage, then Roush's paychecks would've been slashed to the bone and he'd never accept that. Fortunately, he didn't need to. Free from want, Edd and his family maintained their comfortable small-town life during the height of the Depression. As a result, 1933 seemed like any other year when the local newspaper mentioned another mini-milestone for Mary — an appearance in her high school's junior class play.

Though home foreclosures and bank closings increased at an alarming rate, the national news wasn't all bad. Prohibition ended in 1933, which put smiles on some faces, Roush's included. Baseball staged its first all-star game, as nearly 50,000 watched the American League win a 4–2 decision at Comiskey Park. An aggressive innovator named Larry MacPhail took over as Cincinnati Reds president, quickly goosing the floundering franchise toward a brighter future. This was also the year that Gus Greenlee chose to start a Negro National League.

So it *was* possible to create something or make money during the Depression. But stealing proved far easier for the brutal criminals who gained national fame in an era of widespread poverty. Bank robberies became so common that it seemed odd if a week passed without one. Yet as a symbol of the foreclosures that left so many people homeless, the bank drew little sympathy from America's downtrodden. To many, such gunmen were modern Robin Hoods and the dust bowl their forest. Living by the gun, these colorful crooks usually died by it, too. In a banner 1934 season for the Federal Bureau of Investigation, agents shot and killed John Dillinger, Baby Face Nelson and Pretty Boy Floyd. Ma Barker bought it a year later.

A kinder, gentler murderers row made headlines in December of 1935 when baseball released the names of 33 nominees for its first Hall of Fame class. These pupils had no school, so to speak, because the Cooperstown HOF building wouldn't open for another three-and-a-half years. It's never too early to start plaque shopping, however. Edd Roush made the list, though he stood little chance of landing a spot on the final 10, not when the field included such names as Ruth, Cobb, Hornsby, Gehrig, Speaker and Alexander. But a never-ending stream of future classes would follow, and Edd had plenty of time to get his due. Or so it seemed.

The Depression rolled on and so did Roush, content in an active retirement. Then along came 1937, a significant year in many ways. Kicking things off, the mother of all floods arrived in January, devastating huge tracts of middle America. Many areas fell under martial law at one point or another, including Gibson County, home to Oakland City and Princeton. But the Roushes wintered in west central Florida where, in an irony for the ages, Edd had become a spring training groupie.

The *New York World-Telegram* said as much in a March 3 story, sent from St. Petersburg: "Looking no older than he did when he roamed center field for the Giants, trim and lithe at 45, Eddie Roush meandered into the clubhouse of the Yankees today and sniffed the familiar perfume of muscle condiments. When Eddie was in baseball, he was the champion holdout and training camp dodger. It was strange, indeed, to see him in a Florida dressing room."

Strange but greatly appreciated, because Edd soon gave reporter Dan Daniel quite a scoop. First, he spoke of little things, such as his new trailer — bought so Mrs. Roush would agree to come south. She hated Pullmans and hotels. Inevitably, a question arose about the 1919 World Series and Edd took a pregnant-pause puff on his cigar before responding, "Well, I am going to tell you something I have kept under my hat for eighteen years. Since I never have told it to anyone, it never has been printed."

He told of that evening after Game Two, when he'd heard about an angry uprising by Black Sox who demanded their promised bribe money. Continuing the narrative, Edd said his well-connected tipster later implied that some Reds players were on the take, too. He described the team meeting before Game Eight, his short speech of admonition toward anyone who dared take a dive, and Hod Eller's revelation that someone offered him $5,000 to lose.

"Have I any suspicions today? Yes, I have, about some of our own men who figured in those defeats in the sixth and seventh games. They are gone and forgotten, so why bring up any names?" He remained hesitant as an old man but mentioned Dutch Ruether on at least one occasion.

In September the *Oakland City Journal* reported Roush was making a bid for "managership" of the 1938 Reds. A *Sporting News* article confirmed the story in greater detail, claiming he came to Cincinnati a day after the former manager was fired. He supposedly sized up the roster, scouted opponents and promoted himself as the natural choice for next Red skipper. About a month later, Bill McKechnie got the job.

With three teams, two pennants and 15 years experience on his managerial resume, McKechnie was the natural choice. True, he hadn't produced a single contender during his latest stint — an eight-season run with the Boston Braves — but he usually squeezed every drop of potential from that talent-starved franchise. Though the Reds did no better than Boston during the Depression years, McKechnie saw enough ability to predict a quick end to their cellar-dweller days.

The new boss still had a hole on his coaching staff, however, and wanted to fill it with an old Hoosier pal. Coming off a 98-loss season, the Reds could place much of the blame on an anemic hitting attack. Who better to whip the 1938 offense into shape than a former batting champion? It seemed like a perfect fit, except for one familiar sticking point — money. Edd also hated the idea of wasting time with a tail-end team, but a decent salary might've made it more palatable. The Reds offered $3,600, which Edd considered a paltry figure that wouldn't even cover his expenses. But McKechnie had an ace in the hole that he didn't even realize; Essie Roush thought her husband needed something to do and encouraged him to take the job.

Things had changed since Edd last wore a Reds uniform, much of it for the better. Attendance increased greatly under Larry MacPhail's reign and he introduced the excitement of night baseball to the major leagues. Best of all, he convinced local radio magnate Powel Crosley to buy the club, a feat of salesmanship that put the franchise on solid financial footing and led to much-needed renovations. Redland Field was quickly renamed in honor of its new owner. MacPhail resigned toward the end of the '36 season and eventually landed in Brooklyn, where he pioneered more night baseball.

The Roush deal went through in early March and Edd reported for Florida duty soon after. He joined fellow coach Hank Gowdy, a former weak-hitting catcher whose expertise tilted toward the pitch and catch department. McKechnie leaned that way, too, so he left most of the hitting tutorials to the old king of swing. But first, he warned Edd to not expect too much from this modern generation of major leaguers. They just weren't as skilled as the players of yesteryear.

Roush soon came to his own harsher conclusion: the Reds couldn't hit, run or throw. Focusing on the first shortcoming, he delivered a dose of tough love to his students: "All bad hitters take the first pitch, wave at the curve and get themselves so far behind there's no way out ... and you all do this. You're all bad hitters and it's no wonder you're a last-place ball club."[2] From that day forward, every player was required to leave the bench swinging. Take three swings, Edd said, and you might hit one.

He also taught them about scientific batting and discouraged the go-for-broke stroke that Babe Ruth popularized. Not that the Reds all became physics experts overnight, but their pre-season improvement was obvious. It carried over to opening day, with the Reds pounding out 14 hits and seven runs at Crosley Field. Unfortunately, the visiting Cubs checked in at 15 and eight, respectively. Some 35,000 fans got their money's worth on that hot, cloudless April day.

Armed with a much-improved offense, the Reds surprised prognosticators by making a legitimate run at the pennant. Catcher Ernie Lombardi led the league in hitting and was named National League MVP. In his first season as starting first baseman, Frank McCormick churned out a league-best 209 hits, batted .327 and drove in 106 runs. After hitting 12 home runs the previous year, outfielder Ival Goodman cranked it up to 30 in '38. With every returnee improving his hitting, the team average increased by 23 points, home runs went up, and strikeouts declined. It can't all be definitively attributed to the new hitting coach, but for the purposes of this book, it's strongly implied.

On the pitching front, Johnny Vander Meer made history that summer. Playing in front of a modest home crowd of about 10,000, the rookie southpaw tossed a no-hitter against the Boston Braves on June 11. That feat put his name on a long list of notables who'd done the same throughout baseball history. When he threw another one four days later, Vander Meer joined an exclusive club of one. Nobody had ever done it back-to-back and nobody has since. The second no-hitter unfolded under a Brooklyn night sky, with the Dodgers staging their first game under artificial lights. Nearly 39,000 fans attended, many of them treating the New Jersey native like a favorite son.

One no-hitter was great, but two made Vander Meer the toast of baseball and a legend in perpetuity. The instant celebrity was besieged by requests for media interviews, and advertisers came knocking with product endorsement offers. He would go on to record a solid season but things never got nearly so exciting again. Vander Meer's final 1938 stats (15–10 record, 3.12 ERA) were almost pedestrian, and over a 13-year career he produced 119 victories, 121 losses. Yet "Vandy" surpasses Edd Roush on most name-recognition scales, all because of one week in June.

Continuing their unlikely pennant quest, the Reds pulled within 1½ games of first on June 28. A six-game losing streak followed, but McKechnie's overachievers stayed in the hunt, launching a late-summer streak that put them in second place, four games behind Pittsburgh on September 5.

This month belonged to the Cubs, however. Trailing the Pirates by seven games on August 31, they went 21–5 over the next 30 days, culminated by 10 straight triumphs and a sweep of the league leaders toward month's end. Chicago moved into first on September 28 and never trailed again. New York edged past Cincinnati for third place, but that 82–68 Reds record looked impressive from a team that was supposed to stink. It also made for the city's first winning mark in 10 years. The future looked bright for McKechnie and Roush.

Edd didn't return in 1939, which is a shame because the Reds took the pennant that year. The national media would've loved *this* story — Cincinnati back in the World Series for the first time since the Black Sox days and Roush there both times. It never happened. Edd helped plant the seeds of success but by harvest time was "gone with the wind," also the title of a new Clark Gable film released that season.

He felt insulted by his next contract offer from the Reds, a $4,000 deal that included a $400 raise. By Roush standards, it was still chicken feed. Before Edd reluctantly signed his stingy 1938 pact, McKechnie supposedly told him he'd get a better future deal if the Reds advanced in the standings and made more gate money. The team improved greatly and attendance shot up by nearly 300,000, so he felt entitled to a far better bump than four C-notes. And that perceived slight cuts deep when the manager is a close friend. Not that McKechnie ran the payroll department, but the Roushes presumed he held enough influence to arrange a fair reward. He certainly arranged a nice enough salary for himself. Edd, on the other hand, was running at a deficit.

"Why, good God almighty, it cost me more money being on the ball club than it did at home. Thunder! Why, I always figured it cost me five or six thousand dollars to be with the club."[3]

Roush retired for the second and final time, though a rumor had him returning to Ohio to manage the Dayton Ducks. That didn't happen, either, and while he lived a simple life at home, the world became dangerously complicated in 1939. When Adolf Hitler ignored an ultimatum to stop his invasion of weakly Poland, France and England declared war on Germany in September. Fortunately, Japan and the United States quickly declared neutrality, so there were at least two global powers determined to share the planet in peace.

As the Depression decade wound toward a close, a baseball legend's life did the same. Feeling the early effects of a disease that would eventually kill him, Lou Gehrig ended a streak of 2,130 consecutive games when he benched himself on May 2, 1939. Doctors later diagnosed Lou with amyotrophic lateral sclerosis, a fatal neuromuscular disorder. More than 60,000 people packed into Yankee Stadium for "Lou Gehrig Day" on July 4 and the guest of honor calmly delivered the most moving farewell address in sports history.

A humble son of German immigrants, Gehrig had lived the American dream and remained grateful for it, even with the Grim Reaper in tow. Though lacking a gift for gab, he stepped up to the microphone and bravely proclaimed himself "the luckiest man on the face of the earth." He died a couple years later, 17 days shy of his 38th birthday. Back in Oakland City, Edd must've felt he made the right choice when he didn't sever Lou's leg during that aforementioned pre-season game. Blocking first base shouldn't be an amputation offense, especially for a good guy like Gehrig.

Bushwhacked by Japanese warplanes at Pearl Harbor, the United States finally became a full-fledged combatant at the end of 1941. Now 48 years old, the Roush twins needn't have worried about getting invitations to *this* party. Their generation put the Kaiser in his place, now the next one bore responsibility for the Asian emperor and Austrian paperhanger. Of course, nobody was completely insulated — not with neighbors' sons risking their lives in distant lands or civilian rationing on the home front. Some might've even felt a twinge of regret about the horrific firebombing of German cities and nuclear destruction in Japan. But as Edd Roush used to say about an entirely different topic, "You needed to play that way or they'd run you out of it, one or the other. Now which is the best, you run them or they run you?"

The torch of local celebrity soon passed to a resident of nearby Petersburg, where Gil Hodges seemed to have a bright baseball future. In 1947, the former Oakland City College student-athlete joined the Brooklyn Dodgers. He became a beloved borough figure, spending 11 seasons there before the team made its heart-wrenching coastal shift to Los Angeles. Anchoring first base, Hodges played alongside some of the biggest names in baseball and became one himself. Jackie Robinson, Duke Snider, Roy Campanella, Pee Wee Reese, Don Newcombe, Carl Furillo, Preacher Roe, Johnny Podres ... and a certain burly Hoosier with huge hands.

During his 17-year career, Hodges strung together seven consecutive 100-RBI seasons and played in seven World Series. On the flip side, he was also notorious for falling into horrible, incurable slumps. After a famous 0-for-21 flameout in the 1952 Series, his woes carried over into the following spring training. He'd soon get some friendly advice from a familiar Florida snowbird, Edd Roush. The two met briefly during a spring training game in Bradenton, where Edd offered free swing analysis. Said Hodges, "He told me to stand closer to the plate and to keep my bat cocked as I follow the outside pitch, the better to take or swing at the last second."[4] His batting average leaped 48 points in 1953 and he eclipsed the .300 mark for the first time.

Ten years later, Hodges hung up his spikes and became manager of the Washington Senators. After five unsuccessful campaigns in that baseball graveyard, the clouds parted and a ray of destiny shone down on him — he was named manager of the New York Mets. Taking over a young franchise known for futility and 100-loss seasons, he quickly turned things around. In his second year at the helm, the 1969 Miracle Mets stunned baseball by winning the N.L. pennant, then stunned it again by dominating Baltimore in the World Series. Leading a light-hitting underdog to the Promised Land, Gil Hodges became a New York icon for the second time, once as player and now as fearless leader.

The Roush brothers got into big trouble during the summer of 1949. While coaching an Oakland City Junior Legion team, they became embroiled in an on-field brouhaha that led to their arrests for assault on a minor. It happened at a local diamond and the opponent was county rival Princeton.

The Roush account: Edd did not strike the boy in question, a 16-year-old catcher named J.D. Pegram. The trouble started when Princeton's manager became confrontational about Oakland City's physical brand of play. What's more, the boy attacked Edd, kicking his leg with a spiked shoe. A punch seemed forthcoming and Fred entered the fray to prevent said youth from landing the anticipated blow. One Princeton newspaper report had Edd striking young Pegram and Fred rushing in to kick the kid as he sat. In that corner of the county, folks remembered the Roushes as villains of the affair.

What really happened? An eyewitness version comes from Bill Marshall, a local attorney and town historian who played center field for Oakland City that day. He says it all started after a violent collision at the plate, with Pegram getting bowled over by a base runner who'd tried to stretch a triple into a home run. When the catcher's father came on the field and accused Edd of teaching dirty tactics, a physical confrontation ensued. Marshall remembers the adult combatants engaging in a series of slashing leg kicks.

"Edd was backing him up.... J.D. came up (from) behind and when he reached out for Edd, Fred spun him around and knocked him like that. I mean Fred cold-cocked him! Fred said, 'A 16-year-old kid is big enough to hurt somebody and I'm not going to let anybody hit Edd.' And, of course, when he knocked him down, that's when the Princeton fans all came out of that third base bleachers. And then Fred picked up that ball bat. That stopped the fight. He was urging, 'Come on, you son of a bitches!' Oh, he was a mad looking guy!"

The game was called off, authorities ordered the grounds cleared, and everybody left peacefully. Everybody except the Roush brothers and town marshal Paul Gross, the latter planning to apprehend the former. While the twins collected equipment and loaded it into a truck, Gross approached and declared, "Edd, Fred, I'm gonna have to put you under arrest." Edd looked him in the eye and said, "Go to hell." Then he turned away and continued loading. When the Roushes finished, they got into the truck and drove off.

The law caught up with them later, however, and both were arrested. It seems charges were eventually dropped against Edd, but Fred's case went to trial, with testimony from players, coaches and spectators. Found guilty in justice of the peace court, Fred drew a fine of $10 plus court costs. He appealed to circuit court but later entered a guilty plea to a charge of assault and battery upon a minor. Maybe his defense was becoming more trouble — and costly — than it was worth. A new judge imposed the same sentence: $10 plus costs.

Embittered by the entire experience, the twins did not return to coach in 1950 or any other year.

21

The Long Way to Cooperstown

He had gray hair and he looked a lot older than the rest of the base-ball players working out in the St. Louis Cardinals camp here. And yet, he could still pick them up — grounders and liners from the bats of young Cardinal players. He wore an old Cincinnati Reds uniform and a glove that had seen plenty of wear. A big wad of tobacco bulged his mouth and colored his teeth, which had many gold inlays. Most of the Cardinal players did not know who he was.—1947 spring training story from St. Petersburg[1]

Equipped with a puffy little first baseman's mitt that barely covers his right hand and looks like something Cap Anson might have earned by saving box-tops, he takes his place at shallow shortstop as the Braves take their batting practice. House-wreckers like Hank Aaron and Ed Mathews send whistling shots through the infield, and Edd Roush, sexagenarian, scoops them up deftly in his fat little glove.—1960 Bradenton report by Jack Mann, Newsday.[2]

For someone so critical of modern baseball, Edd sure spent a lot of time around the Grapefruit League. But this made him no more hypocritical than a swallow returning to San Juan Capistrano, or a salmon to its spawning grounds. Ball players gravitate to ballparks. Bopping around team camps over the years, Roush wasn't a typical spring training spectator. He became an official, in-uniform greeter for reporting players and involved himself on the practice field, too. Shagging balls wasn't beneath this legend, who did it effortlessly with an old-fashioned, undersized glove. How could young players *not* benefit from witnessing the lasting effects of fundamentals well learned? Edd also offered occasional batting tips to anyone willing to listen, and the Milwaukee Braves thought enough of his insights to make him a volunteer spring coach during the 1950s.

In '52 the Roushes decided to retire their rolling home and put roots into Florida soil. They settled south of Tampa, building a country house on the outskirts of Bradenton, a town that reminded them of Oakland City. When Edd said he built something, he wasn't speaking figuratively, like an architect. Assisted by one helper, the Roush brothers created most of that two-bedroom home with their own hands. Descendants would remember it fondly, along with the property's bountiful orange trees. Yet even with permanent property in the Sunshine State, Edd and Essie remained part-time residents, always returning to their Hoosier home for the warm months.

As a long-time spring training site of major league teams, Bradenton had baseball in its blood and retired players in its neighborhoods. Bill McKechnie lived there and his familiar, friendly face proved a major factor in drawing Edd to the area. Home to the Boston Braves for eight years, Bradenton retained its position when the franchise shifted to Milwaukee in 1953. A year later, Edd was doing his typical spring thing when a slender black rookie caught his eye. He could tell right away that this kid had something special. Propelled by wicked wrist rotation, baseballs just flew off the guy's stick during batting practice. "There's a hitter!" Edd thought to himself.

After practice, he approached manager Charlie Grimm — the same man he'd viciously spiked in 1931, but those wounds, figurative and literal, had long since healed. When Grimm said the youngster was scheduled for demotion to the minors, Edd advised him to take a second look. Even at the tender age of 20, this prospect seemed ready for the majors.

The starlet in question was Hank Aaron, a man destined to knock Babe Ruth off history's home run pedestal. Grimm put him in the lineup for a March 6 game and he singled in both plate appearances. A few days later he hammered a 425-foot homer, his first in a major league uniform. Edd's endorsement was only the first break for young Aaron; the second occurred in an ankle belonging to Bobby Thomson. That spring training injury created an outfield opening that Aaron grabbed and never let go. Twenty-three years later he retired with 755 home runs.

The 1950s marked Edd's second decade of Hall of Fame rejection by the Baseball Writers Association of America (BBWAA). He received two votes during the very first balloting in 1936, leaving him 168 short of induction, but that came at a unique time when baseball was thick with kings and short on thrones. The electorate consisted of a couple hundred experienced baseball writers, each allowed to select as many as 10 players or none at all. To win, a candidate had to receive votes on 75 percent of the ballots and few legends ever achieved it on their first try. Roush found himself trapped behind a backlog of historic talent.

Yet somewhere along the line, less accomplished men began passing him from behind. Ross Youngs? Nice career, but it didn't compare with Edd's. Smokey Joe Wood? Same story. Dizzy Dean? An unforgettable character who pitched spectacular ball for three short years, but longevity made Roush a far better candidate.

In 1954, the baseball writers elected Rabbit Maranville and his .258 career batting average. Though owning a mark 65 points higher, Edd placed 12th out of fifty-plus candidates. He would eventually move toward the top of those lists, but still couldn't reach the mandatory 75 percent mark.

Ty Cobb spoke out against the perceived injustice, putting Roush on a short list of deserving graybeards that also included Eppa Rixey, Sam Rice, and Joe Sewell. "I say put these great stars of the past, who were shamefully omitted for lo these many years, on the Hall of Fame rolls while they are still living, even if it means relaxing your admission rule," Cobb said while watching a spring game in Phoenix. "They can be tightened up again after these injustices have been rectified."[3]

A new decade arrived with Edd Roush at number one among all candidates. Sitting atop the 1960 list, he looked down on some of those names that once looked down on him. Yet his 146 votes fell way short of the 202 required for election. "I've been runner-up four or five times," he grumbled. "Now, I'll probably never get in. I'll be past the 30-year limit when the writers vote next (in 1962) and that means I'll be shifted to the old-timers group. That practically leaves me without a chance."

In truth, Roush's chances improved tenfold when his case went before the "old-timers group." Better known as the Veterans Committee, this small assemblage focused on players from the distant past who'd been retired for at least three decades. Its knowledgeable presence counteracted the age discrimination of BBWAA voters, who knew little about their elders. On January 28, 1962, Edd J. Roush received unanimous approval to join the immortals at baseball's Hall of Fame. Bill McKechnie made it, too, reuniting buddies in yet another stop on their pastime path. The Bradenton City Council soon renamed fields after each man.

Not everybody saw it as a happy ending. Usurped by younger candidates during previous elections, Roush reversed roles and became the usurper in 1962. He cut to the front of a line that consisted mainly of long-dead ancients, waiting to pass from purgatory to baseball heaven. McKechnie's ascension seemed particularly curious, as he'd been a non-factor during previous pollings.

Also named to the class of '62 were two beyond-reproach selections made by the Baseball Writers Association. Their names — Bob Feller and Jackie Robinson. All four would share the spotlight during a July induction ceremony, but long before that day, Edd had it all to himself in Indiana. Bursting with pride over its decorated native son, Oakland City hosted a summer celebration called "Edd Roush Days." One day wasn't enough for his rare achievement, so officials set aside two.

On Saturday, June 16, the festivities kicked off with a parade led by an

Oakland City honored its hometown hero with an "Edd Roush Days" celebration after he was elected to the Hall of Fame. Edd and Essie traveled by convertible in a parade (Roush Family Collection).

American Legion color guard, plus high school bands from Oakland City, Winslow and, ironically, Mount Olympus. Behind them were floats, fire trucks, saddle horses, motorcycles and antique cars. The local high school's athletics field was dedicated with a new name — Roush Field — and Edd threw out the first pitch before a Junior Legion game. Day one concluded with a barn dance.

Sunday's schedule proved less hectic and more cerebral. They held a big chicken fry at the local park, then followed it with a series of tributes by various guest speakers. Edd heard praise from the Oakland City College president, superintendent of public schools and mayors of both Princeton and Petersburg. Representing the baseball world was Rube Bressler, a Reds teammate during the glory years. It would be hard to top that hometown homage, but baseball gave it a try the following month at the charming village of Cooperstown, New York.

Ya had to make a speech in Cooperstown there and I told 'em, "This beats anything I ever saw. You got a Hall of Fame here for what? Ya can't get in it. Nobody can get in it. Ya gotta be out 30 years before the (Veterans) committee gets ya. You play till you're 40, and 40 and 30 is 70. You're 70 years old before you're put in here by the committee. Most the fellas I played with are dead." So the next year, they changed it to 20 years, see.

> Now then, they try to put everybody in there. The writers and everything else goes in there now. Some of them never even played baseball. Umpires and so on. Why thunder![4]

On the morning of July 23, more than 4,000 people watched with reverence as baseball's Hall of Fame inducted four new members into its pantheon. For the record, this is the text of Roush's acceptance speech:

> Ladies and gentlemen, I'm glad to have been put in baseball's Hall of Fame. And I want to thank the committee that voted me in this year. This is quite a place. I spent most the day yesterday looking things over in the Hall here. It's quite a place but I'm glad I'm in along with the rest of the fellows and I want to say thank you to all of you.

What about that strong critique of the whole selection process? Was it just a figment of an old man's imagination? No, octogenarian Edd remembered his sermon perfectly well but confused the pulpit. His message reached the masses through newspaper interviews. Contacted by United Press International on the day of his election, he sounded almost disinterested: "It's all right but sometimes these things come too late. It takes them too long to vote on these players. Waiting 30 years after a man becomes inactive to vote him in is too long. By that time a lot of men are not around any more."

On induction day, Edd was placidly cordial. He'd already made his point. Sitting in attendance was an eclectic array of baseball folk, including the widows of John McGraw, Christy Mathewson and Eddie Collins. Honus Wagner's daughters were there, too, along with Frankie Frisch, Joe Cronin, managers, general managers, team presidents and assorted league officials.

After Roush's brief opening act, the star of the show spoke next. Fifteen years removed from breaking baseball's color barrier, Jackie Robinson became unofficial valedictorian for the class of 1962. He gushed over the induction honor, paid tribute to his father figure, Branch Rickey, and thanked the people across America who helped him through tough times. Elated about getting elected in his first year of eligibility, Robinson said he never expected it all to come so quickly.

Edd was overshadowed again, and understandably so. How could the media *not* swoon over the poster child for civil rights and social evolution? Hitting a baseball was difficult enough without the hopes of an entire race tied to the outcome, and the game provided ample pressure without a minefield of racial epithets. One player endured it all. Jackie Robinson was never just a baseball player during his career, and he still transcended the sport in '62.

McKechnie delivered the shortest speech of the day: "Somebody's got this batting order in shape. I never was a third hitter. Mr. Commissioner,

The class of '62 posed for pictures after Hall of Fame induction ceremonies in Cooperstown. From left, Roush, Jackie Robinson, Bob Feller and Bill McKechnie (National Baseball Hall of Fame Library, Cooperstown, New York).

ladies and gentlemen, anything that I have contributed to baseball I have been repaid today seven times seven. Thank you very much."

He never would've made the Hall on his playing record but reached the stars as a manager, piloting three different teams to pennants and winning two World Series. Spending a quarter-century in the managing business, McKechnie was a venerated veteran, better known by the nickname "Deacon," and his calm, fatherly approach earned a generation of respect bordering on adoration.

Nobody could ever mistake that demeanor for weakness, however. Twelve days before the induction ceremony, the 75-year-old confronted two hooded robbers at his Bradenton home and attacked one with a lamp. After deflecting and absorbing several return blows from an iron pipe, McKechnie ran to his bedroom to retrieve a shotgun. When he returned to the living room, the assailants had fled.

Bob Feller talked last and longest, happily rambling from one tangent to another. Though youngest of the bunch, he'd lived a fascinating life. Raised on an Iowa farm, he became a teenage wunderkind and the hardest thrower since Walter Johnson. Finishing his pitching career with 266 triumphs, Feller would've shattered the 300 mark if he hadn't spent four prime years in the navy during World War II.

After the final speech concluded, photographers closed in for a posed group shot of the inductees, with Roush and McKechnie as bow-tied bookends. The younger inductees sported long ties, Robinson standing next to Edd, Feller alongside Deacon Bill.

Life returned to normal for Edd, and within a couple weeks he presided over a town board meeting at city hall. They spent most of their time discussing the finer points of securing a new, 150,000-gallon water tower, but also touched on topics such as engineering specifications, finance bonds, and advertising bids for eight-inch pipe. The headlines didn't grab attention like a Cooperstown weekend, but Oakland City cared about it and so did its Hall of Famer.

Besides, *everything* ranked as trivial compared to what was brewing off the coast of southern Florida. Not terribly far from those spring training diamonds, two superpowers would soon rattle doomsday sabers during October's Cuban Missile Crisis. The Soviet Union had secretly sent medium-range missiles to its island ally, spy planes spotted the launch sites, and President John F. Kennedy insisted on their removal. His ultimatum fell on deaf ears.

War seemed a distinct possibility, and in 1962 that meant something entirely different from all previous combat. Hiroshima and Nagasaki got a taste of it in 1945 at the birth of the atomic age, and now the fission arsenal was so large that better bombs could descend like raindrops. Both sides took aim but the Soviets eventually backed down and global catastrophe was averted. Had things gone bad, Edd's adopted state would've sat near ground zero.

In a year that saw Roush honored in multiple states, an unknown author named Lawrence Ritter began criss-crossing the country in search of old-time ballplayers. Many were dying off in obscurity and taking their memories to the grave. It was a race against time, though in Edd's case, he needn't have hurried. Four years and 75,000 miles later, *The Glory of Their Times* hit bookstores with mesmerizing narratives from the familiar and not so familiar. Included among the cross section of 22 ancients were Paul Waner, Heinie Groh, Rube Marquard, Sam Crawford and Fred Snodgrass. There was a section on Roush, who described the 1919 World Series, his days with the Oakland City Walk-Overs, the climb toward pro ball, Federal League interlude, Reds glory years, and his relationship with John McGraw. These were the same stories he would tell for another two decades.

Toting his omnipresent tape recorder, Ritter arrived on Edd's Florida doorstep in 1964 and their lengthy, cordially comfortable interview produced several pages of book copy. Much of those conversations did not make it into print, however, and one particular omission stands out as insightful self-analysis on Roush's stoic nature:

> I was never much on excitement, never got excited much about anything. Get more or less a little thrill if you get a base hit, you know. Feel good, happy. But a lot of people jump up and down and holler and whoop. Why, I could go to a basketball game, baseball game or any other kind of game and I never see any reason to jump up whooping like that. Well, people are just that way. Maybe something's wrong with me.

The audiotapes also illuminate Mrs. Roush, with Essie coming across as an engaging host, confident conversationalist and assertively classy lady. She chimes in often — sometimes offering food or drink to her guest, other times commenting on topics of baseball, family or friends. Deep into the session, as Edd explained how Burleigh Grimes tipped off his pitches, Essie interrupted, "Come on and have a martini with me." She wasn't talking to her husband, the dedicated beer man. It was Ritter who she saw as a potential partner for her refined palate, and he accommodated her. Essie worried she hadn't added enough gin but her guest proclaimed it perfect. Amidst the sips, Edd continued the dissection of Grimes.

His wife jumped back in when the conversation shifted to that brief and frustrating coaching stint. Nearly three decades after the fact, they still seemed to resent the minimum-wage treatment. Though general manager Warren Giles controlled Reds finances back then, both Roushes believed that Manager McKechnie could've coerced a better distribution of the wealth in 1938 or at least a fair contract offer the following year.

EDD: "The trouble of it was McKechnie had a $25,000 contract, (or) so they told me...."

ESSIE: "And he was supposed to be a friend!"

EDD: "Plus incentives, $5,000 for a first division finish and $5,000 if they drew over a certain number of attendance. In other words, he got $35,000, (coach Hank) Gowdy and I got $3,600."

RITTER: "That's bad."

ESSIE: "Well it was disgusting, that was all. Edd only went back because he liked Bill and he wanted to (coach) for him there. I thought that was the raw treatment."

RITTER: "But you're still friends."

ESSIE: "Oh well, what are you gonna do about it? Sure, we're friends. Bill comes over here and eats with us and we go over there and we're together."

RITTER: "Ever ask him why?"

ESSIE: "No, I've never asked him."

EDD: "No, ain't no use. What the heck?"

While Ritter came to be considered a friend, the local sports editor became that and more. Kent Chetlain formed a bond with Edd that continued long after he left the newspaper business and ended at the grave. A former sports editor of the *Sanford Herald* and *Orlando Evening Star,* he departed journalism briefly when Tropicana offered him more money to install and service orange juice vending machines. Next came a transfer to the company's home office in Bradenton, where he served as a truck dispatcher. Returning to the newspaper business in 1957, Chetlain latched on as a reporter with the *Bradenton Herald.* He became head of the sports department in '62, organizing election coverage for the Roush-McKechnie ticket to Cooperstown.

Away from the office, Kent would discover Edd also deserved induction into the alcohol ingestion hall of fame. The old guy could drink a sailor under the table. "How he didn't get cirrhosis of the liver, I'll never know," Chetlain said. "That guy drank beer like people drink water. I'd go over to his house and we'd start in and we'd sip a little and sip a little and first thing you know, we'd gone through a six-pack and he'd keep going. I've never seen anybody like him. Pabst Blue Ribbon — he had the guys deliver it by the case."[5] Yet Edd still frequented taverns, where he could shoot the breeze while imbibing.

Over the years, Chetlain absorbed a treasure trove of Roush history and anecdotes. Some made it into print, some didn't. He wrote the story about Edd singling out a young Hank Aaron, but never publicized an uncomfortable exchange regarding family lineage. "I was driving to McKechnie Field and I asked Edd, 'Are you part Indian?' He didn't say a word. Essie said, 'Where did you hear that?'... Back in those days, people were just very conscious about that. It was considered a sin. Of course, I don't think Edd really particularly cared one way or the other. But he didn't say anything. Total silence, and I knew I said the wrong thing."

The mute one supposedly had Indian ancestry on his mother's side, perhaps a grandmother or great-grandmother. He certainly sported his share of deep, dark tans.

It's just one of many stories from Chetlain's mental archive, some he witnessed first hand and others supplied by the legend. There was the time in 1968 when he arrived at a local television station with Roush and Joe DiMaggio in tow. They were there to promote the Bradenton Hall of Fame Banquet, an annual gathering of old-timer inductees that Edd helped organize. DiMaggio, of course, was the larger celebrity, but the sports anchor could barely get a word out of him. Silver-tongued Roush saved the day, regaling viewers with tales of the 1919 World Series.

Frequently attending games together at McKechnie Field, Edd and Chetlain seemed inseparable during spring. But only one of them paid much attention to what transpired on the diamond. With its shrunken strike zone and casual pace, 1960s baseball offended the sensibilities of an inflexible purist. Edd spent most of his time in a windowless press room, drinking free beer and holding court with reporters or whoever else passed through. Sometimes he'd run across other golden age alums, such as Dutch Ruether, Heinie Manush, Paul Waner and Bill Terry. Ballparks attract ballplayers.

Though clearly the lesser of the two facilities, Roush Field still saw its share of sporadic spring action. Located alongside Interstate 41, it was the former training site of the Louisville Colonels, a Triple-A team from Kentucky. Some big league clubs later made use of it, too, though on a limited basis. The bare-bones Roush ballpark eventually fell into disrepair and was replaced by public housing, but not before serving as a youth baseball launching pad for a generation of Bradenton children.

Chetlain left the *Herald* in January of 1969, returned as sports editor at the end of 1972, and exited for good a couple years later. He entered local politics, serving three terms as Manatee County commissioner, and continued a profitable side interest in real estate. But even though they took the boy out of the press box, nobody could take the press box out of the boy. Chetlain remained a baseball fanatic and Roush confidant. One day, he would pass along the stories told to him.

—Jim Thorpe? You couldn't keep him around for long because he'd get into drunken brawls and injure teammates.

—One day at the Polo Grounds, John McGraw ordered Edd to swing at a first pitch. Though it sailed over his head, he dutifully followed directions and improvised a lumberjack stroke. Swinging his bat like an axe, he knocked the ball over the right field fence. Upon Roush's return to the dugout, McGraw remarked, "That was the damnedest home run I ever saw. Why did you swing at that pitch?" To which the plain-spoken Hoosier replied, "Well, you told me to swing at the first pitch and I did."

—Informed that a ballpark attendant refused to let Essie drive into the players parking lot, Edd left the diamond with bat in hand and menacingly ordered the man to open his gate. He did so quickly. The game came to a halt during all this because Roush was due to hit next.

Chetlain could go on and on.

22

Looks Good for His Age

Why, good God! They got the colored fellas in baseball in the National and American League and everything's one-handed, one-handed, one-handed. Now they're all one-handed ballplayers. We (caught) with two hands. That (one-armed) ballplayer St. Louis used to have would be right in style now.[1]

For the better part of eight decades Edd Roush dodged every inside pitch from a headhunting hurler named Father Time and kept hustling. By the end of the 1960s, his healthy streak reached 76 years, seven months. Not everybody was so lucky during a nerve-wracking decade that saw superpower staredowns in Berlin and Cuba, assaults on civil rights demonstrators, death in Vietnam and high-profile assassinations of John F. Kennedy, Martin Luther King, Malcolm X, and Robert Kennedy. Across the pond, Winston Churchill died of natural causes at the ripe old age of 90.

But there was epic achievement, too — namely the rapid development of an American space program that culminated in 1969 with Neil Armstrong and Buzz Aldrin taking a stroll on the moon. A few weeks later, counterculture took center stage when a half-million hippies descended on upstate New York for the three-day Woodstock Music and Art Fair. An all-star roster of rock musicians made this happening go down in history under one word: Woodstock.

In May of that same year Edd Roush was voted the greatest player in Reds history. Crowned by an electorate of sportswriters and broadcasters, he topped a historical all-star team that included Ted Kluszewski, Heinie Groh, Ernie Lombardi, Eppa Rixey and a still-active player named Pete Rose. Why make an all-timers list at this particular moment in time? Baseball was celebrating its 100th year as a professional sport, and it all started in 1869 in Cincinnati.

Fun as it was to muse over the past, Edd and Essie stayed rooted in the present. They became great-grandparents when Susan Allen Dellinger gave birth to a son in December of 1967. Unlike the Roush lineage that preceded him, little Jade Dellinger would be all Gator, no Hoosier. Growing up around Tampa, he spent lots of time with Edd, better known as "Daddaw." Jade seemed to inherit some of those athlete's genes, making all-state in high school soccer and all-conference for football. He dabbled with the little white ball, too, but eventually abandoned that sport.

"To be in pee-wee baseball leagues and (on) the first day of the season your great-grandfather, a National Baseball Hall of Famer, arrives to throw the first pitch, it sort of overshadows anything you

An elderly Edd gets a kiss on the cheek from his wife, Essie (courtesy of the Willard Library Archives).

could do in knocking the ball off the tee," Jade said. "So I sort of made a real conscious decision at a very early stage that baseball would not be my sport."[2]

Athletics were important to Dellinger but not all-important. He developed a strong interest in art and became an independent curator. Organizing exhibitions for the University of South Florida's contemporary art museum, his career path might've seemed a polar opposite from Edd's former profession, but the two were actually interrelated. Dellinger's first experience with museums came at the Baseball Hall of Fame.

"My grandmother, Mary Roush Allen, made a real point of taking me by the hand as a child and saying this was really an important place and that it was important to us, the family, because of Daddaw's relationship (to baseball). Seeing your great-grandfather's dirty used shoes — baseball spikes in this case — or hat that he wore really had a kind of profound effect on how I thought about museums.... I think it's largely because of him that I got involved in museums and also involved in collecting."[3]

Dellinger owns strong memories of his great-grandmother, too. He remembers Essie as someone who liked to read and was interested in culture, learning, and personal growth. Forbidding everybody from smoking in the house, she was very much about setting rules. "I think in a weird way, she wore the pants in the family," he said. "I think it was a lot about her expectations of Edd, that he had the success he did and he made the money he did.... He was always in a way living up to her expectations of him. And she was very interested in (life) experiences."[4]

Dellinger used to tag along with Daddaw when old players gathered in Cooperstown and Florida. Begun in 1964, Bradenton's Hall of Fame Day became quite a show and Edd often served as event chairman or co-chair. Still dripping with charisma, scores of legendary retirees would arrive for their banquet, dressed nattily in suits and ties. Earlier in the day, they'd get an official introduction at a spring training contest.

Old-timers games were social affairs, too. Roaming center field until his early 70s, Roush was a regular at the annual March of Dimes charity contest in nearby St. Petersburg. After Edd singled off a particularly famous pitcher as a 75-year-old, Essie Roush was heard to shout, "I'll bet that's the first hit Bob Feller ever gave up to a great-grandfather."

A huge honor awaited in 1970, or so it seemed. Edd was chosen to throw out the first pitch for the All-Star Game at Cincinnati's brand-new River-front Stadium, before some big-shot politician swept into town and took the job. It was the 37th president of the United States — Richard Milhous Nixon. The day wasn't a total loss for Roush, however. He got an audience with the commander in chief and they exchanged autographed baseballs. Edd also received a nice on-air mention by famed broadcaster Curt Gowdy: "Edd Roush and wife Essie Mae of Oakland City, Indiana, have been married 56 years, which is something in this day and age."[5]

Among other things, that particular day included a buxom kissing bandit named Morganna, who'd become famous for running onto playing fields and smooching athletes. She tried it again in the top of the first, jiggling her 44-23-37 figure toward testosterone. But a security officer tackled her first and she didn't seem at all interested in kissing *him*. Escorted off the premises by police, Miss Morganna Roberts must've made her strip club proud.

History did not record whether Roush studied the sordid scene, but it's probably safe to assume he limited all longing glances to the missus. Though she'd never require handcuffs, Essie could be fun, too. An Oakland City tavern owner took notice when she made a rare appearance at his establishment, joined her husband and ordered a double shot of whiskey with a beer chaser. Don't mistake classy for dull.

In 1972 Edd made a ceremonial plate appearance before the April 18 home opener of the Evansville Triplets — a Triple-A franchise and farm club for the Milwaukee Brewers. On the mound was Mayor Russell Lloyd, poised to throw the more traditional first pitch, but who says there can't be a first swing, too? Wearing a suit, tie and dress shoes, the 79-year-old stepped to the plate and coiled into that old faithful batting stance. Lloyd's throw came in tight, with the batter gracefully avoiding the brushback.

Declaring an executive do-over, the mayor tried again and still couldn't get it near the plate. Edd waited for something to rip but the wildness continued and he never got a chance, which was just as well. "I'm glad he didn't get any over," he said. "If I would have hit the thing I might have hurt somebody."[6]

On July 1, Edd played a couple innings in an old-timers game, held in conjunction with the Fourth of July Festival in little Ferdinand, Indiana. Five days later, he spent part of his afternoon doing yard work at his house. Essie told her beloved to take it easy but he dismissed the notion, saying he needed action to keep in shape. Edd suffered a stroke the following morning. Though listed in serious condition, the patient had shown signs of improvement by July 10. "He was able to walk a little bit today and able to shave himself with an electric razor," Essie told the *Evansville Courier*. "He seemed much better today."[7]

Indeed, the old man still had many good years ahead of him. He would continue telling his story to new generations of yesteryear fans, autograph hunters and budding baseball historians. Some might get a look at his trophy room, with a collection of career mementos displayed in an antique glass-front cabinet. When newspaper or magazine writers came calling, it usually resulted in a huge feature spread, full of hard-edged quotes and devoid of powder puff clichés. Uninhibited to the end, the man remained a great interview.

In time, Edd became the gatekeeper of baseball antiquity, the guru atop Mount Cooperstown. At first a booming tenor in a white-haired chorus, his voice became one of few, and then finally the lone cry from the dark. He simply outlived everybody else. That superior heart kept pumping, the brain stayed sharp and his tongue continued lashing. To one and all, Edd proclaimed that modern players couldn't hold a candle to the men of his day. Accurate or exaggerated, those types of inflexible edicts were as old as baseball itself.

Ty Cobb said his generation's standouts were better than overhyped legends like Joe DiMaggio, Stan Musial, Mickey Mantle, Ted Williams and Willie Mays. Expressing a similarly dismissive opinion about Cobb and crew was player-turned-evangelist Billy Sunday. They had nothing on his 1880s contemporaries, such as Ed Delahanty, Sam Thompson, Cap Anson or Mike "King" Kelly. Anson took it a step further, declaring Cobb and Honus Wagner would've had a hard time cracking the lineup on his old pennant-winning team in Chicago. Follow the chain back far enough and there's undoubtedly some silver-maned caveman, grunting nostalgic, "Cro-Magnon swing club like girl compare to Neanderthal."

Edd moved up the seniority ladder as his HOF peers died off during the 1970s. Ray Schalk, Zack Wheat, Max Carey, Sam Rice, Red Faber, Harry Hooper, Rube Marquard, Casey Stengel ... all his elders and all gone. Younger contemporaries expired, too.

Inside baseball and out, times were changing. Kicking off the decade, Ohio National Guardsmen killed four students during a war protest at Kent State University. More Americans walked on the moon, NASA sent unmanned craft toward other planets and President Nixon resigned under fire from the Watergate break-in scandal. The Roushes lived through it all. Then Edd experienced the worst kind of change in 1978 when Essie passed away at the age of 86. Life went on for the man who'd loved her and, a couple of months later, he smiled when a fresh-faced future author dropped by unannounced for a chat about the past 85 seasons.

Long after his 12-year reign as Oakland City mayor came to an end, Bob Robertson remembered the day he got blindsided by a concerned constituent. Angry about excess water in the city sewer system, Edd leaped in with spikes flying—figuratively speaking. "He cussed me up and down," Robertson reflected. But the tempest passed and they were soon on cordial terms again. "He was a cantankerous booger when he wanted to be but then he was O.K. the next day. He said it the way it was."[8]

When out-of-towners arrived for an audience, the mayor sometimes guided them to Edd's house himself or asked police officers to handle it. Though not exactly a household name outside his hometown, "Roush" resonated with a sizeable sect of the baseball world. He was a hidden treasure and local source of pride. Oakland City scheduled another Edd Roush Day in 1982; this one fell on his 89th birthday and included a spot of honor for his brother. The town newspaper even ran a feature story about Fred, shining a spotlight on the less talkative twin. Readers learned of his own baseball career, which began with a 1916 Kitty League stint in Dawson Springs, Kentucky. Next he traveled to Michigan to play minor league ball in Saginaw, and then Grand Rapids.

Fred would eventually hang up his spikes and go to work in the coal mines. After quitting subterranean labor, he began traveling to Bradenton for winters and found menial spring training employment at McKechnie Field. (One writer called him "Milwaukee's Man Friday.") Fred built a house at Oakland City in 1962 and, 20 years later, an *Oakland City Journal* reporter arrived on that doorstep for the rare interview. Though he needed a walker to get around, his mind sprinted through time, all the way back to child-hood:

"We ran a dairy farm east of town. We'd peddle milk in town for 20 cents a gallon. Sold it in pints or quarts ... whatever you'd want."

"Kids from town would come over and we'd play ball. All the time. Guess we did it more than anything else."

"Daddy bought us a glove apiece so we'd stop smoking and jumping trains. They were both right-handed gloves, but Edd was a lefty, see? So by gollies, Edd just learned to throw right-handed. Got pretty good at it too."

Much was left unsaid in the brief profile. For instance, neither journalist nor interviewee mentioned a thing about Fred shooting his brother in the face. It happened during a bird hunting trip in the fall of 1921, with Edd taking pellets to the lip, cheek and thumb. Fortunately, the injuries proved minor. As a young man, Fred suffered a lasting leg injury in a farming accident and never could run fast after that. With a healthier body, he might've gone a lot further in baseball.

Fred's draft number came up in World War I and he reported to Louisville for military training. Thirty years later, he served as president of the eighth annual 335th Infantry Company E reunion, held at the "Edd Roush farm." Fred got married in October of 1918, became a father the following year and an ex-husband in due course. Already separated, Eloise Whitman Roush filed for divorce in '21, claiming that Fred abandoned her to pursue a baseball career in Michigan and disregarded family responsibilities upon his return.[9]

Toward the end of the 1940s, he joined his brother to coach Junior Legion youngsters. Though in their mid–50s, the Roushes often participated in practice games between their teenagers and town adults. "Edd usually played first base and I think Fred played third," recalled Bill Marshall, stalwart outfielder for the youngsters. "Fred looked damn good at the plate. Stood up there and he hit the ball hard."

The "other" Roush sometimes sold used major league baseball equipment, brought back from spring training. He didn't charge much. For a young local named Phil Buyher, the signature purchase was a Hank Aaron bat, circa 1956. He used it with pride until a crack formed.

Edd obviously opened a lot of doors to his sibling, most notably a wonderful gig as batting practice catcher for the Cincinnati Reds. Fred also joined the local bank's board of directors, serving alongside his brother. Throw in the investment advice with outright financial gifts and one seems almost like a ward of the other. Did the family's super-achiever inherit all the brains, drive and talent?

"A person doesn't want to sell Fred short," Marshall emphasized. "Fred was plenty smart, and Edd may be right. If it had not been for that injury, maybe Fred could've been just as good as Edd."

Yes, the Hall of Famer greatly respected his brother's baseball ability. If he'd only stuck to catching, Edd lamented, he might've made it to the majors, regardless of slow feet. Ponderous backstops were nothing new but Fred couldn't resist dabbling at other positions, where quickness mattered. In the end, that may be why he rated only an assistant mayor's cap on his 89th birthday while Edd wore the "honorary mayor" hat. Both received keys to the city.

The *Oakland City Journal* published a slew of congratulatory messages from local businesses. Herb's Hide-Away ran one such ad, accompanied by a phrase in quotation marks: "Are You Going to Drink That Beer or Let It Set and Get Hot!" It was an inside joke, easily deciphered. As long as he could walk — and he never couldn't — Edd always wore a path to various drinking establishments. The American Legion became a common destination in two states. He was known to grow more irritable with a snoot-full but advanced age sometimes produced a similar effect during sobriety.

After Stan Covaleski died in 1984, 90-year-old Roush became the oldest living Hall of Famer. And despite his verbal shredding of current baseball, he still inspired reverence from people who loved the game. Fan letters continued to arrive in droves, and Edd continued reading them. His contemporaries hadn't forgotten about him, either; in February of '83, Roush was named National League manager for an old-timers game. More impressively, he also received an invitation to a mid-summer gala in Chicago — site of the 50th annual major league All-Star Game. They held it at Comiskey Park, the same place where Edd made his major league debut 70 years earlier.

In celebration of the game's half-century birthday, officials brought in a slew of former superstars, including most of the cast from the first All-Star Game in 1933. It was a Who's Who of greatness — Ernie Banks, Cool Papa Bell, Joe DiMaggio, Bob Feller, Whitey Ford, Hank Greenberg, Al Kaline, Ralph Kiner, Juan Marichal, Willie Mays, Johnny Mize, Stan Musial, Brooks Robinson, Frank Robinson, Duke Snider, Warren Spahn and more. Roush showed up, too, gazing across the grounds where he'd competed against Cobb, Speaker, Eddie Collins and Home Run Baker. Brief and inauspicious as it was, his White Sox audition marked the beginning of something glorious. He'd also won a World Series in this park, belting two doubles and catching three fly balls in the clinching game.

Edd could've been forgiven if he closed his eyes and retreated to the heady days of youth. During a 1933 old-timers game, he captained a team with an aged veteran who played barehanded at first base. Nobody used gloves in this guy's day and he wasn't about to start now. Brightly attired in a red cap, long blue pants and red socks, he always stood close to the bag during his two-inning stint. By the summer of '83, Roush had become that man, inconceivably ancient and increasingly irrelevant.

Though a knowledgeable minority never forgot the name "Roush," a majority of modern fans never heard of it. Cobb, Ruth, Hornsby, Walter Johnson — those men still resonated with the casual follower but they were dead. Among the living, crowds gushed over heroes like Musial, Mays and DiMaggio, but not the 90-year-old from Oakland City. His elder statesman's status, however, did create some publicity on a national stage, as various newspaper stories singled out the oldest of the old. Slightly younger and also in attendance was 89-year-old Burleigh Grimes, Edd's former teammate and opponent. Six other octogenarians showed up, too.

The younger legends, and a few not so young, took the field for an old-timers game that pitted the National League versus the American. Mays made a couple trademark basket catches in the outfield, aged Lefty Gomez bounced warm-up pitches to the plate, youngish Billy Williams hit a two-run homer off Hoyt Wilhelm and the National League won, 6–5. Before the contest began, Enos Slaughter signed an autograph for Dale Murphy, an all-star outfielder from the Atlanta Braves.

Afterward, many more modern standouts went signature hunting, including three-time N.L. batting champ Bill Madlock of the Pittsburgh Pirates. Halfway to a fourth crown, he reverted to a star-struck kid and dashed from one childhood hero to another. On and off the field, it truly was an afternoon of special memories. One day later, the American League snapped an 11-year losing streak with a 13–3 triumph.

Edd's daughter lived with him in his later years and she fiercely defended her father from incursions, real or exaggerated. There were stories of Mary Allen placing short time limits on conversations or playing "finders-keepers" with baseballs that arrived by mail for autographing. Though Edd's mind remained pretty sharp to the end, she cast a wary eye toward those who might intrude on dad for personal gain.

Autographs became major currency during his old age and it seemed fishy when balls arrived in bulk. "I'm sure it was a dealer who wanted balls to sell," Jade Dellinger said. "...And usually he wouldn't be upset by it. My grandmother would have a fit. She'd be like, 'Keep 'em! If they send them to you, we keep them.' And, of course, he would be much more inclined to sign the first three of them and send them all back."

Allen wasn't some lowbrow bully, flexing muscle in a fit of female machismo. She had a master's degree and used to teach physical education at colleges in Florida, West Virginia and Oakland City. In her 60s, she replaced her mother as the next strong, smart woman in Edd's everyday life. Allen served as his right arm in many ways, yet often kept folks at arm's length.

Nothing changed for the innocent baseball-carrying youngsters who sought out autographs, and he still had final say on who he talked to and for how long. But woe to the wayfarer who rubbed Mrs. Allen the wrong way. A previously mentioned mayor claimed that her abrasiveness derailed a movement to build an Edd Roush monument. He described her with the "B" word and it wasn't "baseball."

Long after Edd's death, Allen still towed the line. Convinced that only family should make any money off her father's name, she refused to be interviewed for this book. Make no mistake about it, the gal was her daddy's daughter. Like the old center fielder at contract time, she would not budge.

23

Last Call

When you think of the Cincinnati Reds, what name comes to mind first? Edd Roush? Johnny Bench? Mine, and I'm not saying that to be boastful. That's the way it is.—Pete Rose, 1988[1]

I should have been dead a long time ago.—Edd Roush, 1980[2]

A century's worth of harsh sunlight registered on his face, with that oft-bronzed skin puffy and wrinkled like cooked pie crust. Muscle and bone that once propelled him to amazing speeds could barely beat gravity, and his arthritis deteriorated to near-crippling levels. Edd Roush's body was quite simply worn out, an inevitable side effect of a spectacularly long and active life. Yet even as he moved into his early 90s, the old man refused to embrace a sedentary lifestyle. When spring training approached, instinct and habit still carried him toward McKechnie Field. Edd loathed the play but couldn't resist the stage.

Heading into the Grapefruit League season in 1987, Edd must've felt like a foreigner on his own soil. With a growing emphasis on situational relief pitchers, baseball continued its evolution away from the game he remembered. Players had changed, too, along with their bank accounts. The average major league salary was about $410,000 in '87, with dozens achieving millionaire status. Edd earned $23,333 at his high-water mark and had to fight management for every penny. Modern players raked in money while agents and union reps did all the heavy lifting.

Roush suffered a heart attack before a March 24 contest between Pittsburgh and St. Louis. Initially refusing medical attention, the 93-year-old eventually allowed his daughter to take him to the hospital. Baseball's oldest knight would hold that unenvied title awhile longer. He was still kicking a year later, healthy enough to leave in a huff after seeing what they'd done to the previously dark, crowded and windowless pressroom. In an off-season renovation, workers removed the infamous Roush couch, painted the wall a cheerful color and installed a couple windows with views of the field. Edd hated it.

On March 21, 1988, Kent Chetlain took Roush to a game between the Pirates and Texas Rangers. They parked and started across the lot, one holding the other for support, when Chetlain suddenly realized that he'd left his scorebook in the car. His enfeebled friend didn't need to be traipsing back and forth across parking lots so he went back on his own, telling Edd to hang onto a parked truck in the meantime. But that withering arthritis made a simple task impossible. Seven weeks away from his 95th birthday, the former athlete extraordinaire couldn't bear to stand motionless. It was too painful. He had two options — keep moving or sit down. "I got to keep going," Edd gasped.

The two men headed in separate directions, with Chetlain backtracking to the car, retrieving his things, and then locking the doors. When he looked up Roush was running, moving as fast as those wispy legs could carry him, which wasn't very fast at all. Approaching the finish line of a nine-and-a-half decade marathon, ancient Edd had no kick at the end. And yet he ran. Behind the bloodshot eyes that witnessed a nation come of age was a mind imprinted by images of swifter former selves. Of the child hurrying alongside horse and wagon when delivering milk in early morning's soft light, the teenager dashing between farm and city while courting his lady love, the man exploding down big league basepaths like a gazelle.

It seemed Edd Roush ran to or through the best times of his life. Now he was running away. In one last bull-headed refusal to succumb, he slow-sprinted from the relentless, grinding pain. All his former comrades had permanently escaped their infirmities, most long ago. Bill McKechnie died in 1965 and Bedford Bill Rariden barely made it past the start of World War II. Edd's father fell from that telephone pole while the first war was winding down, his mother passed away in '51, and he lost Essie 27 years later. Loss and longevity went hand in hand for the Roush twins. Then Fred died at a Princeton hospital on Valentine's Day, leaving Edd as the last of the old guard.

Five weeks later, he ran. Even at a slow pace, it made for dangerous exertion on a brittle heart. Chetlain raced after Edd, overtaking him at the base of the stairs leading to the pressroom. Struggling to catch his breath, it seemed the old-timer had almost stopped inhaling. Chetlain escorted him up the stairs and into a seat, then brought him a beverage. While attempting to take a drink, Roush slowly tilted over and Chetlain grabbed his forehead to keep it from striking a table. He lifted his friend by the armpits, trying to move him to a couch. Edd mumbled something and spit out his false teeth.

An off-duty doctor arrived on the scene and told Chetlain to lay the victim on the floor. The physician could not detect a heartbeat. By that time, emergency medical service technicians were on the scene and a crowd began forming, with some young Texas ballplayers watching from the adjacent clubhouse steps. Using a portable defibrillator, EMTs attached electrical clamps and jolted Edd back to life. His warrior heart beat again, but not for long. It stopped once more, prompting another jolt to get it pumping. Then came another stoppage and another shock. He needed to be in a hospital, so they loaded him into an ambulance, driving across the outfield to a gate exit.

Edd jumped out along the way, donned a pancake glove, then joined his father and brother for a game of catch. The 1919 Reds were there, too, and a few Black Sox even made the cut. Grinning in an ego-free dugout was John McGraw, holding a 48-ounce bat in one hand and a written apology in the other. Edd Roush was dead on arrival at Manatee Memorial and legend has it that he shed his mortal coil while the ambulance passed over center field — a storybook ending for the man who became a legend on major league middle pastures.

Chetlain remembers the chariot traveling a slightly less poetic path: "Yeah, well maybe the ambulance got over to center field, but it was mainly in left field."[3] Still, his final appearance came at a ballpark, with the last out recorded in outfield grass, and that was poetic enough. They went ahead and played their pre-season game that day, with the Rangers taking a 1–0 decision on Ruben Sierra's home run. Occupying the leadoff spot for Pittsburgh was a lean young prospect with two fair seasons behind him and a spectacular future ahead. His name — Barry Bonds.

After visitation in Bradenton, the body was brought home to Oakland City for a March 26 funeral. No Reds representatives attended either gathering, nor did they even send flowers. When Ted Kluszewski died a few days later, team officials flocked to his funeral in the Cincinnati suburbs. About 30 years younger than Roush, he still had lots of living connections to a not-so-distant past. Edd was an antique biplane, barely making a blip on modern Reds radar. Or an overlooked elderly janitor, jingling rusty keys to six cities — Cincinnati included — but still locked out.

Burial took place in a family plot at Montgomery Cemetery, a fitting resting place for the man who served on its board of trustees for 30-some years. Edd became chief caretaker of the grounds and was frequently seen mowing grass there. Shortly after his death, Mary Allen put the Roush estate for sale at auction. It was a collector's dream, featuring the possessions and property of baseball's oldest Hall of Famer. In addition to pastime memorabilia, there were vintage firearms and furniture, hunting knives, grandmother Roush's cane-bottom chair, mother Roush's butter molds, steel traps, a crosscut saw, straight razors, ties, cancelled checks ... and that was just for starters. A nearly 95-year-old accumulates a few things over the century.

In the year 2000 Oakland City hosted yet another Edd Roush Day—this one posthumous. Held at the school now called Oakland City *University*, the event featured photo, audio and memorabilia displays, plus appearances by Roush descendants, all out-of-towners who arrived to pay homage to "Daddaw." Traveling north from Florida, his daughter was now a feisty octogenarian. She told a couple stories from the old days, proclaimed pride in her native hometown and played matchmaker while introducing three strapping grandsons. "And girls, they're all single," she said.

Edd made a final appearance at Evansville's Bosse Field in 2006, not as an apparition but in the form of a six-inch statue, awarded to the first 750 fans for an August 25 Frontier League game. Complete with a detachable bat, the handsome bronze-colored item showed Edd in uniform with a large "E" on his jersey—a tribute to those seasons on Evansville rosters in 1912 and 1913. They held games at a different site back then, though Bosse sprung up soon afterward. It's the third-oldest ballpark in the country, behind Wrigley Field and Fenway Park, and countless prospects made minor league pit stops there before landing in the majors.

Yet none ever crafted a more inspirational moment than aged Edd in 1972.

Edd Roush slides head-first into third base during an old-timers exhibition game at Bosse Field in Evansville, Indiana. He was 79 years old at the time (courtesy of the Willard Library Archives).

Running the bases during an old-timers game that preceded a Triple-A contest, the 79-year-old brought fans to their feet by diving face-first into third base. He beat the throw, got up laughing, dusted himself off and waved to the cheering crowd. There's a picture of the slide, showing him dirtying a Milwaukee Braves uniform while aiming his body toward the outside corner of the bag.

Flash forward 34 years, with hundreds of cloned figurines bearing mute witness, and a center fielder fittingly makes the pivotal play in an Evansville Otters victory. Top of the ninth, one out, bases loaded and a single pulls the visitors within one run. Another man tries to score on the same hit but Dale Mueller fields the ball in center, cuts him down at the plate, and the home team prevails, 3–2.

Somewhere, Edd J. Roush must've been smiling. Either that or shaking his head and critiquing the man's throwing mechanics, but go with the first thought. He had a great smile.

Chapter Notes

Prologue

1. "Where Originality Counts in Batting," *Baseball Magazine*, August 1927, 397.
2. *New York Times* obituary, March 22, 1988, B4.

Chapter 1

1. George Ade, "What We Can Learn from Kenesaw and Will," *American Magazine*, November 1922, 19.
2. "Tony Admits Roush Is Hard Man to Fool," *Evansville Courier*, September 24, 1919, 8.
3. Casey Stengel, *Casey at the Bat: The Story of My Life in Baseball* (New York: Random House, 1962), 241.
4. Ty Cobb, *My Life in Baseball: The True Record* (Garden City, NY: Doubleday, 1961), 228, 232.
5. *Ibid.*, 198.
6. *Ibid.*, 269–70.
7. *Ibid.*, 280.

Chapter 2

1. Author's interview.
2. "2,000 Barrels Oil Daily," *Oakland City Journal*, September 7, 1909, 3.
3. *Oakland City Indiana: Celebrating 150 Years* (Evansville, IN: M.T. Publishing, 2005), 123, 189.
4. Lawrence S. Ritter, *The Glory of Their Times: The Story of the Early Days of Baseball Told by the Men Who Played It.* The Enlarged Edition (New York: Quill, William Morrow, 1984), 223.

Chapter 3

1. Works Progress Administration, *Henderson: A Guide to Audubon's Home Town in Kentucky* (Northport, NY: Bacon, Percy and Daggett, 1941), 75.
2. *Ibid.*, 73.
3. *Ibid.*, 23.
4. "Hens Move Up into Tie for Fifth Place; Hurrah!," *Henderson Gleaner*, August 18, 1911, 5.
5. "New Players Spell Money to Club," *Gleaner*, August 18, 1911, 5.
6. "Game Today to Be for Blood," *Gleaner*, August 22, 1911, 5.
7. "Chickens Use Big Stick and Rout the Invaders," *Gleaner*, August 29, 1911, 5.

Chapter 4

1. Author's interview.
2. "Truthful Tale about Debut of Eddie Roush," *The Sporting News*, October 3, 1918, 2.
3. "Roush's Home Run Wins Game in Fourteenth Frame," *Evansville Journal-News*, August 2, 1912, 10.
4. "Truthful Tale about Debut of Eddie Roush," *The Sporting News*, October 3, 1918, 2.
5. "Rausch's Long Drive Wins for the Yanks," *Henderson Gleaner*, August 14, 1912, 5.
6. Author's interview.

Chapter 5

1. "Jim Scott on Slab, Weaver with Bat Blank Red Sox, 1–0," *Chicago Daily Tribune*, August 21, 1913, 13.
2. "Sporting Review," *Lincoln Daily Star*, September 30, 1913, 7.
3. *Ibid.*
4. "Cornhuskers Triumph Over Gopher Squad," *Lincoln Daily Star*, October 19, 1913, 1.

Chapter 6

1. Author's interview.
2. "Why I Signed with the Federal League," *Baseball Magazine*, April 1915, 62.
3. Babe Ruth with Bob Considine, *The Babe Ruth Story* (New York: E.P. Dutton, 1948), 21.
4. John McGraw, *John J. McGraw: My 30 Years in Baseball* (Lincoln: Bison, University of Nebraska Press, 1995), 160.
5. "Big Leagues Ordered to 'Play Fair,'" *Indianapolis Star*, March 4, 1914, 10.
6. "Hoosier Manager Refuses to Include Roush in Trade — Braves Practice in Cold," *Indianapolis Star*, March 21, 1914, 10.

Chapter 7

1. Author's interview
2. "Brookfeds Routed by Hoofeds in Twin Bill," *Indianapolis Star*, August 23, 1914.
3. "Long Cy Squeezes Out Victory on Phillips Day," *Star*, September 21, 1914, 10.
4. "Team of Macks May Play Hoofeds," *Star*, October 9, 1914, 7.
5 "Hoosiers Challenge World Series Winner," *Indianapolis News*, October 9, 1914.

Chapter 8

1. "Hoofed Outfit Again Looking Like Champions," *Newark Evening News*, March 24, 1915, 29.
2. "'Surpasses Them All,' Says Gilmore of Opening Outburst for the Feds," *Evening News*, April 17, 1915, 31.
3. "Sinclair, Thoroughly Angry, Ready to Fight Organized Baseballdom with Its Own Contract Weapons," *Evening News*, April 30, 1915, 35.
4. "Great Enthusiasm — Great! Is Verdict of in the Air Man at 'Votes' Game," *Evening News*, June 26, 1915, 27.
5. *Ibid.*
6 "Sport News And Views," *Evening News*, July 12, 1915, 14.
7. "Peps Soar to Top Peak on Wings of Home Run Clouts by Roush and Esmond...," *Evening News*, August 23, 1915, 17.

Chapter 9

1. John McGraw, *John J. McGraw: My 30 Years in Baseball* (Lincoln: Bison, University of Nebraska Press, 1995), 250.
2. Frank Graham, *The New York Giants: An Informal History of a Great Baseball Club* (New York: Putnam's, 1952), 85.
3. McGraw, *My 30 Years*, 250.
4. Ray Robinson, *Matty: An American Hero* (New York: Oxford University Press, 1993), 153.
5. "Giants Get Their Bitter Daily Dose," *New York Times*, May 9, 1916, 12.
6. "Comment on Current Events in Sports," *Times*, June 17. 1916, 8.
7. "Manager Mathewson Is a Believer in Making Men Think for Themselves," *Cincinnati Enquirer*, October 1, 1916, 4, sec. 3.

Chapter 10

1. From Edd Roush file at the National Baseball Hall of Fame Library.
2. "Wingos Finally Win a Contest," *Cincinnati Enquirer*, March 11, 1917, 18.
3. "Homer by Roush Defeats Dodgers," *New York Times*, September 23, 1917, 3, sec. 9.

Chapter 11

1. Taped interview at the National Baseball Hall of Fame Library.
2. Gibson County estate records.

3. "The Art of Big League Trading," *Baseball Magazine*, July 1918, 262, 308.

Chapter 12

1. Author's interview.
2. "How They Did It," *Cincinnati Enquirer*, July 7, 1919, 10.
3. "Reds Twice Victorious Over Giants Before Record Crowd," *New York Times*, August 14, 1919, 16.

Chapter 13

1. Author's interview.
2. "Faith in Moran's Team Grows Because of Easy Victory Over Cicotte," *Cincinnati Enquirer*, October 2, 1919, 9.
3. "White Sox Who May Grab Series 'Kale,'" *Evansville Journal-News*, September 28, 1919, 7, sec. 2.

Chapter 14

1. "Huge Times Square Crowd Sees Game," *New York Times*, October 2, 1919, 14.
2. Eliot Asinof, *Eight Men Out: The Black Sox and the 1919 World Series* (New York: Henry Holt, 1963), 66.
3. *New York Times*, October 2, 1919, 13.
4. "Roush's Catch Spells Marne for Sox Hopes; Brooding Silence Falls on Windy City Fans," *Cincinnati Enquirer*, October 3, 1919, 9.
5. *Ibid.*
6. "Scores Posted in Cincinnati Schools," *New York Times*, October 3, 1919, 11.
7. "Roush and Kopf Are the Stars in Second Battle for the World's Title," *Cincinnati Enquirer*, October 3, 1919, 7.
8. "Reds 'Lucky,' Says Kid," *New York Times*, October 3, 1919, 11.
9. Edd Roush's re-creation of discussion during author's interview.
10. "That Old Fighting Spirit Comes Back to White Sox," *Chicago Tribune*, October 4, 1919, 18.
11. "Ahern Thinks Stockyards Enough to Beat Reds in Chi.," *Evansville Press*, October 3, 1919, 7.

12. "That Old Fighting Spirit Comes Back to White Sox," *Chicago Tribune*, October 4, 1919, 18.
13. "Eller and Williams to Oppose Each Other in Fifth Game of World's Series," *New York Times*, October 6, 1919, 20.
14. "Wizard of the Mound," *Cincinnati Enquirer*, October 7, 1919, 9.
15. 1919blacksox.com and bioproj.sbr.org.
16 "Fullerton Loses Faith in Baseball Figures After Fourth Defeat of Sox," *Cincinnati Post*, October 7, 1919, 21.
17. "Carelessness by Reds Gives Sox Game, Cincinnati 'Blowing' Four-Run Lead," *Cincinnati Enquirer*, October 8, 1919, 1.
18. "What Is Wrong with White Sox? Gleason Asks," *Chicago Tribune*, October 7, 1919, 21.
19. "White Sox and Reds," *New York Times*, October 9, 1919, 14.
20. "Smallest Crowd of Series Sees American Leaguers Triumph in Seventh Game," *Times*, October 8, 1919, 12.
21. *Ibid.*
22. "The Reds Great Feat," *Cincinnati Post*, October 10, 1919, 4.
23. Author's interview.
24 "In the Wake of the News, by Jack Lait," *Chicago Tribune*, October 10, 1919, 19.
25. "Reds Pound Three Hurlers for 10–5 Victory and Title," *St. Louis Post-Dispatch*, October 10, 1919, 31.
26. "No Evidence That My Players Threw Games — Comiskey," *St. Louis Post-Dispatch*, October 11, 1919, 8.

Chapter 15

1. Author's interview.
2. "Why World's Series Games Are Often Ragged: An Interview with Ed Roush," *Baseball Magazine*, November 1920, 579, 611.
3. "Reds Prove Easy Prey for Giants," *New York Times*, August 4, 1920, 12.
4. "Roush Swung Biggest Bat of All," *Times*, March 6, 1960, S2.
5. "Start Quiz to Save Baseball from Gamblers," *Chicago Tribune*, September 5, 1920, 2.

6. "Sox Suspected by Comiskey During Series," *Tribune*, September 27, 1920, 1.

7. "Two Sox Confess; Eight Indicted; Inquiry Goes On," *Tribune*, September 29, 1920, 2.

8. *Ibid.*

Chapter 16

1. "Asks 5-Year Term for the White Sox," *New York Times*, July 31, 1921, 9.

2. "Came Near Blows at Baseball Trial," *New York Times*, July 18, 1921, 16.

3. "More Evidence Against Ball Players Gone," *New York Times*, July 24, 1921, 5.

4. "Confessions Enter Trial of White Sox," *New York Times*, July 26, 1921, 17.

5. *Ibid.*

6. "White Sox Players Are All Acquitted By Chicago Jury," *New York Times*, August 3, 1921, 1.

Chapter 17

1. Author's interview.

2. "Groh Defies Judge Landis," *New York Times*, June 12, 1921, S1.

3. "More Honors Fall to Swat King," *Cincinnati Enquirer*, July 26, 1921, 8.

4. "Moran Asks Every Red to Toe Scratch," *The Sporting News*, January 19, 1922, 2.

5. "Holdout to Play with Reds," *Cincinnati Enquirer*, July 24, 1922, 1.

6. "Reds Pull Funny Stuff to Amuse Woodlawn Crowd," *Washington Democrat*, October 5, 1922, 1.

7. Author's interview.

8. "Outfielder Agrees to Terms," *Cincinnati Enquirer*, April 15, 1923, 26.

9. "Roush of Reds Looks for Long Hitters to Decide It," *Danville* (Va.) *Bee*, October 4, 1923, 9.

10. Author's interview.

11. "Captain Jake Loses Last Battle," *Cincinnati Enquirer*, October 10, 1924, 17.

12. Author's interview.

13. "Eddie Roush Is Appointed Field Captain," *Cincinnati Enquirer*, March 9, 1925, 14.

14. "Flying High After Years of Struggle, Birds Finally Nest Atop NL," *St. Louis Post-Dispatch*, May 3, 1992, 9, sec. F.

Chapter 18

1. Author's interview.

2. "Peerless Pair," *New York Herald Tribune*, January 30, 1962.

3. "McGraw Challenges Ruling by Heydler," *New York Times*, April 1, 1927, 17.

4. Author's interview.

5. *Ibid.*

6. "Rain Greets Giants on Return to Camp," *New York Times*, March 12, 1929, 33.

7. "Cohen and Welsh Hit Home Runs as Giants Defeat San Antonio Bears, 8 to 2," *New York Times*, March 10, 1929, S5.

8. "The Last of the Great Place Hitters," *Baseball Magazine*, October 1929, 493.

Chapter 19

1. "Roush's Wailing 'Woice' Sure to Echo Shortly," *New York American*, January 12, 1930.

2. "Edd J. Roush Makes Several Statements," *Oakland City Journal*, April 8, 1930, 1.

3. "Former Outfield King Ignores Boss' Order to Show Up at Camp," *New York American*, March 25, 1930.

4. "'I Got Out Before Age Got Me,' Says Roush, Happy in Self-exile," *Olean* (N.Y.) *Herald*, August 16, 1930.

5. Author's interview.

6. *Ibid.*

Chapter 20

1. "Ed Roush Regrets Absence of Bunt, Hit-Run in Majors Today," *Charleroi* (Pennsylvania) *Mail*, July 5, 1938, 7.

2. "Today's Players Poorly Trained, Says Hall of Famer," *Evansville Sunday Courier and Press*, April 15, 1973, 2-C.

3. Author's interview.

4. "Roush, 60, Tells Gil How to Shake Slump," *New York American*, March 28, 1953.

Chapter 21

1. "E. Roush Rare Old Timer; Lives On Savings from Baseball Days," *Bradford* (Pa.) *Era*, March 20, 1947, 17.
2. "Nobody Is Elected to Hall of Fame? 'Why Heylll…'" *Newsday*, February 5, 1960.
3. "'Speed Old Time Stars into Hall'—Cobb," *The Sporting News*, March 25, 1959, 1.
4. Author's interview.
5. Author's interview

Chapter 22

1. Author's interview.
2. Author's interview with Jade Dellinger.
3. *Ibid.*
4. *Ibid.*
5. "Nixon Autographs Ball for Roush," *Oakland City Journal*, July 23, 1970, 1.

6. "Aging Hurler Lloyd Wild in Triplet Debut," *Evansville Courier*, April 19, 1972, 26.
7. "Edd Roush Improved After Slight Stroke," *Evansville Courier*, July 11, 1972, 15.
8. Author's interview with Mayor Robertson.
9. Pike County court records.

Chapter 23

1. "Pete's New Refrain: 'Rose Is a Red, My Love, Rose Is a Red,'" *Chicago Tribune*, July 14, 1988, 2, sec. 4.
2. Author's interview.
3. Author's interview with Kent Chetlain.

Bibliography

Aaron, Henry, with Lonnie Wheeler. *I Had a Hammer: The Hank Aaron Story*. New York: Harper Paperbacks, 1991.

Alexander, Charles C. *Breaking the Slump: Baseball in the Depression Era*. New York: Columbia University Press, 2002.

Allen, Lee. *The National League*. New York: A.S. Barnes, 1952.

_____, and Tom Meany. *Kings of the Diamond: The Immortals in Baseball's Hall of Fame*. New York: Putnam's, 1965.

Amoruso, Marino. *Gil Hodges: The Quiet Man*. Middlebury, VT: Paul S. Eriksson, 1991.

Asinof, Eliot. *Eight Men Out: The Black Sox and the 1919 World Series*. New York: Henry Holt, 1963.

Boyd, Candy Dawson, et al. *America and Its People*. Glenview, IL: Scott Foresman, Pearson, 1989.

Broeg, Bob. *Superstars of Baseball*. St. Louis: Sporting News, 1971.

Brown, Warren. *The Chicago White Sox*. New York: Putnam, 1952.

Bucek, Jeanine, editor. *The Baseball Encyclopedia*. 10th edition. New York: Macmillan, 1996.

Burk, Robert F. *More Than a Game: Players, Owners & American Baseball Since 1921*. Chapel Hill: University of North Carolina Press, 2001.

_____. *Never Just a Game: Players, Owners and American Baseball to 1920*. Chapel Hill: University of North Carolina Press, 1994.

Burnett, Gene. M. *Florida's Past: People & Events That Shaped the State*. Sarasota: Pineapple Press, 1991.

Carney, Gene. *Burying the Black Sox: How Baseball's Cover-up of the 1919 World Series Fix Almost Succeeded*. Dulles, VA: Potomac, 2006.

Cobb, Ty, with Al Stump. *My Life in Baseball—The True Record*. Garden City, NY: Doubleday, 1961.

Cook, William A. *The 1919 World Series: What Really Happened?* Jefferson, NC: McFarland, 2001.

Creamer, Robert. *Babe: The Legend Comes to Life*. New York: Simon & Schuster, 1974.

Creigh, Dorothy Weyer. *Nebraska: A Bicentennial History*. New York: W.W. Norton, 1977.

Curren, William. *Big Sticks: The Batting Revolution of the Twenties*. New York: William Morrow, 1990.

De Chambrun, Clara Longworth. *Cincinnati: Story of the Queen City*. New York: Scribner's, 1939.

Debono, Paul. *The Indianapolis ABCs*. Jefferson, NC: McFarland, 1997.

Dellinger, Susan. *Red Legs and Black Sox: Edd Roush and the Untold Story of the 1919 World Series*. Cincinnati: Emmis Books, 2006.

Desmond, Kevin. *A Timetable of Inventions and Discoveries*. New York: M. Evans, 1986.

Dewey, Donald, and Nicholas Acocella. *The New Biographical History of Baseball*. Chicago: Triumph, 2002.

Ellis, Edward Robb. *The Epic of New York City*. Tokyo: Kodansha International, 1997.

ESPN Sports. *ESPN Sports Century: 1900–*

1929, 1930–1959, 1960s, 1970s, 1980s. 1999.

Faulkner, Virginia. *Roundup: A Nebraska Reader.* Lincoln: University of Nebraska Press, 1957.

Field Enterprises Educational Corporation. *The World Book Encyclopedia.* Chicago: Field Enterprises, 1975.

Frommer, Harvey. *Shoeless Joe and Ragtime Baseball.* Dallas: Taylor, 1992.

Furer, Howard B. *Chicago: A Chronological & Documentary History.* Dobbs Ferry, NY: Oceana, 1974.

Gannon, Michael. *Florida: A Short History.* Tallahassee: University of Florida Press, 1993.

Goff, Richard, Walter Moss, Janice Terry, and Jie-Hwa Upshur. *The Twentieth Century: A Brief Global History.* New York: Knopf, 1986.

The Gleaner. *A Pictorial History of Henderson & Henderson County.* 2004.

Graham, Frank. *The New York Giants: An Informal History of a Great Baseball Club.* New York: Putnam's, 1952.

Green, Harvey. *The Uncertainty of Everyday Life, 1915–1945.* HarperCollins, 1992.

Gropman, Donald. *Say It Ain't So, Joe: The True Story of Shoeless Joe Jackson.* New York: Kensington, 2001.

Heylar, John. *Lords of the Realm: The Real History of Baseball.* New York: Villard, 1994.

Holway, John. *Voices from the Great Black Baseball Leagues.* New York: Da Capo, 1992.

Honig, Donald. *Baseball America: The Heroes of the Game and the Times of Their Glory.* New York: Macmillan, 1985.

_____. *Baseball When the Grass Was Real: Baseball from the Twenties to the Forties, Told by the Men Who Played It.* New York: Coward, McCann & Geoghegan, 1975.

James, Bill. *Whatever Happened to the Hall of Fame? Baseball, Cooperstown and the Politics of Glory.* New York: Simon & Schuster, 1995.

Kahn, Roger. *The Boys of Summer.* New York: New American Library, 1973.

_____. *A Flame of Pure Fire: Jack Dempsey and the Roaring '20s.* New York: Harcourt, 1999.

Klingaman, William K. *1919: The Year Our World Began.* New York: St. Martin's, 1987.

Klotter, James C. *Our Kentucky: A Study of the Bluegrass State.* Lexington: University Press of Kentucky, 1992.

Knepper, George W. *Ohio and Its People.* Kent, OH: Kent State University Press, 1989.

Langford, William M. *Legends of Baseball: An Oral History of the Game's Golden Age.* South Bend, IN: Diamond Communications, 1987.

Leary, Edward A. *Indianapolis: The Story of a City.* Indianapolis: Bobbs-Merrill, 1971.

Liberman, Noah. *Glove Affairs: The Romance, History and Tradition of the Baseball Glove.* Chicago: Triumph, 2003.

Longstreet, Stephen. *Chicago, 1860–1919.* David McKay, 1973.

Madden, W.C. *Baseball in Indianapolis.* Charleston, SC: Arcadia, 2003.

_____. *The Hoosiers of Summer.* Indianapolis: Guild Press, 1994.

Madison, James H. *The Indiana Way: A State History.* Bloomington: Indiana University Press, 1986.

Martin, John Bartlow. *Indiana: An Interpretation.* New York: Knopf, 1947.

McCarthy, Kevin. *Baseball in Florida.* Sarasota: Pineapple Press, 1996.

McCutchan, Kenneth P. *At the Bend in the River: The Story of Evansville.* Woodland Hills, CA: Windsor, 1982.

McGraw, John. *John J. McGraw: My Thirty Years in Baseball.* Lincoln: Bison, University of Nebraska Press, 1995.

Morlock, James E. *The Evansville Story: A Cultural Interpretation.* Evansville, IN: self-published, 1981.

Neft, David, Roland T. Johnson, and Richard M. Cohen, editors. Text by Jordan A. Deutsch. *The Sports Encyclopedia: Baseball.* New York: Grosset & Dunlap, 1974.

New York State Historical Association. *The Empire State: A History of New York.* Ithaca, NY: Cornell University Press, 2001.

Nolan, Jeannette Covert. *Hoosier City: The Story of Indianapolis.* New York: J. Mesner, 1943.

Olson, James C. *History of Nebraska.*

Lincoln: University of Nebraska Press, 1966.

Patry, Robert P. *City of the Four Freedoms: A History of Evansville, Indiana.* Evansville: Friends of Willard Library, 1996.

Rabb, Kate Milner. *No Mean City.* Indianapolis: L.S. Ayres, 1922.

Reidenbaugh, Lowell, and Joe Hoppel. *Baseball's Hall of Fame: Cooperstown, Where the Legends Live Forever.* New York: Grammercy, 1999.

Rhodes, Greg, and John Snyder. *Redleg Journal: Year by Year and Day by Day with the Cincinnati Reds Since 1866.* Cincinnati: Road West, 2000.

Riess, Steven A. *Touching Base: Professional Baseball and American Culture in the Progressive Era.* Urbana: University of Illinois Press, 1999.

Ritter, Lawrence. *East Side, West Side: Tales of New York Sporting Life, 1910–1960.* New York: Total Sports, 1998.

_____. *The Glory of Their Times: The Story of the Early Days of Baseball, Told by the Men Who Played It.* New York: William Morrow, 1984.

_____. *Lost Ballparks.* New York: Penguin, 1994.

Robinson, Ray. *Matty: An American Hero.* New York: Oxford University Press, 1993.

Roseboom, Eugene Holloway, and Francis Phelps Weisenburger. *A History of Ohio.* New York: Prentice-Hall, 1934.

Roush, Walden F., editor. *The Roush Family in America, Volume 4.* Strasburg, VA: Shenandoah, 1979.

Ruth, Babe, with Bob Considine. *The Babe Ruth Story.* New York: E.P. Dutton, 1948.

Smith, Red. *Red Smith on Baseball: The Game's Greatest Writer on the Game's Greatest Years.* Chicago: Ivan R. Dee, 2000.

Sports Illustrated. *Sports Illustrated 2005 Almanac.* New York: Sports Illustrated Books, 2004.

Stengel, Casey, and Harry T. Paxton. *Casey at the Bat: The Story of My Life in Baseball.* New York: Random House, 1962.

Stormont, Gil R. *History of Gibson County, Indiana.* B.F. Bowen, 1914.

Stradling, David. *Cincinnati: From River City to Highway Metropolis.* Charleston, SC: Arcadia, 2003.

Stump, Al. *Cobb: A Biography.* Chapel Hill, NC: Algonquin, 1994.

Tygiel, Jules. *Past Time: Baseball as History.* New York: Oxford University Press, 2000.

Wolf, Dave. *Amazing Baseball Teams.* New York: Random House, 1970.

Wood, Allan. *Babe Ruth and the 1918 Red Sox.* San Jose, CA: Writers Club Press, 2000.

Works Progress Administration. *Henderson: A Guide to Audubon's Home Town in Kentucky.* Northport, NY: Bacon, Percy & Daggett, 1941.

_____. *Stories of New Jersey.* New York: M. Barrows, 1938.

_____. *They Built a City: 150 Years of Industrial Cincinnati.* Cincinnati: Cincinnati Post, 1938.

Wright, Gregory. *Prince Town: A Pictorial History of Princeton, Indiana.* Evansville, IN: M.T. Publishing, 2004.

Newspapers

Bradenton Herald
Brooklyn Eagle
Chicago Daily News
Chicago Tribune
Cincinnati Enquirer
Cincinnati Post
Cleveland Plain Dealer
Detroit Free Press
Evansville Courier
Evansville Journal-News
Evansville Press
Hamilton Journal-News
Henderson Gleaner
Henderson Journal
Hopkinsville Kentuckian
Indianapolis News
Indianapolis Star
Kansas City Star
Lincoln Daily Star
Louisville Courier Journal
Newark Evening News
New York American
New York Times
Oakland City Journal
Pike County Democrat
Princeton Clarion-News

Sporting News
St. Louis Post-Dispatch
Syracuse Herald
Terre Haute Post
Washington (IN) *Democrat*
Washington (IN) *Herald*
Washington (D.C.) *Post*
Winslow Dispatch

Magazines

The American Magazine
Baseball Magazine
Literary Digest
Sporting Life
Sports Collectors Digest

www.ingramcontent.com/pod-product-compliance
Ingram Content Group UK Ltd.
Pitfield, Milton Keynes, MK11 3LW, UK
UKHW041842150726
7214IPUK00015B/127